Baseball's Canadian-American League

Baseball's Canadian-American League

A History of Its Inception, Franchises, Participants, Locales, Statistics, Demise and Legacy, 1936–1951

by

David Pietrusza

FOREWORD BY
JOHN THORN

McFarland & Company, Inc., Publishers
Jefferson, North Carolina, and London

The present work is a reprint of the library bound edition of
Baseball's Canadian-American League: A History of Its
Inception, Franchises, Participants, Locales, Statistics,
Demise and Legacy, 1936–1951, *first published in 1990 by
McFarland.*

LIBRARY OF CONGRESS CATALOGUING-IN-PUBLICATION DATA

Pietrusza, David, 1949–
    Baseball's Canadian-American League : a history of its inception,
franchises, participants, locales, statistics, demise and legacy,
1936–1951 / by David Pietrusza.
        p.   cm.
    Includes bibliographical references and index.

    ISBN 0-7864-2529-6 (softcover : 50# alkaline paper)

    1. Canadian-American League—History.   2. Baseball—
United States—History.   3. Baseball—Canada—History. I. Title.
GV875.C36P54   2006
796.357'64'0973—dc20   89-43627

British Library cataloguing data are available

Cover photograph: The Quebec Braves (courtesy National Baseball
Library, Cooperstown, New York)

Manufactured in the United States of America

*McFarland & Company, Inc., Publishers
  Box 611, Jefferson, North Carolina 28640
  www.mcfarlandpub.com*

To the memory of my father, Daniel Pietrusza,
who first told me about the Can-Am League

Acknowledgments

I would like to thank the following individuals for help in researching this book: Eddie Sawyer of Valley Forge, Penn., Frank "Spec" Shea of Naugatuck, Conn.; John "Whitey" Tulacz and Joseph A. Gunn of Poughkeepsie, N.Y.; Albert S. "Sam" Nader, Alice Nader, Steve Salata of Oneonta, N.Y.; Paul A. Tamburello of Pittsfield, Mass.; Barney Hearn, Frank M. Leary and Leo Pinckney of Auburn, N.Y.; Leonard Amdursky, Robert O'Brien and Raymond H. Haynes of Oswego, N.Y.; Mike Naymick of Stockton, Calif.; John Pollard of Dayton, Ohio; Dr. Isadore I. Kaplan and John M. Swistak, Jr., of Rome, N.Y.; Alex T. Duffy of Watertown, N.Y.; Norman K. Hibbs, Carrol Belgard, Francis Mason, Persis Boyeson and Frederick Erwin of Ogdensburg, N.Y.; Howard "Red" Ermisch of Sarasota, Fla.; Jack Minnoch of Sioux City, Iowa; Frenchie Bordaragay of Ventura, Calif.; Malcolm "Bunny" Mick of St. Petersburg, Fla.; Ben Huffman of Luray, Va.; Hal White of Venice, Fla.; Lynn Lovenguth of Beaverton, Oregon; Brownie Blaszak of Orlando, Fla.; Carl DeRose of Pinole, Calif.; Merritt Clifton of Richford, Vermont; Arthur Horsington of Marcellus, N.Y.; Tony Ravish and Edmund Yasinski of Hudson, N.Y.; Harold Erickson of Osprey, Fla.; Herbert Schultz and Addison Jones of Kingston, N.Y.; Charles Tiano of Woodstock, N.Y.; Dale Long of Palm Court, Fla.; Edward D. Dwyer of Batavia, N.Y.; Charles Harmon of Cincinnati, Ohio; Danny Carnevale of Buffalo, N.Y.; Harry Dunkel, Albert "Duke" Farrington, John Coakley, and Loren Stewart of Gloversville, N.Y.; Phil Connoly, George "Jigger" Thompson and William Evans of Johnstown, N.Y.; Daniel J. McConville and Michael Benson of New York City; Gene Benson and Larry Kimbrough of Philadelphia; Jim Riley of Rockledge, Fla.; Frank M. Keetz, Guy Barbieri, Eber Davis, Donald Decker, Wally Habel and Charles Watson of Schenectady, N.Y.; Charley Baker of Mariaville, N.Y.; Henry "Pat" Hoysradt of Ancram, N.Y.; Monsignor Griffith J. Billmyer of Canton, N.Y.; Robert McConnell of Wilmington, Del.; Dick Kaufman of Mohnton, Penn.; Richard Puff of Slingerlands, N.Y.; Mayor Lawrence Lee, Timothy Lee and Raymond Lee of Smiths Falls, N.Y.; Mayor James A. Durrell and Walter and Ruth Masters of Ottawa, Ontario; Si Miller of Cornwall, N.Y.; Emil Graff and Ronald White of Perth, N.Y.; Phil Marchildon of Etobicoke, Ont.; J.R. "Jack" Griffin of Brockville, Mass.; Francois Dupuis of Sainte-Foy, Quebec; Herbert L. Shuttleworth II, Spencer and Hilda Fitzgerald, Archie McKee, Francis "Dutch" Howlan, William Fennhahn, Harold McMullen, James and Grace Bergen, Bill Tuman, John Shuler, Robert McCullough, Joseph A. Zawisza, Joseph A. Pepe, Paul J. Constantine, Richard Karabin, Edward Rusik, Bill Pope, George Sandy, and Judge Robert J. Sise of Amsterdam, N.Y.; Austin J. Knickerbocker of Clinton Corners, N.Y.; Stanley "Packy" Rogers and Clyde Smoll, Jr. of Elmira, N.Y.; Vic Raschi of Geneseo, N.Y.; Jim Cullinane of Rochester, N.Y.; Steve Wilski of Albany, N.Y.; Henry Biasatti of Allen Park, Mich; and Patricia A. Basford of Scotia, N.Y.

I would also like to thank the Amsterdam *Recorder,* the Rome *Sentinel,* and the Gloversville-Johnstown *Leader-Herald;* the Cities of Ottawa, Perth, Brockville, and Cornwall, Ontario; Little League, Inc., of Williamsport, Penn.; the Diocese of Ogdensburg; and the able staffs of the National Baseball Library in Cooperstown, the New York State Library in Albany, the Schenectady Public Library, and the Pittsfield Public Library.

Contents

Foreword

What could have possessed David Pietrusza to memorialize this "late, lamented league," as he calls the Canadian-American circuit, some 40 years after it breathed its last? What momentous events occurred on its fields? Which legendary players played here? How many scandals fixed the nation's eyes on the league's member cities and towns?

The answer to all of the above is that these are simply the wrong questions to apply to minor-league baseball, and that the author has wisely pursued the right ones: What is the real story of baseball in North America? How is small-town enriched by its baseball heroes, even those who are not homegrown but imported from elsewhere? How does one measure a baseball team's impact on the lives of cities and citizens?

For such concerns we are well advised not to look to a metropolis like New York or Los Angeles, where baseball is but one attraction of a massive entertainment industry, but rather to places like Perth and Gloversville and Brockville and Oswego. In these Can-Am sites the line between professional and amateur was not sharply etched, and players were propelled by dreams in the same way as their youngest adoring fans. Previously unexplored, this *terra incognita* of baseball now has a worthy chronicler.

When the minor leagues began to shrivel up in the early 1950s with the advent of nationally televised major-league games, it presaged the death of North America's small-town claims to attention, among them a particularity of place. Television, telephone, and the global communications network have homogenized much of what once was vibrantly unique. In 1950 a baseball fan could root for one of the 16 major league franchises and (more likely, *or*) the minor-league team that was closer to home. In all likelihood at that time no more than 20 million Americans had *ever* seen a major-league ball game; on one October night only 25 years later, 65 million would be viewing a single World Series game on television. Something was gained with electronic innovation, certainly, but something was lost, too.

This book bemoans what was lost by a relative handful of towns and people—though, by extension, all of us—and celebrates the joys of an afternoon at the ballpark with heroes who were flesh and blood and large

as life, not mere pixel clusters. In so doing, the author has caught the tail
of a comet now blazing back into view after 40 years in the darkness: the
notion that in baseball as in so many other things, small is beautiful and,
in its own way, big. Minor-league baseball has embarked an another boom
phase of its cyclical history.

In 1988–89 the Buffalo Bisons of the International League drew more
than 2.3 million fans to an elegant new stadium. Overall minor-league attendance, which had fallen below 10 million in the mid-1960s, rose to more
than 23 million—still some distance from its peak of 42 million in 1949, but
decidedly on the rise and a 77 percent increase over its figure only a decade
past. Even Class A franchises—the equivalent of the Can-Am's Class C
status—can sell for a million dollars. While the major leagues continue to
play coy about expansion, minor leagues continue to add clubs. Such Can-
Am sites as Oneonta, Pittsfield, Utica, and even Watertown (a Can-Am
dropout after the 1936 season!) are today represented in the New York–
Penn League.

So David Pietrusza's *Baseball's Canadian-American League,* like
Homer's *Odyssey,* takes a serendipitous, winding route that ends where it
began: home. For while the Can-Am League may be late and lamented, it
is with us still in spirit, at any bush-league park, where baseball's
anachronistic charms are best enjoyed.

JOHN THORN

Preface

When I was growing up in the economically hard-hit Mohawk Valley mill town of Amsterdam, New York, my father would tell me wondrous tales of a long-vanished enterprise called the Canadian-American League.

It was a story of minor league ball, of something seemingly to me as mythic as some long vanished civilization.

We could still stare at its ruins, the incredibly high, green wooden fences of its local home, Mohawk Mills Park. We could still view its functionless, rusted light towers and scoreboard. It stood there, in faded, brooding glory, a silent witness to happier times — not only for baseball, but for our community as well.

I played ball — rather poorly, but enthusiastically — on a rock-strewn diamond just beyond those fences and never failed to wonder about what had once gone on within. It was difficult to imagine the great crowds that had once gathered there — and such figures as Mayo Smith, Vic Raschi, Spec Shea and Lew Burdette who had toiled on its once manicured field.

I always thought I'd look a little deeper into this Canadian-American League.

Little did I know.

What started out as an article grew into this volume, a book going beyond the written records as found in a dozen local newspapers to the fascinating pleasures in oral history.

I spoke with men and women about events of over a half century ago. Some recollections were crystal clear. The detail was amazing. The enthusiasm heartening. Others were hazy, sometimes inaccurate, but these gentlemen had been there, so I listened, and sifted and learned. Quite often there was a real joy in their voices, and the pleasure that minor league ball brought to a lot of places was very, every evident.

We have lost something.

Minor league baseball once extended virtually everywhere. Author Bob Obojski in 1974 estimated that at one time or another there were 275 minor leagues in 1,200 cities. And in those leagues were 275,000 players.

There was fun at those parks. In hundreds of cities, on thousands of nights, millions and millions of fans gathered, screamed, cheered, went wild, met their friends, met their mates, went home tired, exhilarated, satisfied or infuriated. But they were determined to be there the next night and root again.

Tell me television is better.

This is perhaps the most exhaustive study ever attempted — or perhaps ever will be attempted — of this era of minor league ball. Here is the story not only the major leaguers who played in this league, but also of those who never made it, of their managers and the parks in which they played. Here too is the tale of how the Second World War altered this league; how integration came after that war; how this circuit was organized; how it prospered in the late 1940s and finally, how it died when the times no longer nurtured it.

So here's to the Canadian-American League and all the other bush circuits in the great baseball beyond.

You really are missed.

DAVID PIETRUSZA

Chapter 1

In the Beginning...

"In the Country of baseball, time is the air we breathe,
and the wind swirls us backward, until we seem so reckoned in time and
seasons that all time and all seasons become the same."
Donald Hall, 1976

It is Quebec City, 1942; in the outfield is one-armed Pete Gray. It is Three Rivers Quebec, 1946. Jackie Robinson is still wearing a Montreal Royals uniform, but two black pitchers, John Wright and Roy Partlow, are integrating a second minor league. It is Pittsfield, 1940. Young Jack Kennedy is cheering on a friend and roommate. It's Schenectady, 1948, and a Phillies farmhand named Tommy Lasorda is not yet bleeding Dodger Blue.

The league is the long-gone Canadian-American, and while it lasted from 1936 to 1951 it was a good, solid Class C circuit, churning out its share of prospects and suspects, small-town legends and big league dreams.

It was kid shortstops and grizzled pitchers trying to hang on for one last season. It was managers and ballparks and bus rides to another country that went on forever. It was baseball in a world gone by.

The Can-Am League was typical and timeless as is all that we call baseball, indicative of its era, an epoch slowly fading from view. It functioned when times nurtured it, providing Depression era excitement, bracketing the war years like bookends, going wild in the joy of peace.

It was above all else, simply great fun.

"Back in those days," a veteran minor leaguer once told me, "now you're talking about before television, you cannot envision how important a baseball team was in a community. It was a lot of the entertainment for the townships, the focal point.... It was extremely important to have a professional baseball team, whether it was good, bad or indifferent. Of course, it was better to have a good one, but it was really and truly the center of entertainment."

He wasn't exaggerating. In 1948 when the Can-Am enticed 703,143 regular season customers, it drew 131 percent of the total population of its member cities. That is, every man, woman, and child in those cities went an average of 1.3 times that year to a League game.

Then came television.

1

The Can-Am withered when television raised its antennae, just as 40 other leagues did. But while it lived, it was a splendid institution. If you want to find out why, read on.

Minor league baseball is almost, but not quite, as old as the big league variety, the very first bush league forming in 1877. Its fortunes have waxed and waned ever since. In 1912, 47 minor loops started the season, but by 1918, thanks to the Great War, only one, the International, survived the full year. The Roaring Twenties brought the minors back to life, with a peak of 31 circuits starting in 1923, but the Great Depression had them on the ropes. Twenty-five leagues completed 1929, but by 1933 just 14 remained, and only five were sure of even starting a new season let alone finishing it.

Into the picture stepped new National Association president "Judge" William G. Bramham of Durham, North Carolina. Bramham carried his judicial title despite never having sat upon a bench. His law school classmates bestowed it to honor his dignified manner, a mien that had carried him far in baseball circles — Bramham had simultaneously headed four circuits, the Sally, Eastern Carolina, Virginia, and the Piedmont.

Times were tough, but Bramham was tougher. The Judge put the minors' house in order, weeding out fly-by-night operators, demanding player salary deposits from club operators (an idea bandied about for two decades but never implemented nationally), and at every occasion tightening the proverbial belt.

It wasn't painless. "Some of the players had to move out of hotels and into boardinghouses and waive most of their salaries until after the season," observed Bobby Dews, then a young catcher for the Piedmont League's Durham Bulls. "Like most players I was happy to have the security of a room in a nice boardinghouse during the season. Raw and innocent though most of us were, we weren't dummies and we knew there couldn't be a payday with the stands nearly empty at every game."

In 1933, the worst year of the Depression, every league starting the season finished it. Not only was this a mean Depression era feat, it was praiseworthy period. In the National Association's first 30 seasons, it had occurred just five times.

Bramham kept it up. Between 1933 and 1941 just two leagues folded in mid-season. He saved the bushes but wasn't the type to be merely satisfied with survival. He demanded growth, tersely ordering his newly appointed promotion director, Joseph F. Carr, to "do something about it."

Joe Carr was a man for all sports seasons, being both a founder and ex-president of the National Football League and a former head of the American Basketball League. He attacked his new mission with a vengeance and, like some baseball Johnny Appleseed, founded circuit after circuit. From 1933 to his death in 1939 the number of National Association members skyrocketed from 14 to 41.

Carr was in the right place at the right time, aided by three important factors: night baseball, the farm system, and the Shaughnessy Playoffs.

The first recorded night game came way back on September 2, 1880, at Nantasket Beach in Hull, Massachusetts, between amateur teams representing rival Jordan Marsh and R.H. White department stores. The contest played to a tie, since both sides were in a hurry to catch the last boat home.

It didn't exactly revolutionize events. Other crude experiments periodically occurred (including a gaslit game in Cincinnati), but the significant step was taken at the minor league's 1929 annual meeting in Chattanooga, Tennessee.

E. Lee Keyser, owner of the Class A Western League's Des Moines Demons, announced his intentions to stage the first pro night game. Most thought his plan folly (particularly its $19,000 price tag), but M.L. Truby, millionaire oilman and owner of the Independence Producers of the Class C Western Association, wasn't one of them. Jumping the gun on Keyser, he rigged a hasty system, and hosted the first professional night game versus the Muskogee Chiefs before 1,000 fans on April 28, 1930.

It was a crude affair. Only 20 foot-candles of light shown on the infield and but 10 on the outfield. (The average office environment may have 75.) Coincidentally, on that very evening the black Kansas City Monarchs were also playing a night contest—using the first portable system, a $50,000 contraption—at Enid, Oklahoma, against Phillips University before 3,000 patrons. Des Moines followed suit on May 2, with over 8,000 paying to get in.

As the turnstiles whirled, believers were made. You could even say they saw the light. Within weeks as Joplin, Lincoln, Rochester, Montreal, Indianapolis, Omaha, Sacramento, and Waco had installed lights. Some diehards continued to view it a mere fad. ("There is no chance of night baseball ever becoming popular in the bigger cities, because high-class baseball cannot be played under artificial lights"—Clark Griffith.) The big leagues didn't switch on the power until 1935 in Cincinnati's Crosley Field (the Reds had drawn an anemic 206,000 in 1934). But in the minors there was no such reticence. Clubs that couldn't afford to install a system, rented portable units for select games—and carted their greenbacks to the bank in a wheelbarrow afterwards. By the mid-1930s most minor league clubs had lights, and attendance skyrocketed as people could actually get to the games.

What a concept!

Farm teams weren't exactly new either. As early as 1884 the Boston Beaneaters had one in the Massachusetts State Association. But the Cardinals' Branch Rickey was the first to turn the idea into a multilevel system. His scheme pumped support into struggling minor league clubs. As late as the 1920s the bush leagues enjoyed much more independence, particularly in the high minors, which were actually exempt from any player drafts. Poorer big league clubs such as the Redbirds felt frozen out of the player development market. It was cheaper to own a club than to have to outbid other major league clubs in buying a player from it.

Rickey came up with some badly need cash by selling splintered old Robison Field and moving into the St. Louis Browns' more modern Sportsmans Park. With part of the proceeds he bought 18 percent of the Texas League's Houston Buffalos and then 50 percent of Fort Smith in the Western Association. Talent flowed into St. Louis. The Cards won their first pennant in 1926 and the idea caught hold. Eighteen major league farm teams existed by 1928, five of which belonged to the Cards. It was just the beginning: by 1940 Rickey's Cardinals owned 34 clubs outright and had working agreements with eight more, controlling over 600 players. Other clubs rapidly followed suit. Eventually everyone got into the act, and independent clubs gradually evolved into a distinct minority.

In the process came an era of numerical growth and relative fiscal stability for the once hard-pressed minors.

In 1933 Montreal Royals business manager Frank "Shag" Shaughnessy came up with the idea of a four-team postseason playoff. Prior to that only pennant contenders could sustain fan interest, and a runaway winner could doom a league. Split season schedules with the first half winner going into a playoff with the second half champ had been experimented with earlier. But besides offering no help in runaways, they had another drawback. When one team won both halves — goodbye playoffs.

The Shaughnessy Plan offered a solution. Now any team within sight of even a fourth place finish could attract cash customers. Traditionalists like Judge Bramham hated the idea, but the fans — and income-loving owners — thought it was the bees' knees. Now just finishing in the first division meant something, and the postseason contests drew huge crowds that often spelled the difference between profit and loss.

Aided by these factors Carr left no soil untilled, and in late 1935 he eyed upstate New York and Eastern Ontario. The International League had strong outposts in Buffalo, Rochester and Syracuse. The old Class A Eastern League had flourished from 1916 to 1932 and upstate New York had enjoyed the Class B New York State League (1902–1917) and the Class D Empire State League (1905–1907). Ontario had made several attempts at organized ball, including the Canadian, the Eastern Ontario and the Michigan-Ontario (later the Ontario) leagues.

But area baseball had recently taken several hits. In 1928 the International League abandoned Syracuse. In 1930 the Ontario League fizzled out, and in June 1932 the Eastern League collapsed leaving Albany out in the cold. But soon there were stirrings of life. Syracuse sprung for a new

$300,000 stadium and rejoined the I.L. in 1934. Albany, too, briefly enlisted in that circuit but soon found a more permanent home in the New York–Pennsylvania (now the Eastern) League.

Joe Carr viewed these developments and foresaw a new circuit in the St. Lawrence River Valley. In November 1935 at the National Association convention at Dayton's Hotel Biltmore he contacted two men: William J. Buckley and George "Knotty" Lee. The irascible Buckley was a Rochester insurance man, promoter, and former pro umpire. The volatile Lee was a former minor league player, manager, and league organizer and also Toronto Maple Leafs business manager who had been biding his time as manager of Kingston in the semipro Central Ontario League since 1934. Both were baseball gypsies who'd bounced around the bushes for literally decades. They'd soon be joined by another key figure, a 40-year-old Ogdensburg, New York, priest, Father Harold J. Martin, a veteran semipro organizer and a former pro pitcher. From this rather odd trio, the Can-Am would form.

It wasn't clear whether it would be a Class C or D circuit. That depended on its ultimate population base. Many likely cities were downright podunks. Ottawa was the largest being studied, and it was gargantuan compared to its prospective partners. Smiths Falls, Kingston (this was to be Lee's franchise), Brockville, Carleton Place, and Perth in Ontario; and Malone, Plattsburgh, Ogdensburg, Massena, and Watertown (this was to be Buckley's) in New York were possibilities according to a report in the *Sporting News*. Most were backwaters, to say the least.

Many of the Canadian localities being mentioned—Carleton Place, Smiths Falls, Ottawa, Brockville, and Perth—had belonged to an "outlaw" semipro circuit, the St. Lawrence League. In fact, the Canadian Can-Am teams—and, really, the new league itself—were continuations of those "outlaw" teams. "A lot of the players from Perth came from Philadelphia," says Ronald White. "I was the only Perth boy on the team, most of the rest being Americans. Most of the Smiths Falls players came from around Detroit. You'd get one or two players from somewhere, and they'd bring their friends. The Brockville team was from all over."

That's how Philadelphia-born catcher Emil Graff found himself in a remote place like Perth. "I was at loose ends," he recalls. "I'd torn the cartilage in my knee, tore it all to hell. I was supposed to go to Portland for Connie Mack, and I thought this was the end of my career, and I didn't go near there. Well, the leg got better, and I was coming home from a party on New Year's Eve. I met a pitcher that I used to play with up in the coal mines around St. Clair, Pennsylvania—Pottersville.

"He said to me, 'Where are you playing this year?' I said, 'I don't know whether I'll be playing much.' That was the way I felt. He said, 'You know I'm going to get in touch with you in the spring.' He painted a picture of playing three days a week, fishing the rest of the time. You know, the grand picture. So in spring, I didn't know what to do, so I said, 'I might as well go up there and see what happens.'"

"Emil's the one who came down and got me," says Norman Hibbs, who played for Perth in 1935–36 and was the Can-Am's first 20-game winner, "because I was pitching down in the Philadelphia League at the time. That was quite a league down there, because they all came to play when all of the leagues in the South kind of broke up because of the Depression. So we had some real good players [such as Howard Ehmke]. We had two or three boys the Phillies wanted and Connie Mack's Athletics wanted, but they were making more money playing ball than they could have made in the Big Leagues with their jobs."

The quality of the St. Lawrence loop was fairly high. Future Red Sox and Phillie Oscar "Lefty" Judd, who made the 1943 American League All-Star team and in 1969 was voted the greatest all-time Canadian lefthander, played in Perth, whose manager was former Red Sox and Federal League second baseman Steve Yerkes.

"The League was starting to get pretty good 'imports.' I was one of them," recalls Graff. "When we were in the playoffs local factories would close down for the afternoon." Crowds of up to 1,500 weren't uncommon for those contests.

A league of this sort wasn't an isolated phenomenon. Up in Quebec, a "Provincial" League was holding sway (more on that later), and in the Adirondack Mountains of far northern New York and the Green Mountains of Vermont a semipro "Northern Baseball League" formed in the 1930s. Featuring such teams as the Malone Stars (later the Maroons), the Tupper Lake Rangers, the Plattsburgh Majors, the Burlington Cardinals, and the St. Alban Giants, it imposed team salary limits of $1,500 a month. The Saranac Lake team employed such stars as Hank Borowy, and George Stirnweiss and even piped in play-by-play from Sunmount Park to the wards of the local tuberculosis hospital. The Massena Alcos of that circuit were later to employ Syracuse University ace Jim Konstanty, who as an economy move had been dropped by Malone. For amusement in town, Konstanty would drop into the local newspaper office, sit on the window ledge, and peer down the summer blouses of the local damsels.

Other leagues flourished. "There was a New York Central League here in 1921 and 1922," recalled Watertown's 89-year-old Alex T. Duffy, for whom the ballpark there is now named. "The New York Central Railroad had so much money they didn't know what to do with it, and they formed a [semipro] league comprising Malone, Utica, Rochester, Niagara Falls, Albany, Binghamton. A fine outfit. We were playing Double-A ball. The first year we beat Albany for the championship, and the next year we finished second, and that year Buffalo won it. . . .

"Well, let me tell you, when those paper mills were operating, every small town in northern New York had a paid ball club. That's hard to believe now, but every small town, some of them are ghost towns now, Brownsville, Dexter, Carthage, Velts Mills, all up and down the north, they all had good ball clubs, and they all drew well. A place called Harrisville had a ball club. It had many players who had been up and who had been on the way out, and they drew well. A place called Deferiet, New York, had a ball club, and they imported a lot of former league players, and they drew well. They didn't pass the hat. You had a gate. I think it was 35 cents and 50 cents in the '20s."

So this was an area that knew and loved baseball. After all, 50 cents was a half a dollar back then. And it was ripe for Joe Carr's plan. "Knotty Lee had a lot of good connections in baseball," continues Graff, "and he was quite an entrepeneur, I'd call him. He went around to these different towns and spoke to the people and got them organized because they were baseball conscious then." A group of eight men met in Ogdensburg's McConville Hotel in January of 1936: Lee and Buckley; Walter Gilhooley, sports editor of the Ottawa *Journal;* R.E. Hicks of Perth; Edward "Ted" McKenzie of Brockville; Walter Masters of Ottawa; and Allen Dashner of Oswego, New York.

Ottawa was the site of a second get-together. And then, according to the official league history, on February 5 in Ogdensburg six franchises were distributed: to Lee, his brother-in-law Fred Hammer, and Father Martin in Ogdensburg; Dashner, Ed Owens and Ed Halligan in Oswego; Buckley in Watertown; Don Stapleton in Ottawa; McKenzie in Brockville; and Dr. A.C. Hagyard in Perth.

Contemporary accounts tell another story. In late February the Ogdensburg *Journal* reported that eight franchises had been awarded, the aforementioned six plus Kingston and Smiths Falls. But Smiths Falls announced it couldn't join in until 1937, and the league decided to stay with just six teams, with Lee scampering over to became Father Martin's partner in Ogdensburg.

They elected Gilhooley president and Buckley vice president. Gilhooley was another odd duck. Originally a pro football performer with the Ottawa Roughriders of the "Big Four," he later became an attorney but turned to sportswriting when his law practice was decimated by the Depression and rose rather quickly to the post of *Journal* sports editor.

Of the first six teams, three were Canadian: the Ottawa Senators, the Perth Blue Cats, and the Brockville Pirates. Three were American: the Ogdensburg Colts, the Oswego Netherlands, and the Watertown Bucks. Geographically, it was a very compact set-up.

The three Ontario teams faced a problem the Americans did not, Sabbath blue laws. Ottawa evaded that by scheduling Sunday games in Hull, across the Ottawa River in the Province of Quebec. Again, that may seem backward, but it was only in 1919 that cosmopolitan New York legalized Sabbath ball. Boston waited until 1929 (probably through bribery of the state legislature), and not until November 1933 did the entire state of Pennsylvania okay it (and that was after Connie Mack had threatened to move the A's to Camden, New Jersey!). These statutes were not just aimed at the pros. In Boston in 1911 three small lads were incarcerated for playing Sabbath ball, and in Brooklyn in 1913 four boys were made to stand for 24 hours in a crowded jail cell for tossing a rubber ball in Prospect Park on the Lord's Day.

There were a lot of really quite basic things to set up. The Worth baseball was adopted as official ball. Each franchise paid an entry fee of $50 and deposited $500 (guaranteeing player salaries) with the National Association. Visiting teams were to receive $60 a game, plus 12½ cents for each ticket sold over 400 admissions. If it rained, they would be given $30 to cover travelling expenses. Umpires were remunerated at a rate of $6 a day, $3 if it rained (it clearly paid to start the contest and get through five innings), and were to bear their own expenses.

A player limit of 14 including the manager was imposed, as was a monthly salary cap of $1,400 per team. A salary limit was a time-honored cornerstone of the minor league system, designed to keep salaries low and clubs solvent. "The clubs that made money," observed Tim Murnane, president of the New England League, back in 1904, "were managed by practical baseball men that struck close to the salary limit — the great salvation of the minor leagues." More than once an owner infected with pennant fever would sign some expensive talent, win a pennant, and go broke in the process. As the minors were recovering in the 1930s Judge Bramham repeatedly warned his charges: Thou Shalt Not Violate the Salary Limit!

At first there were some bumps. Weather conditions depressed attendance (in the spring the area is never exactly balmy), and Bill Buckley, who had formed a partnership with Cohoes, New York, undertaker Louis Gorski, faced tremendous roadblocks at Watertown.

Watertown wasn't a bad little town. It had an illustrious sports history, and in fact, was quite a mini-metropolis. "In the '20s and '30s," recalls Alex Duffy, "we had 23 hotels. We had 11 theatres. We had 51 varied industries. We had two big plants employing together 6,000 people. We had street car service, bus service. The New York Central Railroad's St. Lawrence Division was centered here. Everything in the North Country revolved around here. We had five paper mills. Beautiful homes. We had no unemployment, no welfare at all. It was one of the most highly rated small cities in the entire United States."

Yet there was trouble in paradise. The Watertown *Daily Times* wondered aloud whether the town really wanted a pro team, and even quoted a coach at nearby Clarkson College to the effect that the local semipro crews were superior to what they erroneously termed "Class D" ball.

A digression. It's hard to comprehend now, but in the 1930s semipro teams drew very large crowds, could be better paid than the professionals of organized baseball (at least in the lower classifications), and were often believed to be simply better ball players.

So when the Can-Am League appeared in places like Watertown, or Ogdensburg, it was not necessarily taken for granted that the "pros" were any better than what the locals were used to watching. Victories — crushing victories — by Can-Am squads over these competitors were not only satisfying. They were necessary to gain legitimacy in the fans' eyes. Thus, for example, when the Ogdensburg Colts walloped the Malone Stars of the semipro Northern New York League 8–0 in July 1936, it was considered important because it was.

But back now to Watertown. Bill Buckley faced great difficulties in getting his new field at the Fair Grounds in shape, but countered with promotions such as Ladies Day and Boosters Day. Still the going was rough, since the city continued to be as interested in fast semipro teams in nearby Carthage and Deferiet as it did in the Bucks.

And then there were personnel problems. "An example of what we were up against," narrated Bucks field manager Admiral J. "Pepper" Martin, "can be told best by what is now a laughable incident which then seemed very tragic. I was signed up as manager early last May, and as such reported to Watertown to look over my prospective ball club. Upon arrival, I found assembled 24 ball players, few of whom came there with any especially good record. Now we check them very carefully before offering contracts, but those days were pretty much of a hit-or-miss affair. I went on the field and looked over my aggregation and my first request was: 'All pitchers step forward.' Just one boy advanced. Then I said, 'All catchers step forward,' and no one moved. I found myself with 23 so-called fielders, one pitcher and no catcher."

Only 41 fans paid their way in on Opening Day. Cold weather continued to play havoc with schedules and support.

Attendance picked up (it had to), but the Bucks were still mysteriously crying the blues, crowd-wise. Skullduggery was suspected. "The paid admissions as announced by Buckley," alleged the Ogdensburg *Journal* in late June, "are far below the estimates of the crowds as made by other sports followers.

"Bill Graf, high school coach, has said the grandstand will seat at least 2,000. For the last three Sunday home games this grandstand has been more than half filled, yet the paid admissions, according to Buckley, average between 550 and 600."

Canadian-American Baseball League Schedule

	Watertown	OSWEGO	Ogdensburg	Brockville	PERTH	OTTAWA
WATER-TOWN	MONOGRAM RYE					
OSWEGO		FIVE SCOTS				
OGDENS-BURG			DOUBLE DISTILLED RYE			
BROCK-VILLE				MONOGRAM GIN		
PERTH					OLD COLONEL BOURBON	
OTTAWA						V. O. R. AMERICAN RYE

The first Can-Am League schedule, 1936.

The Bucks announced they'd try a few games in the far northern New York village of Massena. After just one well-attended contest there, Buckley abruptly intoned that the franchise would shift permanently to the "Power Village."

With 11,000 people (pretty small for a city, but pretty big for a village) and an economy which had never really suffered a direct hit from the Great Depression (the Aluminum Company of America had made it into a mini boomtown in the 1920s) Massena seemed a good choice. And, supposedly, there was great enthusiasm and support in the town, but if there was, the glow wore off mighty fast. By the time the official opening day occurred (it took time, after all, to organize the big parade from the Opera House to Alco Field) Buckley realized he'd blundered. Attendance was positively wretched. "It was cold up there!" says Joe Gunn, who, you must remember, was coming from Perth, Ontario, and not West Palm Beach.

"A small crowd of fans, about half of them from Ogdensburg, witnessed the game," sadly noted the Ogdensburg *Journal,* "According to reports here, Buckley has decided to move back into the Watertown territory for the rest of the season."

So within two weeks, the team was back home in Watertown, where surprisingly all was forgiven. Buckley was replaced as business manager. The Bucks changed their name to the "Grays," perhaps to protect the innocent, perhaps to eradicate any memory of their departed founder. But

The 1936 Perth Blue Cats. *Standing, left*: **Emil Graff, catcher;** *center*: **Mike Sperick;** *right*: **manager Steve Yerkes.** *Kneeling, second from left*: **Joseph A. Gunn.**

fiscal woes continued. Talk circulated of several players jumping ship. The stench was reaching high places. Joe Carr, himself, came "to straighten out the situation that now exists in the local baseball club" (although the Watertown *Times* was now too discreet to define exactly what the "situation" was). Later that same month—to pick up some loose cash—the Grays played a few home contests in Rome and Carthage, New York (shades of the Punic Wars!). It was a mess of an operation. All told they "officially" drew fewer than 10,000 fans for the entire year.

Other franchises were muddling along. The Brockville Pirates faced financial difficulties and looked like they might fold in mid-campaign or at least shift over to Cornwall but somehow pulled through.

The Can-Am League started out with one major disadvantage. Not one park had any of those new-fangled lighting systems. Two games into the season, however, Oswego decided to install one. Local officials, noted the Oswego *Palladium-Times*, "are convinced that afternoon baseball during the week is a losing proposition financially and if the weather is at all favorable, night games will be initiated next week."

Oswego previously enjoyed organized ball in the International League (then called the New York State League) from 1885 to 1887, the New York State League of the 1890s (the Oswego "Starchmakers"), the Empire State

League (1905 to 1907) and the Class D Central New York League (1910) and greeted the new team with some vigor.

Otis Field, a local semipro field, was made vaguely respectable. Promotions such as "Oswego Night" were staged, featuring such "attractions" as a parade to the park from the Masonic Temple and a performance by the oddly named Whango Grotto marching band. Despite such festivities, Oswego (which finished dead-last) was also rumored to be ready for the moving van, but pulled through.

Perth had been put together on a community basis, behind surgeon, A.C. Hagyard, a huge, rugged man, and featured good players like Norman Hibbs, Emil Graff, .300 hitting third baseman Al Tarlecki (who back home in Pennsylvania had played on a semipro team with his eight brothers!), all-star left fielder Joe Gunn, and Can-Am batting champ Mike Sperrick. They would capture both the pennant and playoffs that first season.

The schedule proved to be as easy as it had been painted for Emil Graff, and that was a problem. "We had two or three days off a week," says Joe Gunn. "Lay around the swimming pools and go into the pool hall and shoot some snooker. In that way—[our landlady] Mrs. Greenlea would bring in all these goodies at night for us—we put on a lot of weight, you know. I weighed as much that year as I ever did—172 pounds. Steve would say, 'You're slowing down. Cut out that stuff!'"

In July, Perth changed its moniker from the "Blue Cats" to the less imaginative "Royals." On Saturday, August 15, they found themselves in a royal cat fight. Steve Yerkes pulled into Ogdensburg with just three players. Five minutes before game time Dr. Hagyard phoned Winter Park, explaining that the rest of the team was marooned 200 miles away in Colborne, Ontario, where they'd been playing with the hirsute House of David under their portable lighting system. Perth had been barnstorming across the province in an effort to raise some badly needed cash.

A furious Knotty Lee demanded and got forfeits for two games. But that was small compensation (literally) for the financial bath he took in losing such lucrative weekend dates. Lee also wanted another forfeit for an earlier game cancelled due to alleged "rain" at Perth. It now appeared the Royals were actually playing the House of David at Sarnia, Ontario, near Detroit, on that supposedly moist day!

Lee was well known through upstate New York horsehide circles. Born in Toronto on May 12, 1877, the lefthander began hurling for the Toronto Athletic Club, a respected amateur outfit of the day, in 1896. His pro debut came on the next-to-last day of the Eastern (International) League's 1898 season, when he calmly one-hit Ottawa. After that he headed south, pitching and playing the outfield for Binghampton, Utica, and Cortland in the New York State League from 1899 to 1901, with the New England League from 1902 to 1906 and with Oswego's Empire State League squad in 1907.

When Lee died in 1962, the Ottawa *Citizen* claimed he "was one of the first users of the now famed spit ball." His grandson Tim recounts that his nickname came from the spitter, which was taught him by an "old, colored pitcher." "His [Knotty's] father," recounts Tim, "said that when he threw a spit ball it developed sort of a twist or knot as it spun through the air. That name stuck with him the rest of his life."

His literally most heart-stopping performance came in the New England League. A blue darter struck him over the heart, knocking him unconscious. He remained comatose for 48 hours, and most reports gave him up for dead.

Later in Toronto, a man accosted Lee, noting there was a ball player with the same name, and if he didn't know better — since the hurler in question was deceased — he'd say Lee was that fellow. Knotty modestly admitted that he was indeed often taken for him.

Lee was no stranger to organizing new leagues. In 1911 he helped form the Canadian League and from 1911 to 1915 managed its Hamilton, Toronto and Guelph teams. The Great War killed the circuit, but peace still reigned south of the border, so Lee headed to the Keystone State where he helped initiate the short-lived Pennsylvania League. In 1919 Lee was instrumental in founding the Michigan-Ontario loop where he piloted Brantford (1919–20) and London (1925).

Knotty was never shy about tangling with the men in blue. In fact, press accounts reveal incident after incident where Lee was tossed from games, and even where his antics led to forfeits. In 1920, for example, former Federal League umpire Lou Fyfe challenged him to an on-field fight. "Lee," noted the *Sporting News,* "needed no second invitation." Both combatants were fined a hefty $50, and Fyfe tendered his resignation from the Michigan-Ontario League.

That 1920 season was certainly eventful. In July the club's owner came down to the bench during a game. It wasn't a friendly visit. Knotty barked at him: "You may own the team, but I'm managing it. Get out." The response was Lee's firing (although the *Sporting News* reported that he'd resigned due to front office failure to back him on player matters). That should have been the end of the tale, but it wasn't. The Red Sox threatened mutiny unless their skipper was reinstated. Within three days he was back on the job.

In 1921–22 Lee served as Toronto Maple Leafs business manager. Along the way he manufactured and sold the "Knotty Lee Special" glove. ("Fields 1000% — Made in Canada." Ironically, he'd been an abysmal fielder.) In 1930 Lee was both president and field manager of London in the Ontario League, which he led to a pennant of sorts as the circuit was

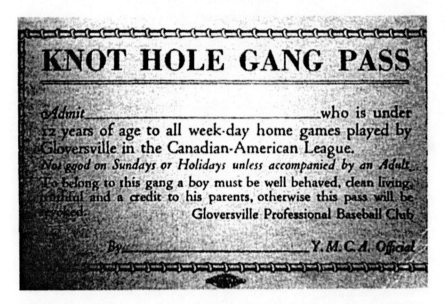

KNOT HOLE GANG PASS

*Admit_____who is under
12 years of age to all week-day home games played by
Gloversville in the Canadian-American League.
Not good on Sundays or Holidays unless accompanied by an Adult.
To belong to this gang a boy must be well behaved, clean living,
truthful and a credit to his parents, otherwise this pass will be
revoked.* Gloversville Professional Baseball Club

By_____Y.M.C.A. Official

"Knot Hole Gang Pass," Gloversville Glovers, 1937. (Courtesy of Bill Tuman.)

collapsing. He was 52 years old, but that didn't stop him from getting into a knock-down brawl with Brantford pilot "Dixie" Walker after a Brantford hurler's alleged balk, and the local constabulary had to wade in and break things up.

Lee also bounced around the old New England League, managing Attleboro in 1928, Haverhill (which moved to Gloucester that same year and then went out of business) in 1929, and Worcester in 1933 (which along with the league went belly up in June). With most of organized ball in ruins thanks to the Great Depression, Lee went semipro, piloting Kingston in the Central Ontario Baseball League.

So Knotty's career saw more than a few horses shot out from under him, but when Joe Carr beckoned, he was raring to saddle up again.

"He had a personality that picked people up, that people liked," recalled Frederick Erwin, who sold tickets for Lee at Winter Park. "He was a hot-headed Irishman, a real Canadian," added writer Daniel McConville, whose father owned the McConville Hotel. As helmsman of the Colts, Lee scorned superstition by wearing uniform number 13.

At Ogdensburg he secured the use of Winter Park with the help of his new partner, Father Harold J. Martin, who insisted that as part of the agreement children were to be admitted free of charge. It was not much of a field. "Lee built the stands himself. He got people to donate lumber," says Carrol Belgard, the team's travelling secretary. "He didn't have any money. Father Martin didn't have any. Fred Hammer from Toronto, Knotty's

The 1937 Gloversville Gloves. (Courtesy of Bill Tuman.)

brother-in-law, he was the one who put the money up. He had quite a bit."

"He never had financial backing," disagreed Knotty's son Lawrence, "that was his problem. What he used to do was he had a good eye for a ball player, and he'd bring in young ones and then at the end of the season he would actually sell the contracts to major league clubs."

Lee's arrival at Ogdensburg was impeded by the U.S. Immigration Service, which detained Lee along with four of his players for the better part of a week just across the border at Prescott, Ontario. Finally local alderman "Billy" Doe advanced the $500 bond necessary to spring them. His reward was a Winter Park ceremony in which a floral horseshoe bearing the legend "Number One Baseball Fan" was placed upon his shoulders.

Teams scrambled to secure help from higher classification clubs. Watertown got players from Elmira and Rochester; Ottawa from Montreal and Toronto. Brockville had many holdovers from their "outlaw" days, but they also received personnel from Albany and signed a pact with the Boston Red Sox for good measure. Oswego affiliated with Buffalo.

"We lost about 13 in a row at the start of the season," adds Belgard. "We had no working agreement, never did. So we had a constant flow of players from around Boston. Father Martin, he had connections in Boston. He was a friend of Joe Cronin. . . . We got Danny Cosgrove, an expert

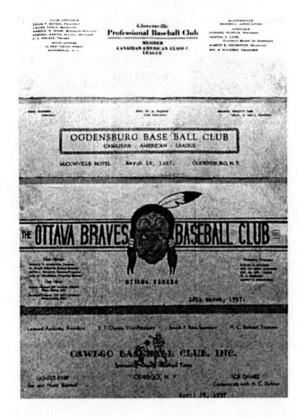

Can-Am League letterheads, 1937. (Courtesy of Bill Tuman.)

first baseman from Boston. He was working for the WPA, digging ditches. He'd been on the job for two days when we called him, and his hands were all blisters, and he couldn't hold the bat. So he didn't work out.

"The top salary limit was $125–$135 a month, although there was more under the table, especially in Ottawa, where they got the biggest crowds.... If we went to Ottawa I would check on the gate to make sure we got our share, and other teams would check on us."

The most colorful Colt of all was hurler Peter "Daffy" Hornozy, who made a fine first impression by informing Lee he would not accept a cent until his first win was notched. It was an offer a frugal manager could not refuse. In his initial appearance Daffy was knocked out of the box but was nonetheless strangely unfazed as he contemplated his next start.

"These Oswego guys are easy," he bragged, "Just watch me burn that ball across so fast they can't see it. Somebody said [Turk] Massic was going to work in the outfield this afternoon. Well, we won't need any outfielders if my fast one is working right."

It was good enough, and he squeezed by to a 5–4 victory, but within a couple of days he was brawling in Ottawa. His banter got the Senators, shall we say, edgy, and a couple of the lads took pokes at him. One connected, giving him a fair sized cut under the eye. Daffy, bloodied but unbowed, calmly whipped out some sheet music, retreated to the team bus, and launched into song!

Lee was suitably impressed and did the only rational thing; he tried peddling him to some other team. The league was equally rational: nobody wanted him. So Knotty went one step further, giving the phenom his release. Hornozy finished his brief yet colorful career with 14 strikeouts, 44 walks, and a 9.54 ERA (the league's worst). Oddly enough he had a winning record for a second division club.

Overall, 1936 was a good beginning for the new league, although perhaps a bit lackluster in official attendance, as for both the regular season and playoffs combined it drew but 65,000 fans.

Leadership changed on December 6, 1937, as Father Martin, now with St. Raphael's mission parish in outlying Huevelton, New York, became league president.

At that same Montreal meeting, agreement was reached on expansion. In 1936 Lee talked of adding Malone and Kingston, and in fact an Ogdensburg-Ottawa contest was scheduled in Kingston to test the waters. However, in February 1937, new franchises were awarded to Rome and Smiths Falls, and Watertown transferred to Gloversville. Rome had originally been considered as the Grays' new site, but having lost that honor to Gloversville, received the expansion slot almost as a consolation prize.

Perth's A.C. Hagyard felt that the new Smiths Falls club, only 12 miles from Perth, made his club vulnerable. He was right. Both cities were among the smallest in pro ball. Perth toyed with the idea of putting some of their games in Watertown. Instead they shared their home schedule with Cornwall, Ontario.

Former President Gilhooley observed that "the circuit should be stronger than a year ago.... The majority of the towns were making their debut in organized baseball and executives and managers had to feel their way. They had a lot to learn, and while some of their experiences brought grief, the circuit should be in a stronger and more secure basis during the coming season."

Toward the end of 1937 there was even talk of a 12-team, two-division confederation. A Mohawk Valley division with Amsterdam, Oneonta, Schenectady, Troy, Gloversville, and Rome was contemplated, as was a northern one featuring Ottawa, Smiths Falls, Brockville, Perth-Cornwall, Ogdensburg, and Oswego.

Look out world, the Can-Am League was on its way.

Chapter 2

Follow the Bouncing Franchise

> "Whoever wants to learn the heart and mind of America
> had better learn baseball, the rules and reality of the game—and
> learn it by watching some high school or small-town teams."
> *Jacques Barzun, 1954*

There's nothing so permanent as a temporary tax increase, nor so transient as a club in a freshly minted bush league.

Teams beginning with flags flying are soon hiking from one scruffy diamond to another, scurrying across the landscape like so many refugees. The Canadian-American League wasn't any better than the norm. It would be a few seasons before stability was established, and before then many were called, few were chosen, and more than one investor had been ruined.

Besides its original six scrappy but largely underfinanced pioneers, the Can-Am roll call consisted of 15 more franchises of varying degrees of fiscal solvency and artistic success. They were:

Amsterdam, New York (1938–42, 1946–51)
Auburn, New York (1938, 1940)
Cornwall, Ontario (1938–1939)
Gloversville, New York (1937)
Gloversville-Johnstown, New York (1938–42, 1946–51)
Kingston, New York (1951)
Oneonta, New York (1940–42, 1946–51)
Perth-Cornwall, Ontario (1937)
Pittsfield, Massachusetts (1941–42, 1946–51)
Quebec City, Quebec (1941–42, 1946–50)
Rome, New York (1937–42, 1946–51)
Schenectady, New York (1946–1950)
Smiths Falls, Ontario (1937)
Three Rivers, Quebec (1941–42, 1946–50)
Utica, New York (1939–1942)

Some were big league farms, well-stocked with talent, such as Amsterdam and Oneonta. Others were rag-bag, independent outfits. Very early

Harold W. Ward, owner of the Gloversville Glovers. (Courtesy of Bill Tuman.)

working agreements were often minimal, dealing with just a handful of players, but eventually grew into a coherent system. Still, as late as 1940, only three of eight franchises (Amsterdam, Gloversville-Johnstown and Ottawa-Ogdensburg) had any kind of pact at all.

Almost all clubs were locally owned, examples of civic pride, backed by prominent local Babbitts, businessmen or just plain fans. There were two exceptions. After World War II Three Rivers was purchased outright by Brooklyn, and for the league's last two seasons the New York Yankees owned Amsterdam.

Here's how each Can-Am franchise, for better for worse, for richer or poorer, took shape:

Watertown/Gloversville/Amsterdam

As the Watertown Grays collapsed Lou Gorski dissolved his partnership with Bill Buckley. Gorski sued, charging Buckley had paid just $50

Admiral J. "Pepper" Martin, manager of the Gloversville Glovers, 1937. (Courtesy of Bill Tuman.)

for the franchise and had made no financial accounting. Lou, a former third baseman in the old Eastern and Michigan-Ontario leagues, lost a reputed $6,000 on the venture.

But he wasn't about to give up, at least not yet.

In 1937 the team moved to Gloversville, largely at the behest of Ottawa's new manager, Jimmy Nolan. Nolan, three years earlier, had played for the Gloversville Collegians, a fast semipro outfit largely made up of Colgate undergrads.

Gorski who saw the handwriting on the wall in Watertown, drove to Gloversville in the summer of 1936, approaching a local attorney and baseball fanatic named Harold Ward about the possibility of a move.

One thing Gorski insisted on was an enclosed park. Ward didn't exactly know how to resolve that, but wasn't about to tell Gorski. "So," Ward later revealed, "without any knowledge of the Fair Association, we drove to the then so-called 'Berkshire Park' and pointed out that 'beautiful' grandstand up there. Lou liked the looks of the grandstand, but looked out front and saw a rough cow pasture. He asked, 'Where's the diamond?' (Persistent cuss, wasn't he?) We promptly built it for him out of thin air."

Gorski failed to see through Ward's bluff and returned in January.

With two feet of snow covering the ground, Berkshire Park looked just fine. The Glovers (a.k.a. the "Mittens" to clever sportswriters) were born.

Gorski pledged to meet the standards of the highly regarded Collegians. There was one contest where the Glovers more than met that goal: on July 26, 1937, when the Pittsburgh Pirates took on the Glovers at Berkshire Park.

"The Pittsburgh club," puffed the Gloversville-Johnstown *Leader-Republican,* "is one major league outfit that is noted for putting as much into an exhibition as it puts into a championship contest. In that respect, the Pirates always have dealt fairly with the public. They use their regular lineup and play to win at any cost, which accounts for the fact that they are in greater demand for exhibition games in minor league towns throughout the country than any other in the major loops."

Whether they really weren't going full tilt, or whether the Glovers were very, very good we'll never really know, but before over 2,000 fans they stunned the Buccos 11 to 8. Even Paul and Lloyd Waner couldn't keep hurler John "Whitey" Tulacz from besting Pirate rookie Jim "Abba Dabba" Tobin. Aiding the Glovers were three straight homers in the eighth frame — a feat they never accomplished in their entire regular-season history.

On the coaching lines were some distinguished personages. Gloversville's George Burns, a former star Giant flyhawk, wore a home uniform. Honus Wagner was there for Pittsburgh. Wagner, who had appeared locally for an exhibition around the turn of the century, observed laconically, "The town hasn't changed much."

Tulacz recalls: "Martin says, 'You pitch the first three innings, OK?' and I says, 'Yeah.' And then, after three innings, he says, 'You want to pitch another one?' Well, to make a long story short, I pitched the whole ballgame. Duke Farrington, he was our best lefthanded pitcher at the time, he had his mother and father and everyone from Detroit in to watch him pitch. He always threw that at me, reminded me of it. I said, 'It wasn't my fault. It was the manager [Admiral Martin].'"

"I was madder than a hornet," fumed Farrington. "I was so damn upset, I ripped my uniform off. The buttons went flying. I threw my glove against the wall right in front of Pepper Martin's nose and it smacked right into the wall. He never even turned and looked at me.

"So I never reported for three days. I didn't go out to the ballpark. When I finally got out there, he tossed me the ball and said, 'You're in there, Lefty.' So I just walked out against Oswego, and I tossed the ball right straight across the center of the plate, and they pounded the hell out of it, and they had four runs in the first two innings. They didn't take me out, and I came in, and I put my fist right through the dugout about two inches from his [Martin's] face, and I just missed a big four-by-four. If I had hit that I wouldn't have to worry too much about pitching. Then I went out and won the ballgame six to four. Oswego started kidding me. They started yelling at me and got me mad at them. Then I started to blast the ball in there.

"They didn't even get a loud foul the last six or seven innings."

After an opening day crowd of 1,479, attendance tailed off, and the team flopped financially with a low of just 140 crossing the turnstiles for one game versus Ogdensburg.

To augment revenues a contest was transferred to Coessens Park in nearby Amsterdam, a bustling mill town noted for its carpets and rumored to be angling for the struggling Brockville franchise, or even Ogdensburg's. Other reports had Amsterdam and Gloversville sharing the Glovers. "I understand," grumbled an irate Jack Minnoch of Amsterdam's *Evening Recorder,* "that Gloversville would have liked to tie up with Amsterdam ... but that Gloversville wanted all Sunday games—Do they think they're in sap country and all they have to do is hang the buckets out?"

Gorski demanded a $3,000 "gift" for the team to stay, later knocking that down to two grand. A group headed by Gloversville Business School manager Albert Houghton was willing to pay, but wouldn't give Lou the cash outright. Instead, they proposed a buy-out but deemed his price "out of proportion."

So Gorski moved to Amsterdam. John Pollard was athletic director of the Mohawk Mills Association, an organ of the Mohawk Carpet Mills, Amsterdam's largest employer. At his urging Lou moved into Mohawk Mills Park.

"We had a semipro team," recalled Pollard. "You'd go out on a Sunday to play a game and you didn't know if you had nine men or seven men. It got to be a headache. In order to draw people I had to bring in teams like the New York Black Yankees, the Homestead Grays, Cubans, Chinese teams. The cost of the visiting clubs was so much there was nothing for the home team. It was tough to get players. Bigelow-Sanford [the rival carpet manufacturer in town] had a nice new field on Locust Avenue, and it was easier for the people to get to."

A Can-Am franchise could answer his prayers. Pollard and Minnoch headed to Ogdensburg to lobby for Amsterdam. The trip was more arduous than either expected. The Scottish-born Minnoch (who saw the *Titanic* being built when he was a lad) spent the night on a pool table, but permission was granted.

Pollard and field manager Admiral Martin then went after a working agreement, travelling to Rochester for a Cardinal tie-in, but the Redwings claimed they were too late. Pollard, though, had a friend who knew Yankee farm director George Weiss. Soon Bronx chief scout Paul Krichell was

John Pollard of the Mohawk Mills Association.

meeting Pollard, and a deal was struck: Amsterdam became a Yankees farm in return for $1,000 a year plus (used) uniforms.

Krichell, the first Yankee super scout, is worth noting. He inked over 200 prospects including Lou Gehrig, Red Rolfe, Charlie Keller, Whitey Ford, and Phil Rizzuto. A former catcher, he was extremely bowlegged. "Paul would have been seven feet tall if it weren't for the two-foot bend in his legs," vowed Lefty Gomez.

Some events augered well. The Jacobs brothers, well known minor league concessionaires, set up shop at Mohawk Mills Park. In return they built a handsome new $600 scoreboard. One hundred and fifteen fans entered a contest to name the new team. Two entrants came up with "Rugmakers," both receiving the whopping prize of ten free tickets to Amsterdam games. Losing entries included such gems as Loom Sox, Rug Sox, Carpeteers, Grass Cutters, and Top Hatters.

August 13, 1939, Mohawk Mills Park in Amsterdam, N.Y.: Area former major leaguers gather at "George Burns Day" to honor former N.Y. Giants star outfielder George Burns, a resident of nearby Gloversville. *Left to right*: Arnold "Lefty" Stone of Hudson Falls, Pittsburgh pitcher; "Bud" Holmes of Gloversville; Jake "Bugs" Reisigl of Amsterdam, Cleveland pitcher; Ed Phelps of Albany, Pittsburgh, Cincinnati, Cardinals, Brooklyn catcher; Jimmy Esmond of Albany, Cincinnati and Federal League pitcher; Melton "Red" Wolfgang of Albany, White Sox pitcher; Bill Cunningham of Schenectady, Washington second baseman; George Burns of Gloversville, N.Y., Giants outfielder. (Photo courtesy of Amsterdam *Recorder,* Val Webb Photo.)

The squad got off to a great start and was pennant bound, but with a major strike paralyzing the town, Gorski couldn't meet the payroll and was set to toss in the towel. "We're at the crossroads," swore Admiral Martin. "It's up to the people of this section to get solidly back of the Rugmakers if they expect the New York Yankees to continue their interest here."

On June 24, with the assistance of Krichell and Father Martin, the team became community owned, Gorski being bought out for just $2,800. That broke down to $1,800 to settle claims such as players' back salaries, with the remainder to cover the franchise itself, the team bus, and all sundry equipment including bats and balls.

Many civic leaders including Mohawk Mills executive Herbert L.

Amsterdam Rugmakers stock certificate issued to Herbert Shuttleworth.

Shuttleworth II took active roles in the new corporation. Capitalization was sought in the amount of $10,000, at ten dollars a share. Quickly the Rugmakers turned themselves around.

"There were a lot of shareholders," recalled Shuttleworth. "Wally McQuatters and I went from house to house to sell shares. If there was an old woman who wanted to own a part of a professional Yankees ball club, we'd sell her a share."

"At any major league park they had advertising," continued Pollard. "So I figured there's revenue in it, and it will dress up the park. It was $125 to $175 for the season, and we paid Harvey, the sign man, $35 for the sign."

Getting advertisers could involve a little hardball. Herb Shuttleworth approached bakery magnate Bud Freihofer to buy a billboard on the ballpark fence: "Bud was a good friend. He was best man at my wedding. I was his best man, but he said, 'We don't do that kind of advertising.'

"'Well,' I replied, 'We don't buy Freihofer's bread for the Mohawk Mills cafeteria!'

"He said, 'How much is a sign?'"

Even though Mohawk Mills didn't charge for the park's rental, the operation was hardly flush. "Anytime a foul ball was hit," says Shuttleworth, "You'd see 20 guys on their feet. That was the Board of Directors, worried about the cost of the ball."

Local ownership continued until January 5, 1950, when the team was sold to the parent Yankees' "Amsterdam Exhibition Co.," under George M. Weiss, who became president of the Rugmakers. "When we finally dissolved the corporation," says Shuttleworth, "we wrote all the stockholders and returned a couple dollars per share."

Meanwhile, folks in Gloversville weren't about to take the loss of their team (particularly to Amsterdam) lying down.

Brockville/Gloversville-Johnstown

Brockville's five owners faced financial woes from the beginning; rumors of a shift to Cornwall circulated as early as 1936. Then whispers emerged of a move to Amsterdam.

"It was a nice little town," says outfielder Barney Hearn, who played there in 1937. "It was one of those Canadian towns that hadn't quite accepted baseball too well." On February 20, 1938, the franchise was forfeited to the league. Community leaders in Johnstown and Gloversville bought the club for a big $400 and it became a revamped version of the Glovers.

A Gloversville-Johnstown combination wasn't exactly new. In 1902–03 Johnstown was in the New York State League, then from 1904 to 1907 Johnstown, Amsterdam, and Gloversville shared a club known by its acronym, the "JAG's."

Key figures in the new franchise included Albert Houghton, who served as its initial secretary and eventually become league president, and Harold W. Ward, who later became league counsel, as well as many bigwigs from Fulton County's predominant leather industry (at one time 95 percent of American gloves were made there). The Reverend C.H.L. Ford, rector of Gloversville's Trinity Episcopal Church, served a turn as president, and in June 1937 married second baseman Hank Gimple and a Miss Margaret Knowles of Chester, Pennsylvania. After the ceremony, Gimple, obviously in a good mood, homered with the bases loaded in his first at-bat as the Glovers beat Cornwall.

Improvements were immediate. "Last year," wrote Jack Minnoch in 1938, "Lou Gorski ... admitted he couldn't raise more than $200 in Gloversville for various improvements to the Glovers' Park, etc. But yet, under a city-wide shares proposition, the Fulton County club has erected a new fence, improved its stand and field and has made other improvements that have run into the hundreds of dollars—and, like Rome, the group doesn't owe a nickel...."

The upturn was temporary. Harold Ward's law partner, former state assemblyman and senator Harry Dunkle, became Glovers president in 1942. He recollects how that came to be: "The baseball team was having an annual meeting, and they were badly in debt. They owed everybody. Badly managed. And two friends of mine called me on the telephone the day of the annual meeting and told me they were getting me elected to take over.... I couldn't get out. They were both clients of mine. They got me hooked into it.

"It was in terrible bad shape, and I sent a letter to all the Big League clubs, looking for a working agreement, and I told them we had money but no ball players. When I said we had money, as soon as I was elected, Sam Rothschild and George Dorfman gave me $500, and I immediately got the thing organized, got a treasurer. Out of all those ball clubs, the St. Louis Browns called on the telephone. They were in spring training, and they told me they didn't have any money, but they had ball players. I said, 'That's what we need.' I made a contract with them, and they gave me no money, but after that they gave me several thousand dollars each year because we did a good job for them."

The rivalry between Amsterdam and Gloversville-Johnstown was fierce, particularly in that first year. A fistfight even broke out in the Berkshire Park stands between a Fulton County man and an Amsterdam woman.

"The people just made you feel at home," recalls postwar manager Jim Cullinane, with one major reservation: "If you didn't beat Amsterdam, they gave you a blast!"

Not only did Carpet City partisans travel to "Gloversville" to root against the Glovers. So did a hard core of Johnstown residents, who just couldn't keep from thinking of the team as strictly a Gloversville phenomenon. "The crew from Johnstown came to all the ballgames," chortles Dunkel, "they rooted for the visiting teams every time. Oh, a lot of jealousy between Gloversville and Johnstown, but I didn't care how they rooted! They had to pay to get in. Must have been 30 to 40 of them. They came early and sat in the same section of the grandstand every game."

The team received some personnel from Brooklyn in 1939 and Albany in 1940–41. In 1942 it switched to the Browns, and in its final two years operated independently, with a few players on loan from the American Association's Milwaukee Brewers in 1951.

Oswego/Pittsfield

The Oswego Netherlands, namesake of the Netherlands Milk and Ice Cream Company, worked with several clubs, including the Indians and Senators. It's president was Leonard Amdursky, a young law partner of local congressman Francis Culkin.

The Nets installed lights in 1936 but in 1939 removed and sold them.

Starting times were termed "admittedly inconvenient," and by 1940 the local press conceded that baseball had "reached the crossroads" in the Lake Port city.

"Oswego didn't draw enough people to pay for the balls," observed Rugmakers' travelling secretary Spencer Fitzgerald.

A WPA project to improve the grandstand and reinstall lights was discussed. Then, the city council considered allocating $7,500 to install arc lights at Otis Field, but "met with considerable opposition among a number of taxpayers...."

Albany produce dealer William V. Connely bought the Nets in the fall of 1940, moving them to Pittsfield, Massachusetts. He originally planned on renaming them the Ponies, but by the time 1941 opened they were the "Electrics."

Pittsfield's long baseball tradition dated back at least to July 4, 1859, when the very first intercollegiate game (Williams vs. Amherst) was played there. In 1862 a nine called the Elms took the field and was noteworthy locally for some time after. For a brief period in 1894 Pittsfield was in the New York State League, and from 1919 to 1930 it fielded the "Hillies," of the old Eastern League, which in the spring of 1925 raffled off a house in the Dalton Avenue section of town, grossing $15,252.51. At that point, some killjoy pointed out the scheme was illegal. Those requesting refunds got them, and ironically the Hillies netted $10,941.92 — more than they would if the scheme had gone through!

At first, events were promising. Connely purchased ten acres of land on Dalton Avenue to construct a new 2,400 seat ball yard, started work, and promised it would be ready for the May 8 opener. All seemed rosy. At a welcoming banquet, a local baker who had unsuccessfully tried out for the team even presented *Berkshire Eagle* sports editor John M. Flynn with a huge cake in the shape of the proposed stadium.

That was as close as it got to completion. Connely had paid $1,000 for the land (which he put in his wife's name) and advanced between $1,000 and $1,300 to the park's contractor, but soon ran out of funds. Work was halted as the builder hit him with a court order, declaring work would resume if Connely came through with partial payment of $7,500.

Because the new field wasn't ready, the Electrics were forced to play at makeshift Dorothy Deming Field, which was hardly impressive. On Opening Day over a thousand fans paid admission and even more lined nearby rooftops. (Most, sniffed the *Berkshire Eagle,* were "not children and many were persons who were not shy of any cash.") But Deming Field's crude conditions discouraged attendance, despite a competitive squad.

Within a month the franchise collapsed. Bill Buckley was brought in as business manager, but it was far too late. Obligations, including the team payroll, were not being met, and Father Martin appointed

Amsterdam's Herb Shuttleworth to investigate the situation. Connely earnestly promised to pay his starving squad and then to honor the remainder of his debts, but soon missed his deadline on player salaries.

The handwriting was on the wall.

Connely first tried unloading the team on a local semipro promoter, but there was little interest in assuming obligations on his unfinished park. Then he attempted to move. Auburn was mentioned, but Sherbrooke, Quebec, was much more attractive than a two-time loser like Auburn. In fact, an announcement was made that the franchise had shifted to the Canadian city. A player revolt loomed, however, as many shocked Electrics (sorry about that) swore they'd quit if the team left town.

The city rallied around its team. Father Martin was absent on a religious retreat up in Plattsburgh. ("He was a great guy," says Herb Shuttleworth, "but every time there was a crisis he was on spiritual retreat!") Shuttleworth, acting as league vice president, informed the circuit that a group of local businessmen stood by to take over the club. He advised the league and National Association President William G. Branham to depose Connely. They did.

Connely blustered about regaining his franchise, and even about placing a Northern League semipro team in Troy, but faded away. The Pittsfield Professional Baseball Corporation was formed, with attorney Paul Tamburello as its president, to pick up the pieces. Tamburello was a hustling young barrister who eventually became head of the Massachusetts Bar Association and in 1972 a Justice of the Superior Court (aided, some asserted, by a timely switch from the Democratic party to the G.O.P.).

The group took over in return for assuming the franchise's outstanding debts, estimated at between $5,000 and $6,000. Within 24 hours, over $2,000 worth of stock was subscribed and the remainder was raised easily enough.

The new team eventually became affiliated with the Cleveland Indians and finally with the Philadelphia Phillies in 1951.

Rome

Prior to the Colonels' birth in 1937, the Copper City held slots in the Empire State (1905) and the Central New York (1910) leagues. The new team's president and business manager, former Can-Am umpire Arthur P. Knight, Jr., a Rome native, put together a syndicate whose names were never made public. Initially, they drew well, with 1,012 opening day paid admissions, but as play faltered so did support. Having used up its working capital repairing League Park, Knight's group was soon flat broke. By early June they had to announce that unless a $750 guarantee was posted with

Paul A. Tamburello, Pittsfield president and league treasurer.

the National Association, the franchise would be forfeited. On June 11 the club was turned over to a corporation headed by Forest E. Richmond, works manager at Rome's Revere Copper & Brass Company.

Next came a more significant change as ex–Watertown boss Bill Buckley conferred with Richmond on February 17, 1938. After his disasterous experience in Watertown, Buckley had spent 1937 managing the Sidney Mines Ramblers of the Class D Cape Breton Colliery League. A month later, the franchise was ceded to a community ownership group headed by a wealthy local surgeon, Dr. Dan Mellen. Mellen, who derived a large part of his fortune from a patent concerning x-rays, named Buckley business manager and announced the purchase of six and one-half acres on which he'd built new Colonels Park. Buckley raised the money to keep the franchise afloat. The Chamber of Commerce even chipped in with a $3,000 gift.

Buckley kept a tight grip on the purse strings. "We had maybe two or three station wagons, and we'd have our equipment or baggage in one of them," notes pitcher Hal White. "I don't think we stayed overnight

Gene Hasson, Pittsfield manager, brought comfort to polio victim Bobby Kidney in 1948. Kidney had been in an iron lung for three years. Around Kidney and Hasson are (l-r): John Masuga, John Kunka, Walter Murray, Joe Bodner, Louis Palmisiano and Ted Myozowski.

anywhere. If we went to Ogdensburg or we went to Cornwall, after the game we'd go back to Rome. Quite an experience. Take four o'clock in the morning, it's kind of cold and windy in those wind-swept station wagons."

The heavyset Mellen assumed sole ownership in 1946 and held control until December 1949 when Copper City Sports Enterprises, under Dr. Isadore I. Kaplan, a long-time team booster, took over. "I guess he wanted to sell out," says Kaplan, "but unfortunately we bought it and lost money for two years in a row and we gave up the sponge."

In 1939 Admiral Martin and the Pirates clashed once more. This time Martin was at Rome, and on July 24, 1939, before 1,976 paying customers, he bested them 7-6.

With the National Leaguers ahead 6-2 going into the ninth, the fun began. "Gus Suhr was playing right field," recalls Rome's shortstop Howard "Red" Ermisch. "Ken Heintzelman was pitching, and Ken could throw hard, and the first pitch I fouled it off into the right field seats. Suhr made believe he could catch it, and he stayed in the seats, and Heintzelman

Luncheon ticket issued to Rome pitcher Art Horsington.

threw me one on the outside, and I hit it into right field where Suhr ordinarily would have been playing, and he came chasing out of the stands, very much embarrassed..."

The game unravelled for the Pirates, and they returned home once again with Grade A egg on their faces.

On August 21, 1942, major leaguers returned to Rome as the Phillies paid a visit to their Rome farm club. With Phils owner Gerry Nugent in attendance, the National Leaguers triumphed 6–4 before 2,112 fans.

The nickname "Colonels" referred to Rome's Fort Stanwix, where during the Revolutionary War the Stars and Stripes were flown for the first time in battle. The fort, under command of a Colonel Gansevoort, refused to crack under the pressure of a 21-day seige by the British and their Indian allies (believed to be direct ancestors of the Utica Braves).

As in Amsterdam, the team nickname was chosen in a contest. Among the losing enties were Rangers, Knights, Romehawks, and Royals.

Until 1942 the team operated independently. Then a Phillies pact was hammered out, but provided little talent. After the war (World War II, not the Revolutionary) a Tigers farm club operated until 1950, although the help Detroit provided was fairly minimal, and in 1951 a tie-in with the Philadelphia A's was in place.

Smiths Falls/Auburn/Utica/Schenectady

The Smiths Falls Beavers was an expansion team owned by the Canadian Pacific Railroad, which operated the largest freight yard between Montreal and Winnipeg in the tiny city. A great rivalry existed between Smiths Falls and nearby Perth. "The people from Perth and Smiths Falls, boy," recalls Emil Graf, "if you were from the other you were a bum."

Technically, the club was owned by the Canadian Pacific Recreation Club which provided diversions for railroad employees. Previously, it had fielded the "Railroaders" of the "outlaw" St. Lawrence League. The new Beavers, under President Andrew Williams and Business Manager Ed McMullen, operated as a Yankees farm under field manager Johnny Haddock.

The new team attracted the curious, and over 200 fans came out just to watch their first practice, but Smiths Falls was too small (9,000 souls) to support a team. The Beavers drew a mere 14,197 in 1937, and forfeited the franchise in 1938.

It was then purchased by some Auburn businessmen, most notably Canadian-born construction magnate (he had managed work on the Chrysler Building) William Bouley, for whom the squad was named.

Auburn held memberships in the Central New York League (1888), New York State League (1888–89; 1897–99), the Empire State League (1906–07) and the Central New York League (1910), but was much better known as National Association headquarters from 1901 to 1934. The city was home to John H. Farrell, long-time secretary of the National Association and president of both the New York State and New York–Pennsylvania (now the Eastern) leagues.

In the 1930s Auburn bided its time by fielding a team in the Central New York Semipro League, along with Oneonta, Oswego, Deferiet, Cortland, and Marksons.

The Bouleys operated independently, but drew only 16,178 and lasted one season. The team stayed afloat that long largely by peddling players to Syracuse, and its management was charged with lacking "promotional ingenuity." Evidently, having the mayor throw out the first ball to the warden of the local state prison was not enough.

A highlight came when Auburn sort of played the Cincinnati Reds. The National Leaguers were scheduled at Syracuse, and for some reason the Chiefs felt compelled to ask the Class C club for help. So they borrowed five Boulies for the clash.

Ambrose Moses McConnell ("a real character and a great baseball booster") transferred the Boulies to Utica in 1939 and began that initial season piloting the squad himself.

A former Red Sox and White Sox second baseman, McConnell had

been voted the most popular Red Sox player of 1908 and led the junior circuit in fielding in 1911. On July 19, 1909, Amby was the unfortunate who hit into Cleveland shortstop Neal Ball's unassisted triple play, the first in major league history. He managed Utica in the N.Y.S. League (1916-17) and in the New York–Penn League (1924) as well as several other minor league teams, including the piquantly named Petersburg Goobers of the Virginia League, which he led to a pennant in 1919 while pacing the circuit in batting. He had a semipro club in Camden, New York, for awhile, but in 1937 returned to Utica, bought Braves Field and ran a semipro team there before securing his Can-Am franchise.

Utica's professional history dates back nearly to the Stone Age. In 1878, only the minors' second season, it joined the International Association. It later enjoyed teams in the International League (1885–87 and 1892), the old N.Y.S. League (1902–1917; called alternately the "Harps," the "Pent-Ups," the "Asylums" or the "Utes"), and the New York–Pennsylvania (now the Eastern) League in 1924. That club, however, transferred to Oneonta on August 1.

McConnell's "Braves" met with some skepticism. The high cost of tickets was blasted, and the media was lukewarm. On top of that they just plain stunk, finishing dead last, with a 45–78 record. Ironically, the team was an immediate box-office sensation, drawing 105,394 of the eight team league's total of 349,513 patrons. Helping the cause was the mayor's designation of Opening Day as a half holiday. Children were excused from school to view the welcoming parade, and many mills and businesses let their employees out early to catch the game (in which the Braves, by the way, were shut out).

That first season, McConnell found himself in hot water, charged with signing shortstop Leo Schoppmyer to two contracts, putting Utica above the league salary limit and thus in serious violation of baseball law. What is interesting is that the boom was being lowered on him by his own partner. Rumors circulated that Father Martin, now a part-owner in the Braves, was prepared to fine McConnell $100 and suspend him for two years.

Martin had not been pleased with the choice of Schoppmyer in any sense, terming him a "troublemaker." He brought the matter to National Association head judge W.G. Branham, but later backtracked, confessing he "may have acted hastily" in fingering Amby. "I did only what I considered my duty as president of the league," stressed the priest, "that I might not be open to a charge of favoring the Utica franchise because I am a partner in it.... Whatever violation of the contract rules existed were of

Opposite: Top row; left to right: **Witte, ss; Martin, lf; Valentine, 3b; Greble, rf; Juelincich, 1b; Zubic, of, c; Mishasiak, p; Kominecky, cf; Ott, p; Munger, p; Kovac, p.** *Bottom row; left to right:* **Lauer, p; Tisko, p; Smith, p; Radakovich, c.**

Utica owner Amby McConnell. (Courtesy of Rome *Sentinel*.)

a minor technical nature, and I find no evidence of any intent to violate the rules."

McConnell denied intent, but didn't deny the facts of the case, writing a rather lame and convoluted apologia to Judge Bramham. The latter wasn't about to drop the matter; he placed McConnell on two-year probation and fined Utica $250. Whether coincidentally or not, McConnell did step down as field manager that year.

Amby died of a heart attack in May 1942. At year's end, as the Can-Am was suspending operations due to World War II, the club transferred to the Eastern League, replacing Williamsport, Pennsylvania. The Utica Boosters gave the Braves $10,000 to aid their transition to the higher league. A year later Father Martin and Mrs. Frances McConnell sold the team to the Phillies for a healthy $35,000. Martin poured his profits back into Winter Park.

Rumors presistently that the Can-Am League heading for Schenectady. In 1937 a 12-team loop was hoped for with the city as a partner. In

1940 it was thought Schenectady might be after the Cornwall franchise, and in 1941 the town was again reported on the verge of enlisting. But it wasn't until 1945 that the Schenectady Baseball Club, Inc., led by two local beer distributors, the McNearney brothers, Pete and Jim, secured a franchise to replace Utica. This gave the Electric City its first pro team since its N.Y.S. League nine of 1899–1904 and its short-lived Hudson River League squad of 1907.

Schenectady was a major catch for the league. It was a bustling manufacturing city of 90,000 souls, home of the huge General Electric and the American Locomotive Company plants. It was prosperous, and it was sports crazy. And it was more than ready for professional baseball.

Jim McNearney, in particular, had long been associated with local sports. The story circulated that in 1910 he pitched for Albany in the N.Y.S. League for a $500 bonus and a salary of $40 a month, big money for those days. He also reputedly hurled for Chattanooga in the Southern League, although no record can be found to support either tale. He certainly did play local semipro baseball and football. Around that time an area columnist wrote: "The dirtiest player in local football is Jim McNearney."

Following his playing days, he bankrolled a series of local semipro squads, most notably the Hedricks (named after a brew put out by Albany's long-time Democratic boss Dan O'Connell). Jim was an active Democrat, and was "in tight" with Uncle Dan. Despite being a beer distributor, Jim supposedly never touched a drop in his life. The Hedricks were later termed, with perhaps some blarney, as being "as good as the professional class A clubs of the day. Crowds of 3,000–5,000 were common whenever they played."

Perhaps.

The McNearneys opened the season on the city's Central Park "A" Diamond, a modest facility, but then accelerated construction on a modern, new McNearney Stadium on Jackson Avenue in the Woodlawn section, near their distributorship.

As in Gloversville, a keen rivalry existed with Amsterdam. "When the Blue Jays played in Amsterdam," recalled Schenectady broadcaster Bill Pope, "there would be something akin to a giant funeral procession heading out on the road from Schenectady to Amsterdam, with a huge line of cars. People would pick up their friends and neighbors along the way."

"The McNearneys were hot headed guys," says Guy Barbieri, who served as Blue Jays trainer, travelling secretary and even groundskeeper. "One time in 1947 coming back from Rome the ball players tore the bus up. They destroyed it, tore the seats up, everything. I was driving, but it was dark, and I didn't see what had happened.

"The next day I pick up the bus, and I see what happened. 'Jesus,' I say, 'The McNearneys are going to fire me. This is it.'

"I went to Lee Riley, the manager, and said, 'I'm through, Lee. I don't even want to see the McNearneys.' You see, he had driven back in the station wagon. He didn't know what had happened either.

"He said, 'I'll tell Pete and Jim.' They hit the roof. They shouted, 'The whole ball club is fired. We're firing the whole club.' Now, this was two weeks before the end of the season, and we're leading for the pennant! Finally, they called a team meeting, and the guys who did it owned up.

"They found a company in Penn Yan that could fix up the bus and sent me out by train to pick it up. So we got a beautiful 'new' bus out of the deal."

In 1948 Jim left the operation in rather dramatic fashion. The McNearneys and the Phils had not gotten off to a good relationship. The 1946 team was poorly stocked and finished a bedraggled seventh. When manager Bill Cronin was replaced by Lee Riley after the season, the brothers were not even informed of it by the Phillies, learning about it from the local press. Then came the big blow up. Jim McNearney occasionally would slip his players a few extra bucks. The Phillies organization got wind of his generosity and sent Minor League Director Joe Reardon to quash it. "You're spoiling our ball players by giving them too much." Reardon ordered McNearney to "stop now."

Jim responded, in his usual cool fashion, by slugging the gentleman, leading to his departure from the Blue Jays and the league.

"You'd think a guy could do what he wants with his money," fumed Jim. "If I wanted to let those minor leaguers live a little better, it was my business."

Veteran Blue Jays hurler Charlie Baker sheds a rather different perspective on Mr. Jim's supposed largesse. "I knew 'em both pretty well, Jim and Pete," says Baker. "Jim was more flamboyant. Jim, if he loaned you ten dollars, everybody in the state knew it. Pete gave you a hundred dollars, and nobody'd ever hear about it. One of those things. In fact when we got in the playoffs with Amsterdam [in 1947], they had a big battle because Pete suggested if we could beat Amsterdam in the series that he'd give each of us a $100 bonus — which was big money in those days — and Jim fought him tooth and nail on it, and finally Pete said, 'I'll pay it out of my own pocket then.'

"And that was the deal, if we beat Amsterdam, we got a hundred bucks apiece, and it wound up we did beat them, and he was right there. He handed out the hundred bucks.

"Jim liked the publicity, but he was tighter with the buck than Pete, and Pete never got credit for anything. I liked them both. I never had any trouble with either of them, but it was like day and night, the difference between the two of them."

But the McNearney brothers weren't always so open with their purses.

"There was a cop on a motorcycle outside the park," Guy Barbieri said, "and when a ball was hit out and a kid would find it Pete would send the cop tearing after this poor kid with the siren and everything. . . ."

"There was a screen all around the grandstand at McNearney Stadium," says ex-Blue Jays Eastern League shortstop Wally Habel, now a Schenectady minister. "It wasn't to protect the fans. It was to save on baseballs."

After slugging Reardon, Jim went back to the distributorship, and Pete become sole proprietor of the ball club. Pete would lead the franchise into the Eastern League in 1951 and then into total dissolution in 1958.

The Blue Jays' nickname came from their parent club. After the 1944 season, the woeful Phillies tried to shake their bad luck (they had lost 90 or more games every year since 1936 and between 1939 and 1942 lost a minimum of 103 games every year) by coming up with a new moniker. Over 600 names were submitted, but a Mrs. Elizabeth Crooks won a $100 war bond and a season pass for "Blue Jays."

Not everyone was enthused. The student body of Baltimore's Johns Hopkins University objected that "Blue Jays" was their nickname and suggested that the National Leaguers call themselves the Philadelphia Cyanocittea Cristatae instead—the bird's correct zoological name. In any case a spate of Blue This and Blue That farm clubs resulted—the Utica Blue Sox (a name persisting to this day), the Wilmington Blue Rocks and, of course, the Schenectady Blue Jays.

Ogdensburg/Auburn

The League returned to Auburn in 1940 when Knotty Lee moved his Ogdensburg Colts to the city.

Lee had his ups and downs in Ogdensburg. One of the more laughable downs occurred in the summer of 1939. "The Ogdensburg Colts," reported the Cornwall *Freeholder,* "almost missed getting paid June 15. Manager Knotty Lee left his bag containing the cash in the hotel lobby. A commercial traveller with similar luggage picked up the bag and departed. Fortunately, he was overtaken at Gouvenour [N.Y.] and the bag recovered."

As 1939 closed, Lee announced that the Colts would move unless a local group bought him out. One reason was a sharp drop in attendance. Another was Winter Park's lack of lights, despite an active lobbying campaign for them by sportswriter Frank Mason. Lee asked $4,000, setting an October 15 deadline. The locals regarded that as excessive, since a raft of player sales to Pittsburgh had left the roster virtually barren. No one took Lee up on the offer, so he moved down to Auburn, which the previous summer had been angling for the faltering Cornwall franchise.

The 1948 Schenectady Blue Jays. *Front:* Charlie Baker (pitcher), Joe Palkovitz (third baseman), Tommy LaSorda (pitcher), Duke Markell (pitcher), Richard Campbell (infielder), Larry Rush (outfielder), Ernest Woods (outfielder), Guy Barbieri (travelling secretary). *Standing:* Lee Riley (manager), Ken Olvesen (pitcher), Mike Genevrino (first baseman), Freddie Speranza (shortstop), Bill Peterson (outfielder), Ray Walters (catcher), Archie Luba (pitcher), Charles Lindquist (pitcher), Stanley Edwards (pitcher), Fred Price (infielder), Charles O'Malley (infielder). *Front:* Pete Lucas (batboy). (Photo courtesy of Guy Barbieri.)

"He had a great sense of humor," related Leo Pinckney, a retired Auburn sportswriter. He needed one: his team was awful, with a .231 won-lost percentage, the worst in Can-Am history. The Falcons at one point dropped 16 in a row. Rome's hurlers whitewashed them three straight games.

"He was something else," said Rugmakers hurler Frank "Spec" Shea. "He'd raise hell all the time. He was quite a guy. I remember him. He was quite an entertainer, I'll tell you. He argued like hell. He'd throw his hat up in the air; he'd beat around. And they'd warn him, you know, about throwing the hat. You're never supposed to throw your hat up in the air. He'd throw it up anyway, and then they'd warn him, and a little later they'd warn him again. He'd have the crowd crazy!"

Lee lost his shirt as the new Auburn Falcons drew a meager 10,040 fans all season. He had to peddle his best player, pitcher Leo Pukas, to Utica for $1,000. Some games were even transferred to other league cities to help the franchise out.

"As far as being helpful to Lee is concerned," noted Amsterdam

Philadelphia Phillies farm director Joe Reardon.

sportswriter Jack Minnoch, "there is no question about the park arrangements being satisfactory. The dean of Can-Am managers is getting free rental for his club and the financiers are paying for the arcs for night baseball. Personally, it appears that Auburn just can't make a go of it and the quicker the league forgets that town the better."

"It was going so bad, he would try anything," recalled Leo Pinckney. One day, Lee got a letter from a pitcher who bragged he had terrific stuff. Lee sent him bus fare, signed him and started him. The prospect hit the first three batters he faced and walked the next seven.

Later, the portly Lee was at Auburn's old Osborne House, the team's headquarters, and was fuming. The young hurler approached, saying with great understatement, "I was a little off tonight."

Lee reached in his pocket, shoved four dollars at him and snapped: "You better be farther off tomorrow!"

Once Lee was asked if anyone was "behind him," meaning financially. "Yeah," he shot back, "the Lehigh Valley Railroad ... it goes behind the park twice twice a day."

Lee was out of the Can-Am League but was far from totally ruined, as he later went into the hotel business in Smiths Falls. "Lee," says Dan McConville, "did very well. He got a lot of troop trains stopping off during the war and would load 'em up with beer and food."

Lee's business success was no accident. He did a little advance scouting.

"I had to take someone, maybe my wife, to the train station in Smiths Falls," Emil Graff recalls, "and I walked over, I saw this fellow standing on a corner, just outside the station. There was a hotel there, and I took a look, and I said, 'Knotty! What in hell are you doing here?' and he started laughing: 'I'm just casing the joint.'

"I said, 'What do you mean?' He says, 'I'm just watching this hotel. I'm watching the action around here. I'm thinking of buying it.' I don't know where the money came from. He had a brother-in-law that was wealthy, that's my hunch.

"Well, he did buy the hotel, and being an entrepreneur, he had baseball pictures of all the big leaguers—Connie Mack and all—hung over his beverage room, and it went over big. He had a good, clean place."

The collapse of the Auburn Falcons helped pave the way for the two Quebec franchises to enter the circuit. The league took over the Falcons for nonpayment of obligations, and at the same time, the Ottawa-Ogdensburg Senators were also in financial straits.

Ottawa

Ottawa enjoyed a long, if sporadic, baseball history, having clubs in the Ontario League in the 1880s, the International League (1886–87 and 1898), the Canadian League (1912–15), the Eastern Canada League (1922–23), and sharing a team with Hull in the short-lived Quebec-Ontario-Vermont League of 1924.

Owner Don Stapleton held the franchise from its inception in 1936, and according to Amsterdam's Spencer Fitzgerald, "was all into sports. He ran the big conventions over there. He had the ball team. He used to put on boxing, wrasslin', hockey..."

It wasn't a bad town to play ball in. "Up there, there was the Parliament buildings," recalls Cornwall's Joe Gunn. "There was about 15 girls to every guy..."

Late '30s Ottawa Senators scorecard.

When Ogdensburg pulled up stakes for Auburn after the 1939 session, the franchise, at the behest of Ogdensburg mayor Francis Burns, moved part of its schedule into that city. The scheme, however, did not work.

On the one hand the Ott-O's were an unlikely candidate for demise, Ottawa was the league's largest city. Pennant winners in 1940, the Senators were one of only three teams with a working agreement. Basically, the Phillies loaded the club with an infusion of talent from the Class D Georgia-Florida League, including manager Cy Morgan. "They were the best team I saw," claimed Fitzgerald, who was in the league from 1939 to 1942. "Boy, they were good!"

But there was a dark side. Prior to 1940 Ottawa had witnessed wretched teams, and attendance had never been overwhelming. Now, because of a lack of lights and the pressures of war they felt unable to continue.

QUEBEC BASEBALL CLUB
April 1942

The Ott-O's planned on moving to Auburn to replace the Falcons which were to be sold to Brockport's William Burns and moved to either Watertown or Niagara Falls. Watertown again proved uncooperative in providing a ballpark. Niagara Falls was still alive, but then Lee and Burns couldn't agree on a price. To complicate matters further, Father Martin suggested Burns return the Falcons/Colts back to Ogdensburg, but Burns wasn't interested. Steve Yerkes was but got nowhere with it.

A somewhat convoluted scenario, to be sure.

Quebec and Three Rivers

Complicating, but ultimately resolving this mess, was the collapse of the Class B Quebec Provincial League, up north in "La Belle Province," Quebec.

Organized baseball had been tried in fits and starts in Quebec Province. Quebec City had enjoyed International League baseball for part of the 1903 season. Quebec and Three Rivers had been members of the Eastern Canada League in 1922 and 1923, and Quebec had been a cog of the Quebec-Ontario-Vermont circuit of 1924. Both cities were part of the new Quebec Provincial League which had fallen apart almost upon its founding in 1940.

It had been a continuation of a six-year-old "outlaw" circuit (known as the Provincial League) that had often attracted jumpers from the Can-Am by offering them higher salaries than the pro circuit legally could, despite a relatively short schedule (varying from between 28 to 72 games). Second baseman Mike Sperrick went over to Granby in 1938. Pitchers Charley Nist, Bill "Lefty" Kalfass, Joe Dickenson, Frank McCaffrey all signed with Provincial League teams in 1939.

It also contained a handful of major league castoffs (such as Kalfass and first baseman Del Bissonette), some black players (including at least one from a barnstorming squad called the Zulu Cannibal Giants!), and one aggregation, the Caughnawaga Braves, made up totally of players from an Indian reservation. On one occasion the Braves were arrested just before a crucial series (crucial for last place, anyway) by members of another team composed of Montreal police officers. In Three Rivers in August 1937 the crowd poured onto the diamond and beat up the whole squad.

The Class B Quebec Provincial League was a lot less colorful than that and died a quick death. Sherbrook and Drummondville folded in

Opposite: **Spring training, 1942. The Quebec Braves at the National Baseball Hall of Fame. (Courtesy of National Baseball Library, Cooperstown, N.Y.)**

mid-campaign, but Quebec and Three Rivers drew exceptionally well and wanted to stay in organized baseball. They approached the Can-Am.

A delegation of J. Emile Dion, president of the Quebec Provincial League and business manager of Quebec, Dr. Jean Rochefort of Three Rivers, Lorenzo Morel of Quebec, and Joe Page of Montreal, a former president of the Eastern Canada League, Chisox scout, and agent of the Canadian Pacific Railway (Page promoted many leagues in order to stimulate rail traffic), came to negotiate.

The two cities were admitted. "I feel we made a wise move in admitting Quebec and Three Rivers," stated Father Martin. "We are doing our bit to cement international relations and we also are helping baseball by keeping it alive in two spots where it otherwise might die.

"I have seen the parks of the two Canadian entries and they are superior to any now in the league both in accommodations and lighting. Quebec drew 110,000 fans and Three Rivers about 90,000 last season under serious handicaps, so I believe we can reasonably anticipate added revenue too."

Not everyone turned cartwheels. Oneonta and Gloversville voted no (or was it "non"?). The great travel distances to the new clubs were a big problem. Some even seriously suggested that the American teams fly to Canada — at the time a revolutionary idea. But as Father Martin noted, high costs and player squeamishness were mighty stumbling blocks.

Quebec manager Tony Ravish recounts: "You'd leave Quebec say at midnight and come into Schenectady at say six in the morning and go to Pittsfield. You'd get there at noontime, just in time to play the ball game. That's a 12-hour drive in those days because they had no turnpikes. It was rough."

"I didn't think the fans knew as much about baseball as we did at the time," contends Blue Jays and Colonels hurler Lynn Loverguth, who was also less than enthusiastic about the trips to La Belle Province, since he had to drive the team bus.

But there were many positive aspects as well. "Quebec was a fantastic town to play ball in," says Bill Fennhahn, who pitched there in 1947–48. "You got to remember, it's a town of about 100,000 people, and if you walked down the street one day, everybody talked to you. The fans were fantastic. If you won a game the night before, well, the next day they sold standing room tickets only. And they were rabid fans. Oh, Lord! I mean everything was rah-rah for the home team and boo-boo — 'shoo,' they used to say — for the opposition, and boy I'll tell you they were fantastic. They

Opposite: **Scorecards for the Trois Rivieres Royals and the Quebec Alouettes. (Courtesy of Guy Barbieri.)**

J. Emile Dion, Quebec sportswriter and director of the Can-Am League's "Star of the Day" Program.

really got you up for a game. It's too bad we couldn't win more games for them because they were fantastic fans."

"If they [the Quebec fans] didn't like a decision by the umpires," says Oneonta catcher Steve Salata, "they'd throw pillows at them!"

"One Sunday night," added 1946 Glovers pilot Ben Huffman, "they had an overflow crowd, and in the first inning we scored 15 runs, and there wasn't anybody out. They threw seat cushions all over the infield. It took them a half an hour to get them off the field.

"So they was excitable fans!"

Three Rivers was pleasant, albeit a lot less cosmopolitan. "Everything looked good up there," remembers 1948 Royals hurler Ed Yasinski. "Well, I was young. It wasn't prosperous. I'll tell you that. It was a paper town. . . . The fans were always good. They were good to you."

So were the local tradesmen. "The kids every time they came to bat, could win a prize," added manager Frenchie Bordagaray, "They gave so many prizes, the merchants did, that the kids ate free most of the time."

Baseball, of course, took on a whole new language up in Quebec —
French. Translations of the positions and baseball terms, as reported in a
Quebec Alouettes scorecard, were as follows:

Pitcher	*Lanceur*	Single	*Coup sur*
Catcher	*Receveur*	Double	*Deux-buts*
First Baseman	*Premier but*	Triple	*Trois-buts*
Second Baseman	*Deuxième but*	Homer	*Circuit*
Shortstop	*Arrêt-court*	Stolen Base	*But vole*
Third Baseman	*Troisième but*	Strikeout	*Retire au bâton*
Left Fielder	*Champ gauche*	Base on balls	*But sur balles*
Center Fielder	*Champ centre*	Error	*Erreur*
Right Fielder	*Champ droit*	Wild Pitch	*Balle passée*

Some stateside fans couldn't quite grasp the idea that their "Quebecqois" rivals were mostly Americans like themselves. "I'd go into Oneonta
or Pittsfield," recalls Tony Ravish, "and they'd yell at me, 'Hey, Frenchy!
We're gonna beat you tonight, Frenchy!' Hey, I've lived around Hudson
[N.Y.] my whole life."

Some segments of the league did not appreciate the Quebecqois way
of doing business.

"Those Canadians," contended Harry Dunkel, "are a different breed
of people than we are, a different breed entirely. They have different moral
standards. Other people I dealt with, their word was their bond. You
couldn't trust these other people. I had trouble with them. When my team
was on the road, playing out of town, we got a certain amount of money.
When they played in Gloversville they got a check from us for a certain
amount of money, based on attendance I guess it was.

Up there in Quebec and Three Rivers, they were politicians. They
gave passes to everyone who came to the ballpark, so they didn't have any
paid attendance. They were sharp in that respect. I can remember rais-
ing hell with them over that. The first time the team came home from there
they said they had a hell of a crowd at the ballpark. I said, 'Where's the
money?' They said, 'They didn't owe us anything.' One of those kind of
deals."

The Three Rivers Foxes ("Les Renards de Trois Rivieres") operated independently prior to the war, but were owned outright by Brooklyn after
the conflict, and their name was changed to the Royals, in honor of the
Dodgers' top farm team at nearby Montreal.

The Quebec line-up had a variety of sponsors: Brooklyn in 1941, the
Rochester Red Wings in 1942, the Cubs in 1946 and the New York Giants
in 1947. Otherwise they operated independently. Known as the Alouettes
until 1949, they changed their moniker to the Braves, and coincidentally

became a great winning squad, packed with highly skilled minor league veterans.

Perth/Perth-Cornwall/Cornwall/Oneonta

One recent guidebook described Perth as "a well preserved small town with a good stock of historic buildings. ... The main street — Gore — is reputed to be one of the finest 19th century streetscapes in Canada." During the summer the River Tay, which flows through its downtown, is graced by gleaming white swans. It must have been a fine little place to play ball.

Prior to the Can-Am League, this picturesque community supported baseball in the outlaw "St. Lawrence League." Attendance was low for Dr. Hagyard's Perth franchise ("We were just too small to support that," admits Ronald White, "we only had 4,000 people."). Part of its schedule shifted to Cornwall for 1937, and then moved over totally in 1938.

"I hear ten years later they were still paying off notes," says Ron White of the original Perth group.

"Cornwall was originally a lacrosse town," says Bisons catcher Emil Graff. "Of course, it's right near the [St. Regis] Indian reserve. It was a lacrosse town definitely, and also hockey, but anyway in the summer they had a lot of the top lacrosse teams down there. When we came in, you know the ball players would fool around with the kids, and the first thing you know we'd go in the morning and get a little league going with the kids, and they got conscious of baseball."

Sometimes the team would stage lacrosse-baseball doubleheaders. "Anything to get 'em in there," observes outfielder Barney Hearn, who played there in 1938.

"It was a big paper town there," recalls Spencer Fitzgerald, "and every evening, whether they would let the sludge out or what, I don't know, but the odor it would kill you."

"When you got to Massena you could smell the vapor, the wood pulp," adds Hearn. "Honest to God, it was horrible."

The climate wasn't exactly pleasant in Cornwall either. "We made the playoffs up there," says Rome shortstop "Red" Ermisch. "It was so cold, we were playing against Cornwall. We had to build fires in the dugout, and when a pitcher would pitch inside, and he happened to jam you a little bit, why then your hands rung and stung for 15–20 minutes, it was so bad. ..."

All sorts of gimmicks were tried to increase patronage — those eclectic lacrosse-baseball twin bills, a softball game with the local hockey team, and what was termed baseball's first "Blue Shirt Night," where all males so attired

Left: **Bobby Brake, Oneonta, won 20 games during regular season and four playoff games in 1948.** *Right:* **Charlie LeBrun, Oneonta, with 2.547 earned run average, topped the twirlers in this department in 1948. He also won 19 games in regular season and two playoff games.**

were admitted for a "nominal fee." It wasn't a big hit (only 119 took advantage) as many Cornwallers suspected a catch.

Things were never smooth financially, however, as a major strike rocked the community and slashed attendance. The franchise tottered, and rumors circulated of a shift to Carthage or Watertown. Reports also floated that the team would shift to Utica, but a disagreement over rent for Amby McConnell's park was the roadblock. The city rallied with a community ownership plan, and Hagyard was bought out by a group of merchants headed by French-Canadian attorney Rudolphe Danis.

"The citizens of Cornwall refused to let their team leave town," noted Amsterdam newspaperman Jack Minnoch, "The first night that Cornwall took over attendance doubled at the Canadian park." Yet the next year the same troubles recurred. The new limited stock company had been capitalized at $4,500, and its seven directors dipped into their own pockets endorsing notes for another $2,750, invested $3,000 for two buses and were responsible for an additional $500 in team debt. They were soon at the limits of their personal finances.

By July 18, 1939, the club could no longer meet its bimonthly payroll and in paid newspaper advertising Danis pled for fan support, touting an upcoming "Booster Night" versus Rome on Thursday, July 20. He urged a minimum of 1,000 fans to show up at one dollar a head for grandstand and fifty cents for general admission. If that didn't happen, a $900 bond posted with the National Association would be declared forfeit on July 31.

The situation stabilized, and the Leafs finished out the season, but manager Steve Yerkes was a casualty. Observing this financial plight, he suggested to the directors that they save some money by removing him, adding there would be "no hard feelings." They agreed, and catcher Emil Graff became manager effective July 31, 1939. January 1940 saw the franchise pull up stakes for good.

The League was in turmoil. Knotty Lee had just transferred the Colts to Auburn. Ottawa was in deep trouble. The Canadian Army was using Lansdowne Stadium for troop encampments, and it was widely rumored the franchise would be purchased by an Oneonta group. Meanwhile Ogdensburg sportswriter Frank Mason was lobbying for the Maple Leafs' purchase to replace the erstwhile Colts. Despite an asking price of $2,500, that team allegedly could be had for just $2,000.

At the league's annual meeting, the Oneonta consortium surprised everyone by purchasing not Ottawa but Cornwall. The Senators had just secured a Phils working agreement, but the recent sale of six of its best players made that franchise less attractive to the Oneontans.

Oneonta was a relatively small city but was serious about its baseball. Previously it had pro ball in the New York State League back in the 1890s and with the 1924 New York–Penn (Eastern) League Giants, neither of which had been a roaring success, but the new "Oneonta Sports Association" made a stock offering and included many a prominent local on its board. A club director, Albert S. "Sam" Nader, later became mayor and owner of Oneonta's highly successful New York–Penn League team. The new team operated independently its first season but after that was a Red Sox farm.

Following World War II Oneonta was artistically the most successful Can-Am franchise, winning multiple championships and playoffs and turning out quality prospects for Boston. When the rest of the circuit was ready to pack it in in 1951, tiny Oneonta was steadfastly ready to carry on.

Kingston

The Kingston Colonials came a calling at the tail end of things, in 1951. Long ago, Kingston held franchises in the Hudson River League (1886, 1903–06) and the New York–New Jersey League (1913). More recently (1947) it hosted a Brooklyn farm in the Class D North Atlantic League under pilot George Scherger.

"It was a great team," remembers Charley Tiano, a retired Kingston sportswriter. "The Kingston Dodgers.... The Dodgers had played a memorial game here in 1944 for a great local catcher, Jack Robbins. We had a Supreme Court Judge that Branch Rickey had managed when he was with the Browns, and he had asked him to come up. The game drew about 6,500 people. Pretty impressive, so they wanted to put a team here."

"We lost $25,000 that year," admits former business manager Addison Jones, "and after the season I went down to Brooklyn with Branch Rickey, Jr. He introduced me to his father, and he said, 'Yes, they cost me $25,000.'" Obviously, El Cheapo was not pleased, and that was it for that circuit. Next came a try at the Class B Colonial League, but that venture also failed, as the whole loop disbanded in July 1950.

Engineer Frederick Ertel was president of the independent Kingston Colonials, which had a miserable record in its short Can-Am League tenure, drawing hardly anyone and going through three managers in its single season.

"It was a great experience," declared the 94-year-old Jones, a former dairy farmer, in 1987, "but it took a lot of money. I could have bought two Cadillacs for what it cost me."

Chapter 3

Adventures of the Bush Pilots

"One of the charms of baseball is that the fans think
they can manage better than the man in the dugout..."
Eddie Sawyer

Behind every team is a figure in the dugout, popping Rolaids, spitting out (or just plain drooling) tobacco juice, mapping out strategy, alternately cajoling and threatening his crew.

That's the manager, the skipper, the pilot, the tall tactician, the—call him what you will—but on Can-Am diamonds there were some pretty fair field generals. Right good, indeed. Amsterdam alone graduated Eddie Sawyer and Mayo Smith, who both captured big league pennants.

So let's start with their stories.

In 1934 Eddie Sawyer signed as a player with Paul Krichell and advanced as far as the Pacific Coast League's Oakland Oaks, before a shoulder injury short-circuited his career. Arriving to manage the Rugmakers in 1939, he was still only 29.

"I could still play, even though my shoulder had never fully recovered from that injury," he once reminisced to author Don Honig. "In those days in the Yankee organization you had to play if you were managing. That way they could get two jobs done for the price of one. Typical Yankee efficiency. They weren't spendthrifts—let's put it that way . . . and nobody questioned their way of doing things. In fact, there was one year every team in the organization, around 18 of them, won pennants. That gives you some idea of the type of ball players we had."

He led the Ruggies to their team's second straight flag and paced the league with 103 RBI's and a .363 average. In 458 at-bats he struck out a mere seven times, the all-time league record. In 1940 the team fell to third place, but Eddie drove in 99 runs (in just 120 games) and hit .329.

Ten years later, Eddie, who in the off-season taught biology at Ithaca College, led the "Whiz Kids" to the Phillies' first pennant since 1915.

He had a phenomonal memory. "If he met you tonight," claims Spencer Fitzgerald, "he'd remember you five years from now. He never bought any school books. He borrowed them." One reading was enough for his powerful mind.

We have some independent confirmation of that. "When the Phillies came to Sarasota to spring training," recounts ex–Rome shortstop "Red" Ermisch, "they were playing the Boston Red Sox . . . and I was in the Sarasota Terrace Hotel, and Sawyer was in the lobby talking to some reporter. He spotted me across the lobby of the hotel, and he came over to me, and he said, 'Your name is "Red" Ermisch, and you played with Rome. You was a shortstop, and you liked to hit the ball back up through the middle.'

"Now, you've got to remember that was in 1939 that he managed in Amsterdam, and this was in the 1950s, and he remembered me after all that!"

"Eddie was a great guy," says "Spec" Shea, who hurled for him in 1940. "I know he was a big help to everybody. You know what he was like? He was like your father. He was the father of the club. Any guy had a problem always went to him. 'Hey, Skip! I got to talk to you.' Jeez, I fell in love with the guy. I thought he was the greatest, and then when I found out that he was going to the Piedmont League and I was going down there with him, I said, 'Holy Cripe!' I couldn't believe it. That was the greatest thing that could have happened to me because he was teaching me a lot of things about pitching that I didn't even know, because he was partly a pitcher and an outfielder. So he told us. I don't know if he was a pitcher or not [sorry, Spec, he wasn't]. . . I tell you, Jesus, he was just one hell of a guy."

Mayo Smith, the Rugmakers' 1949–50 pilot, had been playing Triple-A ball off and on since 1933, leading the International League in 1944 with a .340 mark. He played briefly for the Phils in the war year of 1945, but could muster just a .212 average.

There's a story told about him when he was out in spring training with the 1935 Toronto Maple Leafs. St. Petersburg sportscaster Sol Fleischman was assigned to interview young Mayo and his manager, Ike Boone. Smith, a Florida resident, began by informing Sol and Ike of a huge rattlesnake that had wrapped itself around his axe handle one day when he was out chopping wood in nearby Lake Worth.

"What did you do Mayo? Did you pick up the axe and kill the snake?" inquired Boone.

"No, Ike," drawled Smith into a live mike, "I hauled ass."

End of interview.

In 1949 when Mayo began managing Amsterdam he could still wallop minor league pitching, driving in 116 runs in a mere 119 games. In 1950 he was 35 and slowing down but still plated 53 runners in 66 contests. Unfortunately, his teams had far less ability and finished fifth and fourth.

"Mayo Smith was one of my favorite guys," recalls rival Glovers manager Jim Cullinane, "I thoroughly enjoyed every time we met Amsterdam because of Mayo. It was a great rivalry. He was such a gentleman, and he was such a knowledgeable baseball man. He was just an enjoyable man. There are rivalries that you hate one another, but with Mayo, I mean, while you tried to beat him you didn't want to beat him too bad."

By 1955 he was manager of the Phillies. They had about as much talent as a Class C lineup, and Mayo was canned in mid-1958. Ironically, he was replaced by Eddie Sawyer.

Sawyer got a bellyful of that crew, saw they were going nowhere, and quit one day into the 1959 season. "That's right, after one game," he once said. "I could see that things weren't going to get any better. I made one statement at the time; 'I'm 49 years old and I'd love to live to be 50.'"

Aside from Knotty Lee, the pilot who dominated the Can-Am's early history was Steve Yerkes, a big league second baseman from 1909 to 1915, including a Federal League stint. In the last inning of the 1912 World Series he walked and scored the winning run for the Red Sox on Fred Snodgrass's famed "muff."

Yerkes managed Harrisburg in the New York–Penn League in 1924, before taking a decade-long sabbatical. He'd preceded the Can-Am League into Perth, piloting their squad in 1935.

For the league's first three years, Steve was All-Star manager, bringing Perth to pennant and playoff wins in 1936, Perth-Cornwall to the 1937 flag and Cornwall to a playoff triumph in 1938. When fiscal woes struck the franchise in 1939, he left in mid-season to run his bowling alley. He was hired as Glovers pilot in 1940, but his appointment as Yale freshman baseball coach barred that.

Yerkes was a gentle soul. "He was a very nice man," recalls Ron White. "He didn't swear hardly. Everybody liked him."

"Steve Yerkes," says Graff, "was sort of a philosophical, father figure. He went to Yale. He was a graduate. We used to ride in the bus and we'd get lectures on Tolstoi and all the old figures in history. He was good for the ballclub. He had them laughing. He was educational, you know, and there was no nonsense with him. We could have fun but there was a limit.... He was like a father to me."

One incident that happened to Steve illustrates why managers develop ulcers. "One day up in Ogdensburg," recalls Bison Joe Gunn, "we had the bases full, and I think it was Frank McCaffery on first base. For some unknown reason, he took off for second with the bases full. He got thrown out. They got us out. He came into the dugout, and Steve says to him: 'What in hell were you thinking about?'

"'Well,' he says, 'I had a big lead...'"

Another dugout fixture (aside from the drinking fountain, that is) was dark-featured Admiral (his real first name) J. "Pepper" Martin. Martin certainly got around. In the league's first six years he piloted five different teams — Watertown (1936), Gloversville (1937), Amsterdam (1938), Rome (1939–40) and Quebec (1941).

Martin turned pro in 1921, playing for 11 minor league squads including Pittsfield, Albany, and Birmingham, before joining up with the Can-Am. He claimed that in the 1920s he'd spent a year with the Chicago White Sox, but that wasn't exactly true even though he was under contract to them in 1923–24. He was also a veteran barnstormer, touring with the Detroit Clowns in 1930 and the House of David from 1931 to 1933, as well as playing basketball for that bearded crew. The Can-Am League was his ticket back into organized ball.

"Martin was real strict with those guys," says Ed Rusik, formerly of Amsterdam's Hotel Barnes where many of the Rugmakers lived in the late 1930s, "really strict. Well, he was more like a loner anyway, tough. He wasn't like Sawyer. Sawyer was a friendly man."

"He was a good manager," praised Eddie Sawyer. "Of course, he'd been in baseball his whole life. Because of his connections in baseball he got a lot of players on option from other clubs."

Oswego's Riley Parker (uncle of Salty Parker) never played in the majors, either, but he did later pilot the 1942 Semi-Pro World Champions, the Wichita Boeing Bombers, with the help of former Nets hurler "Windy" Johnson.

"He was a good manager," recalls Emil Graff. "I played for him at Moline [Parker was there in 1930–31], but unfortunately his wife died, and Riley used to bend his elbow, and I think that finished him there [in Oswego] because he started to drink like hell. He played second base in the old Pacific Coast League. A good manager, tough, he was a Hornsby type. If you couldn't hit with two strikes: 'What the hell kind of a ball player are you?' you know. He was tough, he was gutty. He would chew you out, but if anybody else got on you, he wouldn't stand for it. That's the way he was, he'd stick up for his players. You were like kids to him; you did what he said."

The bottle took its toll. "He was kind of a laid-back guy," characterizes pitcher Mike Naymick. "He didn't seem too aggressive. He was a nice guy, but he wasn't teaching the kids. We didn't have anybody trying to teach the game to the kids." He was gone before season's end.

Schenectady's Lee Riley, who led the Blue Jays to a flag in 1947, played and managed earlier for Oneonta and Rome. At Oneonta in 1940 he hit .340. At Rome in 1941 Lee paced the league with 34 homers and also batted a healthy .391. During the war, he was briefly a Phillie, but smote only a microscopic .083. Riley later piloted the Blue Jays in the Eastern League, settled in Schenectady, and worked at the city's Bishop Gibbons High School until his death in 1970. He was the father of Pat Riley, coach of the NBA's 1987 World Champion Los Angeles Lakers, and Lee Riley, Jr., who played professional football for seven seasons with the Giants, Titans, and Eagles.

"He was a real good guy," says former Blue Jays road secretary Guy Barbieri, "there were no problems. Nobody ran to the management and said, 'I can't play for this guy' or gave him a rough time, anything like that. He was a gentleman all the way."

Schenectady appreciated Lee and on his 40th birthday (coincidentally Old Timers' Night) presented the father of six with a purse of $577 and also a pig—which was eaten by all the Rileys in the off-season.

In 1949, the Three Rivers Royals were piloted to a third place finish by George Scherger, who would be an integral cog of Cincinnati's Big Red Machine as a coach in the 1970s. In 1950, his fortunes took a sudden downturn as Three Rivers finished dead last, 50½ games back.

"I enjoyed it. I really did," Scherger once said. "A lot of people considered it tough, the bus rides, the rented rooms.... But the hardest part was telling a kid he couldn't make the ball club. Usually those kind of players—the kids that can't play—they're the ones who really want to play. A lot of times I'd be in tears..."

A helluva major league hitter who managed at Quebec in 1949 was Frank McCormick, the National League's 1940 MVP. Former White Sox outfielder Mel Simons and Red Sox flyhawk Charlie Small managed there in 1942. Star St. Louis Browns' first baseman George McQuinn guided the Braves to the 1950 pennant and for good measure hit .318 and drew 83 walks in just 74 games.

Former big leaguers to man the helm at Three Rivers were Yankees catcher Walley Schang (1941), Brooklyn outfielder Frenchy Bordagaray (1946), Dodger second-sacker Lou Rochelli (1947), and Brooklyn pitcher Ed Head (1948).

The mustachioed Stanley George Bordaragay (he grew it for a bit part in the 1936 film *Prisoner of Shark Island*) was by far one of the more colorful players of his era. A member of the hapless Dodger "Daffiness Boys" of the '30s, Frenchy was also an accomplice of the Cardinals' "Mudcat Band" along with Pepper Martin and friends. He was with Brooklyn again in 1945 when his playing career came to a sudden halt.

"Branch Rickey called me into his office one day," recalls Bordagaray, "and he said, 'I'm going to bring the black man into baseball,' and he wanted me [to manage in the minors], and I said, 'Well, I don't want to go because I have three years to go [in the majors as a player] and besides I don't want to miss the pension plan' [actually the pension was not agreed to until August 1946], and he said I'd get back there in time, but I never did so I lost my pension.

"So that's one thing I've got sour grapes about...."

Originally, he'd angled for the Montreal piloting post ("The habitants would understand me *n'est-ce pas?*"), but as that was to be his first managing job, Branch Rickey wasn't about to start him off so high. "I was supposed to get a lot of jobs," says a still bitter Bordagaray, but I never did get any of them. They make you a lot of promises and everything else but they get you to work for them, but they don't care about you. Rickey was that way too. He was no better than anybody else. So I never did get it, and I never did get anything."

Frenchy wasn't one to take injustice quietly. Once in Schenectady he rushed in from right field, protesting a call. After awhile, the ump ordered him to return to his usual position, but Frenchy merely loitered just a few feet beyond his second baseman.

The arbiter again told Stanley to return to right, but since there is no actual rule defining where "right field" is, he had to defer to the manager's whim. By now, Blue Jay fans were yelling their lungs out, imploring their batter to smash the ball to Frenchy's vacated position. Try as he might, the best he could do was a sharp liner, hit one hop to Frenchy, who calmly threw the pill over to first for the third out, then tipped his cap to the throng, and calmly headed for the dugout.

He reported for duty in 1947 as a player-manager in the South Atlantic League. "I was with Greenville," says Frenchy, "and that's where I met my Waterloo. I was suspended because they brought in a guy to umpire one night. I don't know where the heck they got him from, from some high school or something, and the bases were loaded and I was at bat, and I hit the ball slowly between third and short, and I was three steps across first base, and he called me out. I said, 'How can I be out? I was three steps across!' and I don't know why he did it.

"I got mad at him, and I had a big plug of tobacco, and I was getting up closer and closer to him and pretty soon I choked, and I got goofed up and spit tobacco all over him. It was an accident, but I don't think he thought it was. So they kicked me out of the game, and they suspended me for the rest of the season."

"Maybe I did wrong," commented Bordagaray, "but the penalty was a little more than I expectorated."

"I loved it," Frenchy says of managing. "The St. Paul job came up [in 1948], and Walter O'Malley and Rickey wanted me to go manage St. Paul, but the rest of the people who worked for the Dodger organization, they wanted [Walter] Alston, so Alston got the job. So I said, that's it. I give up, then. If that's the way they're going to work things, why... I was the one who should have got that job, and I never did get it.

"Sour grapes again."

In 1946 Lou Rochelli and Jackie Robinson had been rivals for the second base job at Montreal. Robinson admitted the more experienced Rochelli had every reason to resent him, but he instead took Jackie under his wing, showing him the ropes. "Lou was intelligent and he was a thoroughbred," wrote Robinson. In 1947 Lou was the Can-Am's youngest pilot at just 26.

Washington outfielders Emil "Red" Barnes (1941–42) and John "Red" Marion (1948), brother of shortstop Marty Marion, both piloted at Oneonta. Future Red Sox coach Eddie Popowski managed Oneonta in 1949–50. Popowski had skippered in the bushes for 21 seasons before Boston called him up in time for their 1967 pennant. Owen Scheetz, Oneonta's 1951 skipper, never got to the bigs, but in 1945 he won 19 games in the American Association, and led Oneonta to the greatest winning percentage (.709) in league history.

Braves outfielder John "Bunny" Roser (1938); A's, Indians, and Cubs third baseman Elmer Yoter (1939); Browns catcher Ben Huffman (1946), Brooklyn infielder Stanley "Packy" Rogers (1947); and Nats and Indians catcher Jim McDonnell (1948) all skippered at Gloversville-Johnstown.

"That was my first managing job," says Virginia-born Ben Huffman. "Of course, I was in the service for four years, and I was a playing manager. That's the first bus league I was ever in. That's before they had the good roads.

"At that time, that was a Browns farm, St. Louis Browns, and they didn't have a lot of money, and I was a playing manager, but they didn't give me another catcher. If I got hurt I still had to play. . . .

"One Sunday in Gloversville, we had an overflow crowd and stuck a rope up in back of first base, and I was going after a foul ball. I was just ready to catch it, and that rope caught me round the neck and flipped me around on my head, and I couldn't talk for a half an hour. So I still had to play because I was the only catcher. I caught the rest of the game."

Rogers, a Senators and Twins scout for 27 years, was a fiery pilot, famed for raging at umps. "I put it on for the fans," he readily admits. "When I had trouble on the road, I'd tell 'em, 'Wait til I get you at home, you son-of-a-gun!'" The Schenectady *Union-Star* said "he was the most hooted player at the stadium this year."

It wasn't a new act. In 1941 with Bill Veeck's Milwaukee Brewers he actually went out to second base with a light meter to protest the low visibility at Columbus' old Red Bird Stadium.

"One time I was scoring on a base hit, and I could run pretty good," recalls 1947 League MVP Rugmaker Bunny Mick, "and he was playing third base. He kind of stood up in front of the baseline. When he saw me coming he looked toward home, stuck out his foot and tried to trip me.

"I stumbled, but fortunately, I was able to go ahead and score anyhow. I said, 'I'm gonna get him.' So I'm on second base about two weeks later, and I said, 'I'm going to go at him feet first coming in to third,' and I tried to spike him. I came in, but he was such a veteran ball player that he side stepped me, tagged me out and made me look like a damn fool.

"So he nailed me twice!"

Lee Riley (1941), Phils and Nats outfielder Ed Boland (1946), Phillies pitcher Clyde Smoll (1948–49), and Braves first baseman Clarence "Buck" Etchison (1951) all piloted at Rome. Smoll, making his managerial debut, led Rome to its first — and only — flag.

The 33-year-old Etchison contributed to the team with some sharp play around first, 11 homers, and a .275 batting average. He took over a team, however, with virtually no pro experience and was wise enough to foresee the consequences. At a preseason banquet he told Colonels fans: "The only way they're going to get experience is on the ball field.... You'll do us a favor if you let the players alone and ride me, if necessary.

"If I can't take it I've got no reason being here."

White Sox and Red Sox outfielder and former Red Sox overseer Shano Collins (1942), fiery Detroit, Phils, Yanks, and White Sox catcher Tony Rensa (1946–47), A's outfielder Gene Hasson (1948–49), Nats and Indians hurler Lloyd "Gimpy" Brown (1950), and future Phils Coach Dick Carter (1951) all managed Pittsfield.

Joseph Francis "Shano" Collins, along with Shoeless Joe Jackson and Oscar "Happy" Felsch, had played the outfield for the 1919 Black Sox (honestly, on his part, that is) and managed the Pittsfield Hillies in 1928–29. He was the only *former* major league pilot to work in the Can-Am. His Red Sox experience was pretty dismal, finishing sixth in 1930 and getting off to a horrendous 11–46 start (a .196 percentage!) in 1931 before being canned.

Former coal miner Tony Rensa, wrote Lee Allen, "was so sensitive about his bald pate that he fastened his cap to his head with great wads of chewing gum. Every time he threw off his mask to chase a high foul his cap remained on his head, and he was spared the indignity of titters from the crowd."

"He had a brother [Adam] that pitched for him," says "Packy" Rogers. "Wouldn't blacken your eye if he hit you."

Washington pitcher Walt Masters (1936) and Wally Schang (1939) managed at Ottawa; Braves catcher Bill "Crunchy" Cronin (1946) and Dick Carter (1949–50) at Schenectady; and Senators and A's flyhawk Jim McLeod oversaw the Rugmakers in Amsterdam (1948).

Bill Cronin's case illustrates a manager's need to be diplomatic and public relations minded — among other things.

The 43-year-old Cronin couldn't plead inexperience. A major league veteran, he'd managed Binghamton for two years and had even brought home the 1945 Eastern League pennant. But, according to the *Dorp Sporting News,* he was "a hair-trigger tempered individual" and soon ran into trouble locally.

"A lot of newspaper guys," recalls Guy Barbieri, "didn't think too much of Bill Cronin. . . . They felt he wasn't too friendly with them. The newspaper guys for the first year, they wanted to talk to the players, talk to the manager, and he'd say, 'I gotta go!' and he rubbed the sportswriters the wrong way. They sort of got down on him."

Indeed they did. "Bill may be a nice fellow in some ways," penned one local scribe, "but he simply doesn't have it as a manager. He taught his players little, if anything, didn't command their respect, used the 'poorest' strategy we have ever seen in professional baseball. The Blue Jays' absolute lack of spirit and teamwork was the fault of the manager, we feel."

There were other problems, to say the least. "He was bombed most of the time," recalls Blue Jays hurler Charley Baker, "Stole McNearney's Cadillac a couple of times. Well, he'd borrow it, go on a binge, and, Christ, they'd have the whole state looking for him.

"He had a favorite saying. We lost a lot of ballgames in '46, and he'd say, 'Well, the sun doesn't shine on the same dog's fanny every day.'

"Ol' Bill, he was something. A little banty rooster. He carried a chip on his shoulder. That was him. He'd jump up and down on almost anything."

All that — and a seventh place finish — will get you Lee Riley taking your job in 1947.

One manager never suited up — Rome's Bill Buckley. Bill wasn't your typical skipper anyway, having umpired in the Texas, South Atlantic, Western, Mississippi Valley, Ontario, and Eastern leagues. Buckley returned to the Can-Am League in 1938 to field-manage Rome following his frigid Nova Scotian exile.

"He never got in a uniform, [he managed with] a suit on," notes Colonels pitcher Hal White. "In a way he was sort of like [Connie Mack]. Thin frame. Tall. He didn't want to pay much."

"He looked more like Connie Mack than Connie Mack did," amplified Rome shortstop Howard "Red" Ermisch. "A high stiff collar and wore the same type of clothes. Wore a hat. Wore the same type of glasses, and he was very volatile. He was a very highstrung person.

"He used to have a bug on for a certain umpire named [Paul] Crouch. He used to really go with Crouch hammer and tongs. In fact, I can remember one ball game when we walked out on the field, and we were ready to play, and Buckley saw who the umpire was, and it was Crouch. He started [screaming], 'Murder! Murder! Terrible umpire!' They had to take him off the field and put him in jail!

"He was really something. I really liked him, though. He was a fine, old gentleman. I don't believe he was a very good manager. He was good for the players. He was good for that."

In 1939 Buckley became business manager of the Batavia Clippers in

Jim Cullinane, Glovers manager, received the 1949 MVP Award from Bill Evans of the *Gloversville Leader-Herald* as Pittsfield manager Gene Hasson (1948 MVP) and Glovers' president Bob Rothschild look on.

the new Pennsylvania–Ontario–New York League. He continued to be an irascible, but nonetheless oddly likeable individual. "He was a take-over type of guy," recalls Edward Dwyer, who helped organize that franchise. "He didn't get along with the directors. He didn't get along with the fans or with the people. He definitely knew what he was doing, and he also carried it that way. When he left he took the team station wagon. I think he figured he had more pay coming. He was sort of a finagler, but he was a nice guy to talk to, a gentleman all around."

Before we leave the topic of these Napoleons of the bus leagues, let's discuss the institution of player manager, a profession, like buggy-whip maker, that is nearly extinct. Mayo Smith, Eddie Sawyer, Lee Riley, and George McQuinn weren't the only playing managers in the circuit.

The practice, in the Can-Am as in many, many other minor loops, was certainly ingrained, going back literally to Day One. On the league's very first Opening Day, Watertown's pilot, Admiral Martin, knocked in the winning run with two out in the ninth versus Ottawa in a 7–6 contest.

Martin was more or less a fill-in, but there were some real stars performing in the dual role.

Three Rivers' Frenchy Bordagaray wasn't just Manager of the Year in

1946, he was MVP as well, pacing the circuit with a .363 average. "Cause I was still a big league player," Bordagaray insists to this day, "heck, I should have been."

Eddie Sawyer was batting champion in 1939 with a .369 pace, set the all-time league mark for doubles and finished second in the MVP balloting.

Pittsfield's veteran Gene Hasson was such a slick fielder when he was a rookie with Connie Mack's A's in the mid-1930s that an opposing player asked an umpire to inspect his glove. His career was clearly on the down side in Pittsfield, as he had just spent two lackluster seasons in the Piedmont League, but he captured the Can-Am Triple Crown in 1948 with 27 homers, 106 RBI's and a .368 average, and was named MVP. "He was a fat fella," remembers Guy Barbieri, "kind of chubby. I'll tell you he could hit that ball, though!"

Glovers manager–third baseman Jim Cullinane was 1949 MVP, with 91 RBI's and a .322 average. "I'm a little proud of that MVP," says Cullinane, "because the runner-up was Frank Malzone. I still mention that to people when they question whether I ever played ball."

He played for the "Mittens" for two seasons and went to the Albany Senators in 1942, 1947, and 1948. "When the 1942 season was over, Ralph Kiner and I were both bought from Albany," he recalls. "We were roommates and we got the word at the Hotel Ten Eyck where we stayed. The same telegram bought both of us. I went to spring training with Pittsburgh and I had enlisted in the Naval Air Corps, and I was called while I was in spring training."

"One fall [after the war]," recalls 1950 Glovers hurler John "Lefty" Coakley, "he was working out around his house, putting up storm windows, and a window fell on his throwing hand, his right hand, and he had the finger next to his small finger smashed. And he lost about half of his finger. Now, that affected Jim's throwing in the field. Unquestionably, the guy could hit, hit like hell, but that injury screwed his chances of becoming a major leaguer because he couldn't throw the ball to first base."

The year 1940 is indicative of the practice of player-manager. Oneonta's Lee Riley hit at a remarkable .340 pace. Amsterdam's Eddie Sawyer belted .329, Cornwall's Emil Graff hit .234, and Oswego's Art Funk hit .305, all while playing full time. Others contributed on a part-time basis. The Glovers' "Buster" Blakeney swatted .270 ("he was just a superb shortstop," says Jim Cullinane, "a regular Marty Marion"). "Cy" Morgan at Ottawa-Ogdensburg checked in with .301 mark. Utica's "Lefty" Jenkins hit .257 and pitched nine games besides. Even Rome's Admiral Martin was still at it, pitching in two games, with a decent 3.86 ERA.

In 1939, 5' 7", 160-pound Elmer Yoter creaked along part-time at the Glovers' hot corner. Yoter, an off-season butcher, hit .296 in 2,418 minor

Left: **Elmer Yoter, 1939 Glovers manager.** *Right:* **Ottawa manager Wally Schang, 1939.**

league games, but at age 39 was a mere cub compared to 49-year-old (actually very close to 50) Wally Schang who strapped on his shin guards and batted .327 in 44 games for Ottawa. Incredibly, he even caught both ends of three doubleheaders.

One would guess 1939 was Schang's last hurrah. Wrong. He caught ten games and hit .286 for Three Rivers in the Provincial League in 1940, went behind the plate for the 1942 Augusta Tigers of the South Atlantic League, for the 1943 Utica Braves of the Eastern League, and for the 1946–47 Marion club of the Class D Ohio State League. His last appearance came at the remarkable age of 57!

Schang, by the way, was chosen in 1939 to represent the Can-Am League — as a player — in what can only be called the Minor League's Major Fiasco of 1939.

The intentions were creditable, but the idea was basically half-baked. To mark the dedication of baseball's new Hall of Fame, the National Association was sponsoring a Minor League All-Star game in which the best player from each of 41 circuits would be sent to Cooperstown to compete in a gala contest between two teams dubbed the "Doubledays" and the "Cartwrights."

Sounds great, but many loops couldn't afford the honor, and most of those that could weren't about to rob one of their clubs of the services of its

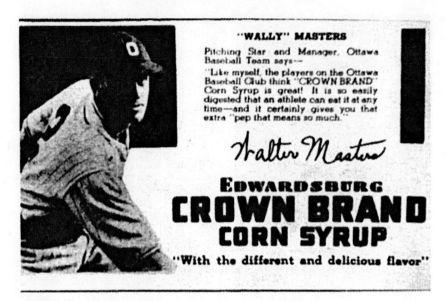

Ottawa newspaper advertisement, 1937.

best player. So on July 9, 1939, at Doubleday Field, a well-tailored but basically untalented band assembled for this unique event — unique because it was not only the first but also the last such festivity.

So Canadian-American Leaguers charged to the rescue. Can-Am pilots suited up and masqueraded as representatives of far-off circuits. Ancient Steve Yerkes, purportedly representing the East Texas League, hobbled around second. Ernie Jenkins, in a Coastal Plains uniform, and Elmer Yoter in Arizona-Texas garb, shared third. Eddie Sawyer disguised himself as a Northern Leaguer and patrolled right. Knotty Lee served as a coach for "Doubledays" manager Mike Kelley. (It was his proudest moment in the game), and Admiral Martin (masquerading as an Alabama-Florida Leaguer) and even ancient Amby McConnell (in Bi-State togs) did bench duty.

Father Martin gave the invocation for the new Minor League exhibit. He might as well have given a eulogy for this misbegotten Minor League All-Star game.

Anyway, back to business. Pitcher Wally Masters was just out of college when he had hurled for Walter Johnson in Washington in 1931 ("They didn't like him much. He wasn't tough enough. His toughest swear word was 'Jiminy Crickets!' you know"). Masters was president, business manager and field manager of the Ottawa Senators in 1936. "I pitched that year," he says, "and played other positions too, even the outfield." He later returned to the major league mound, working briefly in 1937 and 1939 for

Left-right: **Elmer Yoter, Steve Yerkes, Andy McConnell, Knotty Lee, Wally Schang, Eddie Sawyer and Admiral J. "Pepper" Martin at the National Association All-Star Game, 1939, Cooperstown, New York, Doubleday Field. (Courtesy Rome Sentinel.)**

the Philadelphia A's. In 1947, at age 40, he pitched for Ottawa in the Border League, winning both games of a doubleheader.

He also excelled in football, being named to the Knute Rockne All-American team at Penn State, playing and coaching for the Ottawa Rough Riders, and playing for the NFL's Philadelphia Eagles.

Many of these playing skippers were good enough to make the league's all-star squads, such as Art Funk and Eddie Sawyer in 1939, Eddie Sawyer in 1940, Lee Riley in 1941 and 1942, Bill Hornsby in 1942, Frenchie Bordagaray and Ben Huffman in 1946, Lou Rochelli and "Packy" Rogers in 1947, Gene Hasson in 1948, and Mayo Smith, George Scherger, and Jim Cullinane in 1949.

Former Rugmakers catcher Tony Ravish returned to the Can-Am ranks in 1947 as player-manager of the Quebec Alouettes, and for the 1948 season as well. His last playing season, though, was 1947 when he turned in a mere .232 average (he broke his leg in the opening game of 1948 and that was enough of a hint to hang up the mask.)

Ravish was a St. Lawrence College grad who later scouted for 35 years for the Red Sox and Giants (for whom he signed future NL prexy Bill White). Quebec wasn't Tony's first managerial outing: "I had managed in Peekskill, New York, before. I had a helluva year. That first year I won the

The 1948 Schenectady Blue Jays pitching staff. *Left to right:* **Tommy Lasorda, unknown, Charlie Baker, Sam Mayton, Harry "Duke" Markell, Al Oberman, Archie Luba, Ken Olveson. (Photo courtesy of Guy Barbieri.)**

pennant, won the playoffs. I was the all-star manager. I was smart as hell. The following year I wound up in the cellar in Quebec. So a year later I wasn't as smart, but you've got to have the horses."

Often the manager, whether playing or not, was faced with pressure to win from the "front-office." Tony was no exception. "They had 15 directors," he recalls. "The amusing thing was if we lost a ball game every one of them would call me: 'How could, Monsieur Raveesh, you lost?'

"'Well, we lost because we only got two runs, they got three.'

"You couldn't give them a long explanation."

The managers of that era were deficient in one vital area, according to Charley Baker: knowledge of how to handle pitching.

"I can remember when we had the playoffs with Amsterdam [in 1947], he recalls, "and [ex-A's pitcher George] Earnshaw was here [in his dual capacity as the Phillies Director of Instruction and Scout], and he said to me before one of the games, 'Is there anything I can help you with?' In those days, the managers didn't know anything about the pitchers. They were terrible. Riley didn't know anything about a pitcher. . . . They had no idea about when they were tired or to pull 'em out or any of that stuff. They were all hitters, and, you know, they didn't have a pitching coach like you have today.

"I said to Earnshaw, 'Yeah. There's one thing you can help me with. I'm having a little trouble picking a guy off first base.' So he says, 'Come on.' We walked out on the mound, and he says, 'Show me your motion and so forth.' And he says to me, 'It isn't much to correct that.' He straightened out my left foot toward the plate. I was pointing it out toward third base, and he straightened it out towards home plate, and he said, 'You'll be able to spin towards first a lot faster during the game. Try it. It'll take a little getting used to.'

"Well, I picked off Bunny Mick in the eighth inning in a crucial situation, and I picked off somebody else — and I hadn't picked anyone off all year.

"But it was just somebody showing you how to do it. You know, Riley had no idea, the least inkling in the world. Good manager, but he didn't know anything about pitchers. None of them did in those days. Christ, Riley would have pitched me every day! He said, 'If I ever had to win one game and I had anybody to pitch it would be you.' Well, in that Amsterdam series I pitched six out of the seven games. He didn't care.

"It wasn't his arm; it was mine."

Chapter 4

You've Got to Start Somewhere

> "Cut my veins and Dodger blue will flow. When I die,
> I want it on my tombstone: 'Dodger Stadium was his
> address, but every ballpark was his home.'"
> *Tommy Lasorda, 1976*

Nobody plays in the minor leagues thinking that's as far as he's going. Every kid harbors the dream that someway, somehow, he'll make it to the big leagues, get elected to the Hall of Fame—who knows, maybe even get a candy bar named after him.

Just making the show is like hitting the lottery, but obviously it can be done. A decent All-Star team could be made up of Can-Am graduates such as Bob Lemon, Al Rosen, Lew Burdette, Frank Malzone, Vic Raschi, Gus Triandos, Jim Lemon, John Blanchard and Bob Grim. Others were journeymen like Joe DeMaestri, Dick Littlefield or Carl Sawatski. Still more come up for the proverbial cup of java. A large number of Can-Am alumni advanced to the majors, although the progress of many was sidetracked by World War II or Korea.

Here are some of those who made it:

Oswego

In Oswego in 1938, future Hall of Fame hurler Bob Lemon wasn't yet a moundsman, pitching just one game. Instead he hit a creditable .312 as a shortstop-outfielder (it's hard to picture "Lem" as a shortstop, isn't it?).

"I was there the day that Mr. [Alva] Bradley brought him into the ballpark," says Cornwall's Barney Hearn, "and when his father and mother left he was crying, you know. He was just a young boy."

"They knew he could throw," adds Nets president Leonard Amdursky, "because the first basemen used to complain about their gloves. They came pretty fast."

"I was one of a bunch of kids who would throw extra batting practice

Jack McKeon, Gloversville Glovers, 1950.

to him," recalls Nets fan Bob O'Brien. "He was always trying to improve himself."

In Cleveland he would go 207–128, winning 20 games seven times. Lemon was named the *Sporting News* American League Pitcher of the Year in 1948, 1950, and 1954 and to seven All-Star squads.

Also at Oswego in '38 was Mike Naymick, another—albeit a less successful—Cleveland hurler. You'd notice Naymick in a hurry. He stood 6′ 8″ and wore a size 15 shoe. In 1938 he set batters on their ears, posting a Can-Am record of 230 K's in 213 innings.

Mike's first job was in a West Virginia steel mill. His pitching skills for the company nine helped him pull down a big 48 cents an hour. Both Detroit and Cleveland were after him, but he signed with the Tribe and pitched with Springfield in the Middle Atlantic League before joining Oswego.

Jimmie Foxx claimed Naymick threw faster than Rapid Robert Feller.

("I think I could," he quietly states.) He was, however, just a tad erratic, with a league record 37 wild pitches, along with 181 walks. On June 11, 1938, against Auburn, in a game lasting four hours and ten minutes, he issued 11 walks before leaving in the third. (Whatever was ailing the Czech-American Naymick was catching. A total of 47 bases on balls were recorded that game, 29 by the Nets and 18 by the Boulies.)

Mike's size helped keep him out of the service. ("My draft board told me if I was fighting on foreign soil and wore out my shoes, I'd be out of luck. I told them I could fight a Jap or a Nazi as well as anyone else, but they wouldn't take me.")

"He was high with the ball all the while," says Barney Hearn. "Lemon hit Naymick in the head when he was throwing to first one day. Naymick couldn't get out of the way. He had to fall flat on a throw to second base too. Big guy."

"No," argues Naymick, "That's not true. I was never hit in the head by a ball. Someone's trying to exaggerate. I moved pretty well around the mound."

Lemon did give Mike a headache of a different sort. "I'll never forget," says Naymick, "I had a no-hit ball game going, and he dropped a fly ball in the outfield, and he felt real bad about it. I think I'd walked a man and a run scored. I told him, 'Don't worry about it. It happens.'... Bob was a good competitor."

Not only enemy batters were unnerved by Naymick's blazing speed, so were his own catchers. "We finally got a young catcher named Lake, and I'll never forget," recalls Naymick. "I was throwing the ball so hard that he was afraid, and I said, 'Don't be afraid. You'll get used to it,' and in the game I threw a ball right down through the heart of the plate, right around the knees. And it went right between his hands and hit him in the mask.

"I said, 'Oh, what happened?'

"He said, 'Mike, I saw the ball just the time it got to the plate and after that it just disappeared. I just didn't see it.' They had been talking about how fast I threw. Maybe he was a little more afraid in anticipation than he might have been."

And it wasn't just Class C backstops that were edgy. "I remember one catcher [in Cleveland], Hank Helf. I was pitching, and he came in about the third or fourth inning, and he said, 'Hey, you big so-and-so. I've got every sponge that I can put in this glove, and my hand is swollen up like a beefsteak right now!'"

Big Mike still is at a loss to explain why he never made it big. "I don't know," he reflects, "I'll tell you. I'd get there with Cleveland, and hell, they wouldn't let me pitch.... I don't know why.... You lose confidence. You know, when I look back right how, I'm just so disgusted with myself for not being more aggressive and telling them, 'Hey! Either pitch me or get rid of me or something.'

"I could have done a lot for that ball club."

In 1939 the Nets featured All-Star second baseman Frank Skaff, who had played briefly in Brooklyn and then with the A's during the war. One of the few Syrian-Americans ever in the majors, in 1945 with Baltimore of the International League he paced the minors with 38 homers. In 1966 he managed the Tigers, stepping in from the Detroit coach's box.

Pittsfield

In 1946 Pittsfield Electrics third baseman Al "Flip" Rosen ripped the cover off the ball, leading the circuit in homers and RBI's while batting at a .323 pace.

"He was kind of a team leader with the players here," recalls Paul Tamburello. "They wanted a pay raise, but we couldn't give it. We met on the roof of the building, of our office."

Perhaps not surprisingly, Rosen retired as an active player following a dispute with Cleveland management over his salary.

"I can remember Al Rosen," says Schenectady's Charley Baker, who seemed to be one of the few hurlers in the circuit not impressed by Mr. Rosen. "I remember him like it was yesterday. In fact, you know, he had a big reputation, and I can close my eyes and hear [manager] Lee Riley saying, 'Stick it in his ear!' and that was the whole solution. You knocked him down, threw him three curves, and bye-bye Al. He was gone."

"Flip" almost packed it in at Pittsfield. He had to hustle to get into baseball in the first place. No scouts came knocking on his door. He flubbed a try-out with the Red Sox. Then he caught on with the Tribe. After returning from the Navy in 1946, he was promptly cut by Cleveland's Wilkes-Barre and Harrisburg clubs. Scout Laddie Placek assigned Al to Pittsfield: "You'll play there for sure."

But when Rosen got to the Electrics he was again handed a back-up role. Farm director "Buzz" Wetzel happened to be in town and gruffly told all hands: "Anybody who doesn't want to play for Pittsfield can have his release."

Rosen wanted out. When Wetzel saw Al's previous stats, he balked, but Al persisted mightily, and Wetzel gave in.

When Placek learned that Rosen had been released he rushed all over town looking for him, finding him venting his ire on a pinball machine. "Laddie stood beside me," recalled the player they called "the Hebrew Hammer," "and kept repeating, 'You'll be a great player some day, a big star. Stick it out.' He said it over and over. Finally I said, 'Okay.'"

The rest, as they say, was history. Also from Wahconah Park came pitchers Brooks Lawrence and Dick Tomanek, slugging outfielder Jim Lemon, and catcher Hal Naragon. Lawrence was a college football teammate of Jonathan Winters and still managed to win 19 games for the Cards in 1956. He threw the first official intentional walk in history on April 12, 1955. (Prior to that records were not kept on intentional passes.) Lemon coached for the Twins and managed the Senators in 1968. Tomanek's father promised he would walk the 20 miles to Cleveland's Municipal Stadium if his son pitched there. He did. Dick beat the Tigers but won only nine more games lifetime. Naragon backstopped for ten seasons for Cleveland, Washington, and Minnesota and also coached for the Twins and Tigers.

Oneonta

The 1947 Oneonta Red Sox boasted three future big leaguers: Dick Littlefield, Dale Long and Ike Delock. Littlefield pitched for a record ten major league teams. "I've never seen a runner like him," recollects Oneonta catcher Steve Salata. "He was odd because he used to run, and the back of his feet would kick him right in the fanny! I know it sounds ridiculous, but it's the truth, and not just the one side but both sides!"

Long, who hit in a Can-Am League record 28 consecutive contests, homered in eight straight for Pittsburgh in 1956, a mark that stood until Don Mattingly broke it in 1987. Long's other claim to fame came in 1958 when he caught two games lefthanded for the Cubs.

"I was in the Cincinnati organization and Fred Flag released me. He said I'd never make the big leagues. That was in 1947. I made the big leagues in 1951. [After I was released] I worked out with Lynn of the New England League. We played an exhibition game with Boston and I had two doubles. So the Red Sox signed me and sent me to Oneonta. . . .

"What a bus we had in Oneonta! You had to go like this [lean forward] to go uphill.

"Dibble, that was the name of the driver. One time coming back from Schenectady, we were pelting him with wads of paper, spitballs. [Manager] Red Marion wasn't with us. He drove over with his wife. Dibble pulled over and said, 'Cut the _____ out!' He wouldn't drive any further unless we stopped. So we did, and Dibble started up again.

"Rrrh. Rrrh. Rrrh.

"And there we stayed."

Hot-tempered Ike Delock, believe it or not, has the longest tenure for any hurler in Fenway history with his 11 seasons on the mound for the Sox.

The 1949 Oneonta squad was led by 5' 4½" Eddie Popowski, a former House of David player who later coached for the Red Sox, and featured shortstop Joe DeMaestri, catcher Sammy White and third baseman Frank Malzone. White once walloped a home run off the legendary Satchel Paige and kissed home plate in gratitude.

The bow-legged Malzone, who walloped an amazing 26 triples in 1949, married an Oneonta girl. Frank holds a number of unique honors. In 1969 he was voted the All-Time Red Sox third baseman, easily trouncing then 11-year-old Wade Boggs. And in 1952 he finished second in American League Rookie of the Year balloting (Okay, so that meant he lost 23–1 to Tony Kubek. I was hoping you wouldn't look that up).

Oneonta also produced second baseman Ken Aspromonte, shortstop Austin Knickerbocker, outfielders Vance Dinges and Earl Rapp, pitchers Irv Medlinger, Stan Partenheimer, Bob Smith, Emmett O'Neill, and Dick Fowler, and Bosox catcher Eddie McGah.

The only .400 batter in Can-Am annals was outfielder Austin Knickerbocker who walloped the ball at a torrid .406 pace in 1941. The Duke University alumnus got sidetracked by the war, although he managed to appear briefly for the 1947 A's.

"Austin Knickerbocker," contends current Oneonta president Sam Nader, "was the best hitter ever to wear an Oneonta uniform. He would hit line drives to all parts of the field."

"I signed my first contract with the Ottawa Senators," says Knickerbocker, "but I didn't make the team and they sent me to Wausau, Wisconsin, in the Northern League, and I did good enough to get back.

"We held our spring training in Ogdensburg — one of the northernmost towns in New York State. I was a raw rookie, and they only had one game that I recall. I remember hitting three doubles off the left field wall. The next day I found myself on a bus for Wausau, Wisconsin. I couldn't believe that, but I guess I wasn't too adept on the field anywhere, and they didn't know where to play me, so they sent me on."

Dick Fowler's greatest moment came on May 22, 1945, when he no-hit the Browns. "Of [all] the ... no-hitters in the history of the American League," noted the *Sporting News,* "Fowler's had to be the strangest.

"The 6–5 righthander had been out of the Canadian Army only three weeks and was 25 to 30 pounds overweight. He had worked only 11⅔ innings and been pounded for 20 hits, 13 of them in a seven inning effort against the White Sox four days earlier.

"But against the St. Louis team he was invincible..."

His gem was the only instance where a no-hitter was a hurler's only victory of the season. It was also the first by a Canadian.

Fowler, a member of the Canadian Baseball Hall of Fame, settled in

Oneonta in 1946. Employed as a night clerk at the Oneonta Community Hotel for nine years, he died in 1972.

Schenectady

Schenectady's most famous alumnus was future Dodger manager Tommy Lasorda.

"I was there nearly a month," wrote Lasorda in his autobiography, "before my family knew where I was. I couldn't even pronounce Schenectady, much less spell it, so I wrote my family that I was ten miles outside Albany. They thought that was the name of the town, Ten Miles Outside Albany. Only later did I realize that they weren't too sure where Albany was either."

In 1948 young Lasorda was a nearly svelte Phillies farmhand who could throw hard but couldn't quite get the horsehide over the plate, walking 153 in 198 innings. He had a pile of trouble in other departments as well.

Lasorda, for example, had a few problems with unsavory local characters. During the off-season he took a job managing one of Schenectady's largest bowling alleys. He soon quit when he learned it was a front for a bookie joint in the basement.

In Gloversville late in the season, Lasorda was approached in a local pool hall, and offered $100 to throw a game. "Get outta here before I kill you," he growled.

Staked to a six-run first inning lead, Tommy promptly blew it and was showering by the second frame. On the way out his benefactor whispered to him: "You should have taken the money." Tommy went after him with a vengeance.

He could pitch when he was in the strike zone, however. Against Amsterdam on May 31, 1948, he fanned 25 in 15 innings (he also walked 12 and hit 1, while winning 6–5). It was a hell of a game. Lasorda fanned outfielder George Morehouse six times in seven plate appearances. In every inning from the second through the ninth, Tommy got the final out with a "K." In one stretch he punched out six in a row. Yet Lasorda almost lost in the 12th as he allowed two runs, but his teammates promptly tied the score. In the 15th, Tommy singled in the winning run.

You'd think that would be enough heroics for a season, but the left-hander (you just knew he'd be lefthanded, didn't you?) struck out 15 and 13 in his next two starts. The 25 whiffs were a league mark, shattering the nine-inning standard of 22 set in 1942 by Glovers southpaw Earl Jones against Rome.

"Tommy," reminisces Guy Barbieri, "was cocky. I mean when he got

Tommy Lasorda with unidentified teammate, 1948. (Courtesy of Guy Barbieri.)

out there, don't talk to him about anything. He wanted to strike them out. He wanted to strike out every one of them, and he'd come in and he'd say, 'Why that so-and-so, I'll get him next time!' And he was tough, and his ambition he'd say was, 'I'll make the Majors some day.'

"Tommy would fight at the drop of a hat. He wouldn't take any guff from anybody. If there was ball players fighting, he'd be the first one in the scuffle. He'd be the first one in anything."

"He used to coach third base when he wasn't pitching," recalls Eber Davis, then a young Glovers fan, "and when he would shout you could hear him all over the park, with that raucous voice of his. My mother couldn't stand him. She must be rolling over in her grave thinking of him with the Dodgers."

"Tommy was a real dummy when he was here," contends fellow hurler Charley Baker. "He didn't know enough to come out of the rain, but he sure knows now. He was a good pitcher. He had a curve ball that would drop right off the table, but he was 'smart' and a wise guy. One of those types. He and [pitcher] Duke Markell teamed up together, and, boy, they were something else! Nobody liked them.

"In fact, probably the biggest story about him was that he missed the bus going to Quebec, and so he went ahead and got a yellow cab and told him to charge it to McNearney and rode it all the way to Quebec, and McNearney almost died when he got the bill, you know. He was cheap anyway. It was more money than Lasorda's monthly pay, I guess. [Mc-Nearney] almost died. He didn't go for that at all. Should have stayed home I guess. . . .

"Tommy was flamboyant, cocky and aggravating. You name it."

Lasorda's combativeness stemmed in part from edginess and insecurity, as his 9–12 mark wasn't a world beater. Yet he did pitch well against Ed Head's Three Rivers Royals, and Head recommended to the Dodgers that they take a chance on Lasorda. They drafted him for $4,000.

"I was thrilled," says Lasorda, "it was one thing not to be good enough to play for the sixth-place Philadelphia Phillies, it was far more exciting not to be good enough to play for the Dodgers. . . I didn't realize it at the time, but I had just married the Dodgers for life."

Besides Lasorda the Blue Jays also sent up hurlers Barney Schultz (future Nankai Hawks and St. Louis Cardinals pitching coach), Steve Ridzik (the youngest Blue Jay ever and the first to go to the majors), Harry "Duke" Markell, Angelo LiPetri and Lynn Lovenguth, infielder Bobby Micelotta, and catcher Carl Sawatski.

The Paris-born Markell pitched three no-hitters in the minors. He set the all-time Can-Am strikeout mark of 280 in 1948, and later became a policeman, pounding a beat in the romantic Bronx. He hurled two one-hitters, and against Rome in August fanned 21 but was also capable of walking eight or ten per game.

"Markell was the same way [as Lasorda]," adds Charlie Baker. "I remember one night when [Lee] Riley'd run out of pitchers. Everybody had pitched their arms off, and a few of them were hurt or something, and he asked for volunteers, and Markell says 'Well, you want to win tonight, Skipper, let the Duke pitch.' So he put him in. It was against Oneonta. Jeez. They rocked him terrible. Something like 16 to nothing. He kept looking at the dugout. Riley would go back and have another cigarette. 'You wanted to pitch, you got it!'

"He was a heck of a pitcher. He had all kinds of talent."

Sawatski, an outfielder for the Jays, became president of the Texas League but that didn't stop the Phillies organization from cutting him loose in 1946. "I was rooming with Carl when Bill Cronin released him down in Oneonta," recalls Baker, "and he told Cronin that he'd go farther than he ever did, and he went home and got in shape, and I guess he did. That guy could hit a ball a mile. His problem was weight, but making a catcher out of him did it, I guess, got him slimmed right down."

Lynn Lovenguth's debut was particularly gutsy. Inserted against Oneonta with the sacks loaded, he struck out the side. In four innings he fanned eight and gave up but a single safety, then won the contest by driving in two runs. Later that season he came within one pitch of a perfect game.

Danny Carnevale of the 1937 Cornwall Bisons.

Rome

The Colonels promoted pitchers Hal White ("He looked like you ought to be able to knock his ears off, but we didn't" — Mike Naymick); Dale Matthewson; and Lynn Lovenguth. White, who pitched for Rome in 1937–38, led the International League in won-lost percentage and ERA before going on to 12 big league seasons, mostly with Detroit.

"I got out of high school in June," he recollects, "that's why I didn't play much in '37. I got a call from the club in Rome, New York, and so I talked it over with my Dad, and he says, 'Well, if you like baseball that much, go up ahead. They want to sign you? Sign!' So I signed for $100 a month on the window of a pool hall. Quite an experience!"

Did Hal get a bonus? "No sir!" he answers emphatically, "At that time you were lucky to get a salary, but I never regretted it."

The Colonels didn't either as they sold White to Buffalo for a tidy $1,500.

Lynn Lovenguth, who pitched briefly for the Cards and Phils, put in three years in the Can-Am, starting from leading the league with 16 losses in 1946 for Schenectady to pacing it with 21 victories for Rome in 1948.

Perth-Cornwall

In 1937, Perth-Cornwall third baseman Danny Carnevale ("a pretty good player, a hustler," according to teammate Emil Graff) drove in 100 runs while clubbing the ball at a .354 pace. It was the first of four 100 RBI seasons in the low minors. A Buffalo native, Carnevale was signed as a Canisius College sophomore by the Bisons. He never went beyond Buffalo as a player or manager, but surfaced as a coach for the 1970 Kansas City Royals. He also scouted for the A's, Orioles, Royals, and Indians. All told he's spent over a half-century in the game.

Cornwall

The 1939 Cornwall Maple Leafs were very productive and developed outfielders Frank Colman and Whitey Platt, and pitchers Dick Fowler and Phil Marchildon. Marchildon ("He was one of those eager beavers, give me the ball you know," says Emil Graff) and Fowler tied for the AL lead in losses in 1946.

Compared to what happened to Phil in August 1944 that wasn't so bad. Serving as a tail gunner aboard a Halifax bomber in the Canadian Air Force, Marchildon was shot down over the Kiel Canal. He parachuted 18,000 feet into the sea. Of his seven-man crew only two survived. Four hours later, he was "rescued" by a Danish fisherman who turned him in to the Germans, and for nine months he was interned in Sagen, Silesia. Remarkably, before 1945 was out Phil was back with the A's. He'd lost 30 pounds and was really too drained to pitch, but Connie Mack staged a special "Marchildon Night" and 35,000 fans turned out to watch him valiantly go three innings.

"I was up in north Ontario," recalls Marchildon of his start in organized baseball, "and I had played for the Simco Mines, but I moved up to Clayton Mines near Sudbury. I played three years, 36–37–38, up there. My old manager Dan Howley was always trying to get me in with the Toronto Maple Leafs, and I finally got a letter that they were running a tryout camp. I had just pitched a playoff game, but I drove down there anyway.

"Nobody came around after the game, so I drove back up north. It turned out they wanted me though, and they tracked me down and signed me."

"I never had arm trouble, but I had a soreness in my elbow when I got to Cornwall. I went right to the manager.

"It turned out I had an abscessed tooth and the pain went right to the elbow. I went to the dentist and sure enough the pain went away. I won seven games in the 27 days I was with the team." (Keep that story in mind when we move over into the next exciting chapter.)

In 1983 Marchildon was one of the first inductees into Toronto's Canadian Baseball Hall of Fame.

By a strange coincidence, Marchildon, Fowler, Coleman, and Platt all played their very first professional game on the same Sunday for manager Steve Yerkes. Platt homered over the left field fence in his first pro at-bat.

Brockville

The 1936 Brockville Pirates promoted Lithuanian-Canadian pitcher Joe Krakauskas to Washington in 1937. He pitched seven seasons for the Nats and Indians. "He was a big, rawboned lefthander," says Emil Graff, "very good fast ball."

Joe Cambria signed Krakky in 1935, and Clark Griffith was so impressed by the kid's raw talents that he kept him around until December, throwing every day except when it flurried. "He'll make a pitcher some day," swore Griffith. Joe went to 1936 spring training with the big club, impressing most observers with his talent with a knife and fork, but on taking the mound for batting practice, he promptly drilled teammate Red Kress in the "groin" with a fastball.

"If I never see that wild man again it will be all right by me," growled rapidly aging boy-wonder pilot Bucky Harris. They shipped him as far away as they could, which happened to be Brockville.

Stellar work in the Can-Am earned Krakauskas a promotion to Trenton at season's end. He met with curious club officials in his room at the Hotel Milner.

"How's your arm, Joe?" asked business manager Mel Murphy, who had a package of baseballs under his arm.

Joe replied, "How is my arm? Let me see one of those balls."

With that he went into a full wind up, let loose, and hurled the sphere right through the nearest wall. On the other side a woman screamed, and the two visitors left in stunned silence hoping to forget the incident—and they did, until getting the bill from the hotel, that is.

Krakauskas possessed blinding speed. He had 216 K's in 192 innings with Brockville, but walked 166. When he reached Washington, catchers actually refused to work behind the plate when he was on the slab.

But his wildness drove manager Bucky Harris and his teammates crazy. It was the classic case of a talented but uncontrolled young arm. Infielders hated to play behind him, as he flung ball after ball. Harris finally wailed, "He's so pitiful he depresses the rest of the team. The guys won't talk to him."

Mike Naymick, if you're reading this, I'd like you to know, it could have been worse.

Smiths Falls

The Smiths Falls Beavers developed Pirate pitcher Xavier (Mr. X) Rescigno, a Manhattan College graduate who had the all-time best season ERA in the league with a 1.56 mark in 1937. He also completed all 22 of his starts that year. "He wasn't big," remarks Emil Graff, "but he was smart."

Utica

The Utica Braves sent first baseman Reggie Otero (a.k.a. Regino Jose Otero y Gomez) to the 1945 Chicago Cubs, where he hit .391 in 14 games. Reggie paced the Can-Am League in batting in 1942 with a .364 mark. A star jai-alai player in his native Cuba, Otero later managed the Havana Sugar Kings, coached for the Reds and Indians and scouted for the Indians and Dodgers. In 1983 he was elected to the Cuban Baseball Hall of Fame.

Ogdensburg

The Ogdensburg Colts graduated outfielder Maurice "Bomber" Van Robays, who paced all of organized baseball with his 43 homers in 1937. As a rookie, he set the N.L. on fire in 1940, driving in 116 runs for Pittsburgh. After that, the former Detroit area semipro player was bothered by eye problems, went into the service, and never got back on track.

How Van Robays, one of the few players of Flemish ancestry, got to Ogdensburg was a remarkable story. He always dreamt of joining the Tigers and in fact signed with them. In 1935 Van Robays played briefly for two of their farm teams, but was felled by influenza, then by pneumonia. "I was as tall than as I am now," he said as a Pirate star, "but had nothing but skin all over my bones. I was pretty weak and the slightest exertion used me up. It didn't look like I would ever play ball again."

He was out of pro ball for two seasons. "I was through school at the time," Van Robays recalled, "and decided to give baseball one more trial before I would go on to something else. Besides, there weren't too many jobs open for a young fellow and I always loved to play ball. A chap I knew in Detroit who always said I was a hitter, suggested I go to Ogdensburg, New York, telling me they were looking for players. So I went there, and told them I was looking for a job, and they let me try out for the club. I started hitting right away, and soon I was the standout hitter of the league."

He wasn't boasting. Not only did he establish the all-time Can-Am record with 43 homers, but he crashed seven more in seven postseason playoff games. He led the circuit in runs, RBI's, hits, extra base hits, total bases, doubles, and batting average. He finished third in triples.

Not bad for a former 97-pound weakling.

"They had a short left field fence, maybe 260," recalls Graff. "They had some trees outside of that fence, and I used to needle him when he come up to home plate. Of course, we were pretty good friends, and I told him, 'Hell, if I played over here, I'd hit 'em out too.' I wasn't a home run hitter.

"And he'd hit one over those trees and say 'Hit one like that!' He could hit 'em. He was big and he was powerful."

"In a close game in the ninth inning," remembers Carrol Belgard, "Knotty Lee would say, 'Hit one out of the park, and I'll give you an extra five,' He'd hit one, and Knotty would say 'Give him five, give him five.'"

Van Robays died in 1965, "still bitter," opined the *Sporting News,* "over his failure to make the Tigers after a brilliant career on the sandlots of the Motor City."

Gloversville-Johnstown

The Glovers came up with a pathetically small amount of playing talent considering their longevity in the circuit: outfielder Chuck Harmon, Nats catcher Frank Sacka, and Browns pitchers Hal Hudson and Earl Jones. Hudson, Sacka, and Jones were up for just a handful of games.

On September 3, 1942, Jones hurled one of the great games in Can-Am annals. Pitching at Berkshire Park, Earl not only no-hit the Rome Colonels, he smashed Ottawa's Joe Carr's nine-inning strikeout mark of 18 by whiffing 22. "Fans were gaga from the seventh inning on," exclaimed the *Herald.* They carried Jones from the mound and took up a collection for him, which showed where their enthusiasm stopped, as it only netted $70, even with one fellow putting in $22 (one for each K) himself.

Two other Glovers were notable even if they didn't make the majors as players. First baseman Joe Lutz coached for Cleveland and became the first American ever to manage in Japan, when he skippered the Hiroshima Karp in 1975. Reserve catcher Jack McKeon piloted the Kansas City Royals, Oakland Athletics, and San Diego Padres and also served as general manager of the Padres.

McKeon was a $225 a month reserve catcher in 1950. It wasn't exactly a great year. He took one pitch in the noggin and had to be stitched up. He tore up his knee at second base, and nearly got blown up as a result. The team told him to go home to South Amboy, New Jersey, and recuperate. They wanted him to take a Friday trian, but he didn't feel up to it and hung around town an extra day. As Jack was reading the paper the next morning, he saw his home town had been racked by a munitions explosion. Thirty-three were killed. The train got in just two minutes before the blast, and "Trader Jack" would have been 34 (and I don't mean his uniform number).

"I remember one night I was in the bullpen," says Glovers pitcher John Coakley, "and Jack and I were down there, and the mosquitoes were so damn bad that night we started a smudge fire, you know, and the smoke got so damn bad, it permeated the whole ballpark, and the umpire stopped playing the game and made us put out the goddam fire.

"He couldn't hit the ball too good, and he didn't run that well. My plain appraisal of Jack was he was just a mediocre minor league ball player, but he was one of the most personable and intelligent individuals I ever met, and he was glib. He could talk to anyone. I think at that particular point he became a student of the game, and he impressed a lot of people..."

Ottawa-Ogdensburg

The pennant-winning 1940 Senators developed pitcher Bill Peterman, catcher Homer "Dixie" Howell, hurler Paul Masterson (who won 19 games for the Ott-O's including both ends of a June twinbill), infielders Hal Marnie and George Jumonville, and pitcher John "Specs" Podgajny, who advanced directly from the Ott-O's to the Phils that year. It wasn't so much that they were a strong team, although they were. It was that their parent club, the Phillies, was so putrid and their farm system so small, that they were willing to grab any player, anywhere, that looked halfway decent for a tryout.

John Sigmund Podgajny was the best of the bunch. He'd originally been scouted by the Browns organization, but said "no thanks." They offered him $60 a month, but as he was making $100 a month playing semipro, he thought better of it.

Podgajny was hot-headed and often ejected from games. "I remember one time," he recalled, "when I was pitching for the Phillies and we were playing the Cubs at Wrigley Field. I got myself into a jam and Merrill May, our third baseman, walked over to me and said something about not giving up.

"I misunderstood him, because I thought he said I was giving up and not giving my best. Anyway, I grabbed him by the neck and was ready to work him over until some of the guys separated us. May was the most surprised guy on the field. And I felt pretty silly."

Quebec

Because of Quebec's generally independent history (even when they had a Giants agreement in 1947–48, the parent club supplied relatively little), players just didn't advance to the majors. There were a few exceptions, and while his time upstairs was brief, it was appropriate that Roland Gladu was one of those who made it. For if anyone was "Monsieur Baseball" in Quebec Province it was Gladu, player-manager of the Quebec Athletics, who went up to play third for the 1944 Boston Braves.

Gladu, a Montreal native who turned pro at 15, was a veteran Provincial League player in both its organized baseball and outlaw phases. He was also one of the 15 Mexican League jumpers of 1946. Gladu later scouted for the Milwaukee Braves. Author Merritt Clifton termed him "probably the most popular Quebec player ever before Le Grand Orange, Rusty Staub."

In 1949–1950 Quebec featured veteran pitcher Harold "Moose" Erickson, who led the league both years in strikeouts and in ERA in 1950. Erickson started in pro ball way back in 1939 with Lewiston in the Pioneer League, spending several seasons in the Reds organization. Syracuse peddled him to Quebec in 1949. In 1952 Quebec sold him to the Dallas Eagles, and in 1952 he was Texas League Pitcher of the Year, winning 20. The 6′ 5″, 230-pound "Moose" finally made it to the Tigers in 1953 as a 33-year-old rookie, going 0–1 with a 4.73 E.R.A. in 18 games.

Quebec, toward the end of its league tenure, was a team that loaded up with veteran ball players. Players who had enjoyed *previous* major league experience included Frank McCormick, George McQuinn, third baseman "Picollo Pete" Elko, and outfielders Charlie Small and Garland "Butch" Lawing.

Three Rivers

Three Rivers promoted Italian-born A's first baseman Henry Biasatti (Hank was a guard with the 1946 Toronto Huskies of the Basketball Association of America); shortstop Billy Hunter ("always was a good fielder"; says hurler Ed Yasinski, "stick wasn't too good"); Brooklyn hurler Jean Pierre Roy (who hurled a seven inning no-hitter versus Amsterdam in 1941 and later became French-language broadcaster for the Montreal Expos. He jumped to the Mexican League in 1946 to escape the Dodger bench); Pirates manager Larry Shepherd; pitcher George Witt; infielder Danny O'Connell; Cincinnati coach George Scherger, and St. Louis Browns outfielder Pete Gray, whose gritty exploits we will deal with in a later chapter.

Trois Rivieres (Three Rivers) 1947 program cover.

Amsterdam

Not surprisingly, the Yankees Amsterdam farm team supplied the majors with the most talent.

Pitchers were a specialty, as they learned to contend with the very short—but high—left field fence at Mohawk Mills Park.

In 1940 there was Frank "Spec" Shea (11–4; 3.94 ERA), who in 1949 would go 14–5 as a Yankee rookie, win the All-Star Game and two world series decisions against Brooklyn.

Shea was signed off a Watertown semipro team by Paul Krichell, even though, he was underage. He was allowed to finish out the season, and on his 18th birthday he "officially" turned pro.

His first assignment was Amsterdam. "I had a good record in that

Quebec's Hal Erickson.

Collegiate League," he recalls. "You know, everyone was saying, 'Oh, gee. He's a hot prospect.' And the first game I pitched against Gloversville, and they jocked me real bad. They got eight runs in the first inning, and I couldn't get anybody out. I said, 'Professional ball's real tough. . . . I better pack it up and go home.'

"Eddie Sawyer was our manager, and he found out. I was over in the clubhouse packing and he sent someone over to get me and talk to me. He said 'You're not going no place,' and he explained all the things that could happen, you know. If you leave, you're going to get a blacklist from baseball, this and that. So I said, 'Well, alright. I don't know what I'm going to do though.'

"So the next time out I pitched against Gloversville on their home court, and I think it was a two-hitter I pitched and shut them out. And that got me on my way, but the first game I pitched I thought, 'Oh, gee! This is tough.' Like he [Sawyer] said to me after the game, 'Your rhythm, your coordination, was way off. You weren't pitching. You were just aiming and throwing.'

"They had an agreement with me. If I stayed with the club until July 4th, I was going to get a bonus, and I'm sitting in the Hotel Amsterdam [that night] and Eddie Sawyer came down and he said 'I hope you get it because you've done a good job for us so far.' We're sitting there, and he come over and he said 'Did you hear anything yet?' I said, 'No. It's getting near 12 o'clock, and if I don't get it by then, I don't.'

Eddie Sawyer (bottom center).

"So Krichell came walking down the stairs, and he come over and sat right across from us, and I said, 'That's the guy, Ed. I don't know what he's going to do, but I'm going to wait till 12 o'clock, and if he don't say nothing then I'm going to bed.' So, Jesus, about five minutes to 12, he come walking over, and he said, 'Well, we're supposed to talk about a bonus here today.' And Sawyer says, 'Jeez, I hope you're gonna give the kid a bonus. He's helping the ball club, and this and that.' He [Krichell] says, 'Well, he's coming along. He's got to improve and get a little better than that.' Jeez, the Yankees hated to give you anything at that time, so he finally said, 'We're going to take a chance. I'm gonna give him the bonus.' He gave me a check for $250. You're talking about a lot of money. Christ, you'd think it was a big deal!

"You know, it was a funny thing. I was up in Watertown, and the last game I pitched up there I pitched a no-hitter, and he [Krichell] came in to see me and says, 'Jesus, I suppose you think you did a helluva job.' I said, 'Hey. If I can pitch a no-hitter against grammar school kids it would put a feather in my hat. I feel pretty proud of it!' He says, 'Ahhh. That team you pitched against has been on the road, travelling for two days. They didn't get no sleep last night, that's why!'

"They'd never give you no credit.

"That was the last game I pitched up there, and I came home, and I said, 'Jeez, if they don't sign me, I'm going to sign with the Red Sox. But I wanted to play with the Yankees above all, you know, always talked about playing with them."

Shea wasn't exaggerating about Krichell denigrating his work. Back in the late '40s the old scout told the New York *Mirror*'s Dan Parker in great detail how he signed Shea. First Krichell claimed to have had great difficulty in even seeing Spec pitch (no doubt, to cover his underage signing). Watertown, said Krichell, had "one of those glow worm lighting systems with the lights about eight feet off the ground," and on top of that the Collegians' opponent, the Mohawk Colored Giants, were two and one-half hours late in arriving and blitzed out of their minds.

"Between his [Shea's] blinding speed," the old scout continued, "the poor lighting system and the temporary blindness of the Giants, he struck out 22 men and allowed a few hits [oh, really!]. I lost no time in signing him to a Yankee contract after the game [do tell], which was over in jig time [as Al Campanis might remark]."

"Well, I'll tell you, I loved that town," Shea still says of Amsterdam. "That was a real nice town to play in. I lived in the Hotel Amsterdam, a dollar a night, and it worked out real good. In those days we were getting $85 a month. They had these different restaurants that had a meal ticket. They'd punch it out, and, Jesus, you'd have to add everything up what you ordered, so you wouldn't go over, because you were only allowed so much a week. I think a ticket used to cost $7.50, and, Christ, that had to last us a week. It was tough, I'll tell you, on $85 a month. By the time you pay for your food, your hotel, and your clothing and buy a newspaper and pay your dues at the clubhouse and buy sweat shirts and stuff that you had to have you'd be lucky if you could get by. In fact, I got $5 a week sent by my family to survive. You couldn't make it. I'll tell you it was a tough deal."

Vic Raschi was on the 1941 Amsterdam roster, going 10–6. His .667 major league lifetime percentage was one of the best ever. In 1949–50–51 "the Springfield Rifle" won 21 games each year, and in 1951 led the circuit in strikeouts. "My best pitch," he once contended modestly, "is anything the batter lines or pops up in the direction of Rizzuto."

"I would take the ball players up to my camp once a year and put on a feed for them," recalls Herb Shuttleworth. "They only made $80 or $100 a month. They lived on hot dogs and Cokes. Hot dogs and cokes. Some of these boys had never seen a camp, seen a lake. I remember Vic Raschi went on the lake in a rowboat. He didn't know how to row, but he sat in that boat for hours."

"I was just out of William and Mary College, and lived in the YMCA for $6 a week," said Raschi just before his death in 1988. "I got a meal ticket

Scout Paul Krichell (wearing glasses) surveys talent in Amsterdam, N.Y. (Courtesy Amsterdam *Recorder* — Val Webb photo.)

from some restaurant in town for $9 a week.... We travelled in a school bus. I think the only one who had a chance to lie down was the starting pitcher for the next day and he had the big wide open seat in the back of the bus."

"Vic Raschi," adds Spencer Fitzgerald, "was probably one of the nicest personalities. He was a wonderful guy to be around."

Also on the 1941 staff was lefthander Bill Kennedy, who would play for five big league clubs, and tall righthander Karl Drews, who'd hurl for four. Drews was killed at age 43 when a drunk driver mowed him down as he was signalling for help for his daughter's stalled car.

The same year Joe Page, the future Yankee relief star, spent two weeks with the Rugmakers. He didn't pitch for them, however. He was there being rehabilitated, and after a spell Spencer Fitzgerald got a call from George Weiss.

"Is Page still there?" Weiss inquired.

"Yeah, he's here," a puzzled Fitzgerald replied. "He goes down to the whirlpool at the Mill. Then he comes to the ballpark and works out. Yeah, he's here."

"Well, have him call his wife," Weiss growled, "he never told her where he was!"

Lew Burdette was also there in 1947 (9–10 but with a sparkling 2.82 ERA), and was the cream of the crop. The Nitro, West Virginia, native recorded a 203–144 major league record, pitching a no-hitter, and winning three games of the 1957 World Series against his old Yankee teammates, who must have not only regretted trading him away, but also having to throw $50,000 into the deal as well.

"He didn't have outstanding stuff," says long-time friend and fellow Rugmaker Bunny Mick, "but, man, he had courage he hadn't used yet. He was a great competitor."

"Lew Burdette," says Amsterdam alderman Paul Constantine, "used to spend his whole salary playing pinball across from the Mohican Market. He'd play for hours on those machines. Pinball was big then. What were they making? Thirty-five dollars a week? We'd feel sorry for him. We'd buy him meals."

"We knocked him all over the lot every day we played him," says pitcher Charley Baker of the Blue Jays, "I don't know [why]. He sure learned a lot, didn't he? Even I never had any trouble with him. I almost parked one on him in one of the [1947] playoff games there, and I wasn't much of a hitter."

In 1949 righthander Bob Grim had a record for the Rugmakers that was, well, pretty grim, just 6 and 14 with a horrible 5.15 ERA. That wasn't much of a hint that in 1954 he would go 20–6 for the Yanks and be named A.L. Rookie of the Year.

Other major leaguer pitchers to wear a Rugmakers uniform were Mel Queen (1939), Herb Karpel (1946), Joe Murray (1946–47), and Danny McDevitt (1951).

There were some hitters on the squad too.

Kenny Sears, whose father was a N.L. umpire, had signed with Newark for a then princely $5,000 bonus. He could really hammer the ball, hitting .345, clubbing 11 homers (one travelled 490 feet), and driving in 41 runs in 48 games for the 1938 Ruggies. He continued to murder minor league pitching. In 1939 he was MVP of the Class B Piedmont League for the Norfolk Tars. "I saw him, he hit one off of home plate," says Emil Graff, "and he put one over the fence. Hit it on one bounce. When I say 'bounce,' I mean that curve ball bounced off of home plate, and he hit it over!"

Kenny became a Yankees backup catcher until he went into the Navy in World War II. The 1943 American League Red Book described him as "a husky lad," and that was stretching politeness. "They took him to Florida," reminisces Spencer Fitzgerald, "and he always ate, you know. He could hit. They gave him enough money for meals, and after that they'd catch him in some diner!"

"I think he had the feeling that 'My old man's a big league umpire' and that opened all the gates for him," adds Perth's Graff. "I think the Yankees got fed up with him. He was a nice kid though."

"He was the guy who could eat the hamburgers," recalls Rugmakers pitcher "Duke" Farrington. "He could sure blast a baseball, but he was so big and chunky. When he got behind the plate he was a liability to you. You couldn't let him call the pitch. Christ, I'd shake my head all night, you know. I'd try to pitch to him. He was all spread out in back of the plate. He was anything but a help to the pitcher."

"He was a ladies' man," says Ed Rusik. "Sure, he went around in a big convertible, picking up the chicks."

"I was a big kid," confessed Sears as to why he became a catcher, "too fat to move."

In 1942 there was second baseman Allie Clark, one of the few big leaguers to have two pinch hits in one inning, turning the trick with Cleveland on May 30, 1948.

"Two days after he got here," recalls Spencer Fitzgerald, "he got homesick. Sitting by his locker, crying his eyes out. We had to give him car fare home. Three days later he was back though. Geez, you had to babysit them and everything."

Clark's teammates included outfielder–first baseman Joe Collins, who clubbed .341 for Amsterdam and .262 in ten years in the Bronx (he retired rather than accept a trade to the Phils), and Yankees catcher Bill "Moose" Drescher.

Amsterdam also featured outfielder Ford "Rocky" Garrison (1938), outfielder turned pitcher Vince Ventura (1939), first baseman Dick Kryhoski (1946), catcher Gus Triandos (1950), outfielder Zeke Bella (1951) and catcher John Blanchard (1951). Blanchard, who had trouble getting playing time under Casey Stengel (who even spiked him once), launched four consecutive homers for the Yankees in 1961. He wept when the Yanks traded him.

Triandos ("All I remember about Amsterdam is that it was Kirk Douglas' home town") was a veteran power hitter, once swatting 30 four-baggers in a single season. "He could hit the ball about nine and a half miles," recalls the Glovers John Coakley. "Come August when I felt like I was throwing a shot put up there, you looked up and you saw that big Greek up there about six foot six and 240. He looked like he was swinging a telegraph pole. . . . Big, lumbering Gus. He couldn't run, and he was just adequate at catching, but, boy, could that guy ever hit!"

"Big Gus had the reputation for having the record of eating the most Brownie's hot dogs in Amsterdam," says Rugmakers public-address announcer Don Decker, alluding to the wares of a still popular local blue-collar eatery.

Blanchard and Triandos illustrate the difference in attitudes ex-players can develop. The powerful Greek comments bitterly, "What I remember are the lies and the boos." Blanchard, who battled successfully against alcoholism and cancer, feels that "everything about it was special. I loved every minute of it."

Chapter 5

"What, You Never Heard of Bunny Mick?"

"There are a lot of fellas with all the ability it takes to play in the major leagues, but they never make it, they always get stuck in the minor leagues, because they haven't got the guts to make the climb."
Cookie Lavagetto, 1960

Pretty tough talk from a lifetime .269 hitter, if you ask me, and since this is my book you'll hear my opinion whether you do or not.

Life depends on being in the right place at the proverbial right time. A lot of minor leaguers weren't. Hell, in Can-Am days, there were up to 60 bush leagues feeding just 16 major league clubs. The Cardinals alone at one time had 34 farm teams. It was a slippery ladder to climb, and it was a great system to get buried in.

Buried deep.

Here's an example: 1939 Rugmakers flyhawk "Pat" Hoysradt, who hit .351 and led the Can-Am in runs scored, went to spring training with Binghampton in 1941. "They had me batting clean-up all spring and I batted .500, but they sent me down to Norfolk," says the lefthanded slugger. "They wanted to make room for someone who had been up and down with New York and Newark and now he was going to Binghampton. It took away my desire, and I left after a few weeks. That's my only regret. I wish I had been given a chance with Binghampton."

Tony Ravish was promoted with Amsterdam to Akron and wanted a raise: "I led the whole Ohio State League in hitting, not just the team, the whole league, and they wouldn't give you a raise. They were tough."

Many of the most fondly remembered Can-Am players never made the majors. Unlike today, when player development is the minors' *raison d'être,* players back then often remained in a league for years, establishing themselves as fan favorites.

The marks they set were simply astounding. "Jigger" Statz played a record 18 seasons in the outfield with the Pacific Coast League's Los Angeles Angels from 1920 to 1942. Righthander Herman Polycarp "Old Folks" Pillette hurled 23 seasons in that circuit from 1920 to 1945.

Outfielder George Whiteman played in a record 3,282 minor league games between 1905 and 1929. Righthander Bill Thomas had a record 346 wins between 1926 and 1952, despite being unjustly suspended from organized ball for almost three full years (1947–49). Forty-eight-year-old pitcher Earl Caldwell, Sr. actually had his son, Earl, Jr., as a batterymate with the 1953 Lafayette Bulls in the Class C Evangeline League—and led that circuit in ERA.

Oklahoma-born righthander Jodie Phipps, who won 20 games for the 1942 Utica Braves, had 275 victories in the minors from 1939 to 1957 but never made the big show. The mild-mannered Phipps' mark of 2,447 bush league strikeouts is the fifth highest ever. He had one noteworthy quirk, though—kissing home plate after each victory.

One of the greatest-ever home run hitters played for the Oneonta Indians in 1942, yet he pitched that year and never graduated to the majors. He was Bob Crues, and he injured his shoulder soon afterward. Converted to the outfield, he clubbed 69 homers, drove in 254 runs (the all-time organized baseball record) and hit .404 for the 1948 Amarillo Gold Sox in the Class C West Texas–New Mexico League.

Of those long-serving, long-suffering minor league veterans, the longest tenured in Can-Am annals was Oswego's and Pittsfield's Arnie Cohen. The Rochester native was the only person in the league to play from its inception in 1936 to its interruption by the war in 1942, playing in 789 games. A talented but diminuitive (5' 4") outfielder with a fine on-base percentage, Cohen married an Oswego girl and settled in the city. He hit .300 or better in four of his seven seasons. Cohen would do anything to get on base, as evidenced by his league record 16 times hit by pitch in 1938.

Peripatetic outfielder Philip "Barney" Hearn had played previously with the Syracuse Chiefs and for Thomasville and Tallahassee of the Georgia-Florida League. He broke his leg and since management couldn't shoot him, he was released. Knowing Hearn was lame but available, Brockville gave him a call, signing him for 1937.

"We weren't drawing too well at Brockville and [pitcher Paul] Veach and I got thinking about it," says Hearn, "and, my God, we hadn't been paid in a month! So Father Martin was President of the League. We called him on the phone in Ogdensburg, and nothing was done about it. So we screamed to the directors of the club, and I finally got my release and so did Veach."

Cornwall signed Barney in 1938 and then sold him to the parent Buffalo club for the 1939 season. The Bisons farmed him to the Winston-Salem Twins of the Piedmont League in mid-season, and then he found himself with Albany who sent him back to the Can-Am League by optioning him to the Glovers for the 1940 and 1941 seasons. The Glovers then sold him to Quebec for the 1942 campaign. His Can-Am batting averages were impressive—.326, .373, .334, .321, and .286.

The speedy Hearn was a real crowd pleaser. A professional singer in his native Auburn, New York, he wasn't afraid to merge his two careers. "I used to sing in between innings up there [in Cornwall]," he says. "They'd drive up a truck and put me on it, with a piano. You had to be a helluva singer to sing with a piano, alone."

"He had a beautiful Irish voice," confirms Emil Graff, "an Irish tenor that's what he was, but he was a showman. He played the stands. He used to sing at home plate at Ladies' Night..."

He led the Pony League for Jamestown in 1945 with a .345 mark, and after the war he managed Auburn (he'd invested $2,000 in the club) and Kingston in the Border League for five seasons and ended up scouting for the Indians, Yankees, and Mets.

John Grilli was a dominant player in the league for its first three seasons, the first two in Brockville, the third with the Glovers. The Ukiah, California, native had started in baseball with Keokuk of the Mississippi Valley League in 1930. A solid hitter, he led the Nebraska State League in RBI's in 1935. He batted .331, .409, and .323 in the Can-Am, while occasionally taking a turn at mound duty.

"Son of a bitch, he could hit," muses rival pitcher Whitey Tulacz. "Daytime, he'd kill you. I don't care if he was in the big leagues, he could hit big league pitching. But for some reason, he had trouble at night. I think he got beaned one night. He got gun-shy, but he could hit."

Grilli had been plunked, but good. Oswego's Paul Nowak drilled him on August 2, 1937. John suffered a severe concussion, and was out for the remainder of the season.

He was, shall we say, colorful. "Grilli, the Pirates' clowning third baseman–pitcher, kept the [1936 Labor Day] crowd in an uproar with his antics on the mound," noted the Ogdensburg *Journal*. "His antics included throwing a five-cent baseball to start the game, gnawing on an apple in the pinches, and halting the game to consume great quantities of water from the Ogdensburg bench."

It may not have been much of a routine, but it was enough to knock 'em dead in 1936 Ogdensburg.

He had more tricks up his sleeve the next year. "I think [Maurice] Van Robays had hit two home runs off our pitchers when we played in Ogdensburg," recalls Barney Hearn, "so Grilli got ahold of an apple. He pitched to Van Robays. He was the first man up there, and he cried, 'Try this for size!' and he thew up the apple, and, of course Van Robays hit the hell out of it! They fined Grilli and put him out of the ball game."

Rome's 1938–39 shortstop Howard "Red" Ermisch was a 20-year-old from Philadelphia's semipro Quaker City League when he first joined the Colonels. Player recruitment was pretty informal, particularly for a shoestring operation like Rome.

"I had a very close, personal buddy that I went to high school with," Ermisch recounts, "and he played baseball. He had pitched one year up there [Rome], and he came back with the authority to recruit anybody in the Philadelphia area from the semipro ranks to go up to try out.

"They were starting a whole new ball club, and we went up there by bus from Philadelphia, and the first day of practice — you had to bring your own uniform. I had my church uniform, Advent Lutheran Church. The call came out from our manager, Bill Buckley, and his third baseman who coached. They said, 'All infielders hit first!' I grabbed a bat, and I was the second one up there. I remember you got five balls to hit, and I hit five line drives right past the pitcher's ear, and he [Buckley] came running to me, and he said, 'You're a shortstop, aren't you?'

"I said, 'That's the only position I ever played!'

"I never played shortstop. Very rarely in semipro or in the church league.

"I played there the first year at shortstop, and I remember I hit .284, and had the record for double plays. The next year I hit .299 [and made the All-Star team] and was sold to Toronto with Billy Southworth, Jr."

Ermisch had his moments in the league. In one game he homered three times — twice in the first inning with seven RBI's. In the league's first All-Star Game in 1939, he went six for six. But finances weren't always exactly flush.

"The manager came down to sign me as a shortstop," Red, a former Red Sox spring training broadcaster, notes. "He said, 'How does $85 a month sound?' I didn't know doodlysquat. I said, 'I guess that's okay.' Eighty-five dollars a month, and I saved money.

"Course, in those days the families of the fans took care of us. Saturdays and Sundays, we pretty nearly always ate with some Italian family up there with four daughters, who were all beautiful girls. We'd eat breakfast, lunch, and dinner with those people and just had a great time, eating spaghetti, spaghetti, spaghetti, but that's the way they took care of you up there. In fact, you had to find somebody like that because you couldn't eat very well on the money we made."

Slick fielding, slugging outfielder Tony Gridaitis played for Ogdensburg from 1936 to 1938. He'd been a submarine ball hurler with the nearby Deferiet semipros, but soon realized his potential at the plate, banging 25 homers in 1937 and 34 in 1938. In 1938 the righthander led the loop in four-baggers and also in RBI's with 130.

"In those days you got a box of Wheaties for hitting a home run," recalls Leo Pinckney. "Tony had so many in his room he couldn't get his door open."

Gridaitis wasn't satisfied with cereal. When Rome's League Park opened in 1937, he spied a local jeweler's billboard. It promised a shiny gold watch to whoever could sail a homer over it. "That's mine," grunted Tony as he settled into the batter's box, "I always wanted a watch — for nothing." Like Babe Ruth against Charlie Root, he called his shot and took ownership of the timepiece.

Albert "Duke" Farrington, a Detroit native who dabbled in boxing, pitched for Watertown (1936), Gloversville (1937), and Amsterdam (1938). With Amsterdam he set the all-time league mark of 13 consecutive victories. Feelings ran high when Duke appeared at Berkshire Park for the first time as a Rugmaker. A chorus of boos erupted when he took the mound, so loud that he reached into his pocket and put on a pair of black-and-red checkered ear-muffs!

"I learned a lot getting kicked around," Farrington reflects. "I hitchhiked South and I walked in, that must have been the spring of '35, and I went to Fort Worth, Texas. I don't know why I picked out Fort Worth, but I'd been with this travelling ball club [the Detroit Nighthawks], and I wanted to try out for a pro team. When I got there there was a sign: the ball club was in Lake Charles, Louisiana. So I hit the road again. Got down to Lake Charles, and spring training was just starting. They were all trotting around and tossing the ball around, and I walked up to this catcher, and I said, 'Could I get a tryout?' and he said, 'See that guy making the chalk lines over there. That's the guy you've got to see right there. He's the manager.' Del Pratt, his name was. I walked over and tapped him on the shoulder, and I said, 'I came for a tryout.'

"He said, 'What do you mean?'

"I said, 'Well, I hitchhiked down from Detroit, Michigan. I want a tryout.'

"He said, 'A tryout! What do you do?'

"I said, 'I'm a lefthanded pitcher.'

"He said, 'You see all those guys out there, that whole bunch of them there? They're all pitchers. We don't need any pitchers. Get the hell out of here!'

"So I took my glove, and I walked back over to the bench, and I put on a pair of spikes, and I walked out to the mound, and there was a guy sweating. I said, 'The man with the white hair over there told me to start throwing as soon as you get tired.' He said, 'Here, I'm tired. Take it away.'

"So I started wheeling the ball at the catcher. He had a brand new mitt, and it was spring training. Every time I threw the ball in there it was a 'Zapp!' you know, and the guys look around, 'Who the hell's cutting loose the fourth day of spring training?' So the next thing I know Del Pratt was behind me, and I pitched batting practice for three-quarters of an hour. And he finally said, 'Well, if I give you a uniform, will you stick around?'

"I said, 'You can't get rid of me.' So I wound up in spring training with

Fort Worth until they broke camp. When they broke camp they took me in the office, and they said, "You've got the makings of a good lefthanded pitcher, but we have Denton, Rogalski, Selway, and Wade all coming down from Detroit. We've got to make room for them. We can't pay for anybody or have anybody else on the club. So just stick with it, and you'll do all right.' So I hit the road, and I went to Lincoln, Nebraska, and Hopkinsville, Kentucky, and Beckley, West Virginia. I'd pitch a few innings and walk a couple, and they'd say, 'Where'd you come from?' and give me my release, and I'd be gone. . . .

"I went South in the early spring [of 1936] to a baseball school, the Max Carey School or something down there, and in the school I met a fellow named Forrester, and he was from Canada, and when the school broke up I started North, and I went to Detroit.

"I walked in the back door in Detroit, and I asked for a tryout, and they said they don't give kids tryouts. And I said 'Why not?' They said, "We don't even know who you are.' I said, 'Well, you can tell if somebody can throw can't you?' So they gave me a uniform, and I worked out with Detroit for about eight days, and they didn't know what to do with me. I was young, and I had a good, lively arm, and every other day I threw batting practice with the Tigers, and Mickey Cochrane, he was manager of the Tigers, he caught me two days to see what they were going to do with me. Then one day I got a telegram from Forrester asking me if I wanted to join the Watertown club in the Canadian-American League. They needed a lefthanded pitcher. So I went in to the management, and I said, 'What are you guys going to do with me? Are you going to buy me or sign me or what?' So they said, 'What? Just a minute?' So this big guy came over. His name was 'Wish' Egan. He was their head scout, and he said, 'The trouble with you young whippersnappers is you don't know when you're well off. What's your name?'

"I said, 'Duke Farrington.'

"He said, 'Here's fifty bucks for your time, and if you haven't got patience enough to wait until we do something with you, well, go get your own job!'

"I felt about as big enough to stick in a notebox, and I took off for the Canadian-American League."

Farrington, a born salesman, peddled pots and pans door-to-door in Amsterdam and later became a highly successful insurance man. "He could get on an airplane for California," says one source, "and sell a million dollars of insurance before he touched down. Be careful he doesn't sell you a policy!"

"That [the cookware] was in the off-season," says "Duke." "They had some pots and pans called Guardian Service, and they were terrific — $168 a set. I think some of those Polish people down there still have them, still own them. Oh, they were beautiful things, and I used to go and put on a dinner and sell a set of Guardian Service. I remember one month I got 16 or 17 pop-up toasters, Proctor toasters, for selling these things. Some guy gave us a big speech, and I was sold on the health of cooking without water and sold a lot of pots and pans. I gave everybody in the family a toaster."

Everything was looking up for Farrington in mid-1938 as he was reeling up his record string of victories. Detroit, who earlier spurned him, now eagerly wanted his contract, but he wasn't for sale. The Yanks were about to jump him all the way up to Newark.

Then disaster struck.

Sheer bravado caused it. "We were crossing the ferry up in Ogdensburg, and they started to talk how far it was, and I made a foolish bet that I could throw across from the ferry," the lefthander ruefully admits, "and when I did, everything in the back of my neck started to tingle, and the next day I could hardly lift my arm up. So that was really the end of my baseball life right there, but I didn't know it. I finished the season 17 and 4. I started 13 and 0, and my arm was bad.

"When I left Amsterdam my arm was bad. I had a big hole in the back of my shoulder where the muscle used to be. It kind of started to atrophy. I lost all my zip."

Poughkeepsie native John "Whitey" Tulacz pitched for Watertown (1936), Gloversville (1937), and Cornwall (1938). A tough hitter besides, he led the Can-Am in strikeouts in 1937 and ERA in 1936 and 1938. A 5' 9", 170-pound righthander, he left the Can-Am after the 1937 season and began 1938 with the American Association's Toledo Mud Hens. He soon developed a sore arm and was released. Steve Yerkes took a chance on him, and it paid off.

His stats were: a 12–7 mark with a 2.61 ERA, four homers and a .405 average in 1936; 17 and 9, 2.72 ERA, seven homers and .343 BA in 1937; and 18 and 5 with a 2.74 mark, five homers and .247 in 1938. In 1937 he hit ten triples.

"I was down with the Philadelphia Athletics," says Tulacz, "we were working out and Connie Mack got me a room, and I was rooming with some of the big league ball players. In the meantime some of the other guys went off. So while I was there, one of the ball players who went off contacted me and he said, 'You want to play pro ball? You in a hurry to go and play?' And I says, 'Yeah.' You know me, I was a young guy. I say, 'Sure. Why not?' Maybe that was a mistake. Connie Mack was gonna farm me out somewhere."

Tulacz enjoyed great success with Watertown and Gloversville but had one major flaw: a bad arm.

"He had a tremendously strong arm," contends Joe Gunn, a high

Left: **Pitcher Albert "Duke" Farrington, Gloversville Glovers, 1937.** *Right:* **Pitcher John "Whitey" Tulacz, Gloversville Glovers, 1937. (Courtesy of Bill Tuman.)**

school classmate who later played with and against him in the Can-Am, "and I remember when we were in high school. During the summer months they'd hold it, contests like running, batting, and throwing, and I remember he always got the prize for throwing the farthest. He could stand at home plate and throw the ball over the left field fence, but he threw his arm out, and when he was pitching in our league he was more of a junk pitcher, you know, slow curves, placement, and stuff like that. No speed. He couldn't blow it by you anymore. He did well, though. Good curve ball, change up."

"That was one of my biggest problems, my arm," Tulacz admits, "especially in the spring because I was muscular, and it's very hard to relax in the spring. Over the winter months the muscles contract. If I had it to do over again I would never let my muscles contract. I would have gone down to the YMCA and pitch maybe once or twice a week to keep my muscles stretched out. That's the biggest mistake I made.

"Course, I pitched against, my God, big league ball clubs about 15 times, and I did very well against them. It's sort of those things. You come up [sore] in the spring, and it's the wrong time. That's when you should show something.

"I was with Toledo, down in Alexandria, Louisiana. With them we had Dizzy Trout. You remember him? I come up with a sore arm down there. By the way, I played with him, and my son played with his son. My son played pro ball too for awhile. They were together down in Sarasota in the Florida State League and again with Appleton in the Midwestern League.

"I was with Toledo and I came back home. The Cornwall team was coming back North from Virginia and was passing through Poughkeepsie. I was home. Yerkes caught wind of it, and he asked me if I was free. I said, 'Yes, but I have a sore arm.' He said, 'I'll pitch you sore arm and all.'

"So I latched on with Cornwall. I used to pitch only four or five innings because my arm hurt so badly.

"And I always used to kid Steve: 'You know, I'll be in shape by Labor Day.' It just so happened I was with one of the other players, and I bit into a bacon, lettuce, and tomato sandwich. I'll never forget it. I bit into the sandwich, and I felt a pain. One of my teeth had a filling in it, and I said to the owner, 'Call me up one of the dentists in town.' So I went down to the dentist and said, 'See that tooth with the filling in it. Pull it out, will you please?' And he said, 'Why should I pull it out? Maybe its alright,' and I said, "I don't care. Pull it out anyway.'

"He pulls it out, and it was abscessed. I went back to the hotel. I told Steve, 'You know what I said about being in shape by Labor Day? This is it.' That abscessed tooth was causing all the pain in my shoulder. And in two days, I could take a ball and throw it through a wall. It was like night and day."

Now, that story may sound suspiciously similar (if you've been paying attention, class) to what Phil Marchildon said happened to him at Cornwall in 1939.

I offer you, free of charge, five choices:
1. Believe Whitey Tulacz, who offers a wealth of detail.
2. Believe Phil Marchildon, distinguished war veteran.
3. Believe both. (You gotta believe!)
4. Believe neither. (Oh, ye of little faith.)
5. You can try to find that dentist.

"Ogdensburg was our rival," Whitey continues in any case. "Cornwall and Ogdensburg are not too far from each other. I remember one time Duke Farrington was coaching on first base. We were losing 6-0, and he came back to our bench after four or five innings, and he says, 'I think I got their signs.' So he started relaying their signs to us. If he called us by our first name it would be a fast ball. If he called us by our last name it would be a curve, and I don't know how many home runs we hit there that day. I went for the cycle, I'll never forget that.

"I could always hit no matter where I went.

"I was signed by the Buffalo club in the International League [for

1939]. Hal White and I played for them. He and I were managed by a fellow name of George Uhle. He had pitched for Cleveland for years, and they were affiliated with Cleveland. We went to spring training in Plant City, Florida, and, lo and behold, I come down with a sore arm again. This is my downfall every spring.

"I got my arm in half-way decent shape, and after awhile I won two ball games. I beat Newark, and I beat Baltimore. Then we came back to Buffalo, and the team was on the road, and after that they farmed me out to Wilkes-Barre of the Eastern League.

"While I was there in 1939, two weeks before the season ended I came up with a sore arm again! Buffalo recalled me. So instead of going to Buffalo, I went home. Hal White and I both were recalled. He went up to Buffalo and he wound up in the big leagues.

"Some of the managers I had they wanted me to play at third base or the outfield every day, and it seemed like all the clubs I was with needed pitching more than anything else. Maybe if a manager had foresight and said, 'Hell! Forget about pitching. Go ahead and play the outfield,' maybe that would have been a turning point."

Tulacz, like Leo Pukas, Lou Gorski, Dick Kryhoski, Steve Ridzik, John Podgajny, Joe Collins (Kollonige), Carl Sawatski, Dick Tomanek, Paul Masterson, Steve Wilski, Ed Yasinski, Al Tarlecki, Tony Ravish, Alfred Belinsky, Eddie Popowski, and "Packy" Rogers (Hazinski), was indicative of the large Polish-American contingent in league personnel. "I'll never forget," says Rugmaker fan Joe Zawisza, "the time they had Polish day, and Steve Slezak [a local athlete] came on the field with a wheelbarrow of kielbasa!"

Speedy outfielder Torbert "Torby" MacDonald hit .379 and .300 for the 1941–42 Rugmakers. Educated at exclusive prep schools, he was an all–American halfback and captain of Harvard's football team who was later inducted into that school's Football Hall of Fame. He was also young John F. Kennedy's roommate there for four years.

His career bore an eerie similarity to JFK's as he enlisted in the U.S. Navy in 1942 and was given command of a PT boat in the South Pacific.

"On a patrol off New Guinea," noted the New York *Times,* "one day early in the war, his craft came upon five Japanese barges loaded with troops. Four of them were attacked and torpedoed. Mr. MacDonald went after the fifth as it neared an island for a landing. It too was torpedoed but not before Mr. MacDonald's craft was within range of Japanese shore guns. A shell exploded near his craft damaging it. Despite leg wounds, Mr. MacDonald got his crew back to base safely."

He was awarded the Silver Star and Purple Heart, and in 1946 entered the Massachusetts Bar. That same year he managed Jack Kennedy's first campaign headquarters. In 1954 MacDonald upset an entrenched

Republican congressman from the Boston area. In the House he distinguished himself by work on legislation establishing the Corporation for Public Broadcasting and on federally funded campaign financing.

His death in May 1976 attracted national attention because, rather than facing a lingering death, the dying Congressman advised his doctors to "pull the plug" on the life-sustaining equipment. Suffering from massive internal bleeding and hooked up to a maze of tubes, he made his request to his shocked family.

"Do you realize what this means?" asked his sobbing daughter.

"Yes," the Congressman responded.

"You still want us to remove it?"

"Yes."

"He realized he was close to death and this was not the way he wanted to go," an aide told the press. "He wanted to die with more dignity than that."

"He played in the outfield," recalls Amsterdam road secretary Spencer Fitzgerald, "and if the ball was hit on a line or not too high, he was great. He could run, but if it was hit way up in the air, Eddie Sawyer said, he had to get him a helmet."

"You know the story on him?" adds former teammate "Spec" Shea. "He couldn't play under lights. He couldn't hit the ball under lights either. He used to strike out a lot. He went to a doctor about his eyes, and he was having eye trouble. He didn't want to wear glasses, see. Christ, he couldn't see the ball in the outfield. He couldn't see it to hit it. They had to bench him. We were playing mostly night games, you know.

"He was built like Ted Williams, big long legs, and he could go along pretty good. I'll tell you one thing about him. When he hit the ball, he hit it good. But he only hit it in the daytime, and he hit shots, I'll tell you. He was built big; he was a big kid."

"He was a friend of John F. Kennedy," continues Spencer Fitzgerald. "In fact they were roommates at Harvard. Well, one trip we went to Pittsfield. Kennedy and them come up there. That's where I met him. But later on he became an FBI man. He married Phyllis Brooks, the movie actress. He's dead now, but he was typical college. He'd go to mass Sunday down at St. Mary's, he'd have on a beautiful gabardine suit, shirt, and tie—and sneakers on!

"He used to take his books with him. He was going to Harvard Law..."

A far different type of Rugmaker was Florida-born Conklyn Meriwether, who pitched for Amsterdam in 1940. Although his ERA was a poor 5.50, he hit .360. Eventually he switched over to the outfield full-time, and his stickwork propelled him onto the Cardinals' 1946 40-man roster. He never made the Redbirds and bounced around the minors, drifting lower and lower in the minor league vortex. Overall, despite starting life as a pitcher and detouring into the Navy for the 1943 season, he accumulated a creditable total of 279 minor league homers, including a high of 42 dingers with the 1953 Crowley Millers of the Evangeline League.

"The guy was a little tetched to start with. He was lefthanded," says Fitzgerald. "He came up to the ballpark one night, and he was all skinned up, his forehead, his nose, his chin."

"Sawyer said, 'What happened to you?'" continued "Spec" Shea, "'I was standing up on top of my bed and I was trying to change a light bulb in the Amsterdam Hotel.' And he fell off and hit the edge of the bed.

"[Actually] he had all the kids up at the [Harmon Field] pool. He was a hell of a swimmer, you know, and he was going to show the kids how to swim and dive, and he was running out and he hit the board and dove, but before he could catch himself he found out there was no water in it! He really cut himself up good."

"So we're in Oneonta," adds Fitzgerald, "and the first game was getting on. Conklyn was supposed to be getting ready to pitch the second game. He comes out and tells one of the players he's sick. So they find me. I was in the stands. I send him back up to the hotel. It was just a short walk up to the Hotel Oneonta.

"After the game Eddie and I went up to Conklyn's room to see him. Geez, there was nobody there. Sawyer says, 'I think I know where he is.' So, down right in Oneonta was a dance hall. We go in the back door. There's Conklyn, and he's really dancin' it up. After he went out those swingin' doors, I don't think they stopped moving for an hour!"

"He was an acrobat too," says Sawyer. "He was really good. I mean, not particularly as a pitcher, but he was a good athlete, but he was on the flaky side. He could do cartwheels around the ballpark. He was one of the first ball players I ever saw that was a really good gymnast."

"We took him downtown," recounts Fitzgerald's wife, Hilda, "one time after the ball game, and all the way down he was yellin' at all the girls, you know. He just wanted to have a good time, he wasn't like any of the others."

Conklyn didn't adjust well to retirement. On November 20, 1955, just a year after leaving the game, Meriwether, now a carpenter, went berserk, attacking his in-laws with a hatchet at his modest Tavernier, Florida, bungalow. His crippled mother-in-law, Mrs. Martin Ellen Mills, died immediately; her husband, soon afterward. Conklyn's badly wounded 16-year-old brother-in-law survived despite a fractured skull. Sent to prison after a psychiatric exam, Meriwether was paroled in 1975.

A particular Amsterdam favorite was speedy centerfielder Malcolm "Bunny" Mick. Mick was 1947 Can-Am batting champ with a .357 mark, and was, contended the Gloversville *Leader-Republican,* "popular enough

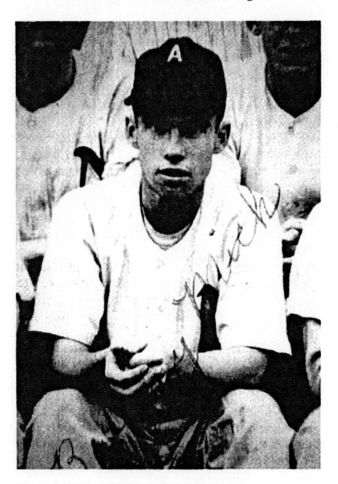

Malcolm "Bunny" Mick.

in the Carpet City to win the mayoralty contest hands down. . . ." To this day in Amsterdam, if you say the word "Rugmakers" people will respond in some Rorschach test–type reflex: "Bunny Mick."

"He was kind of like the Ricky Henderson of the Rugmakers," recalls 1946 Ruggie batboy Don Decker. "He was extremely fast. He was a good hitter for average [years later the Cardinals hired him to teach bunting to Vince Coleman]. A lot of steals. Even stole home on a couple of occasions. He was a very exciting ball player."

"A very, very little guy [138 pounds]," adds teammate Brownie Blaszak, "smaller than Phil Rizzuto. He could run very well, hit the ball consistently. Good outfielder. He had all around speed. He was a very smart, very intelligent player."

Recalls Mick: "When I went with the Yankees before I signed I had to ride my bicycle from Tampa across Gandy Bridge to St. Petersburg, which is 21 miles, to go to my tryout. I went on a bicycle 'cause we didn't have a car. Paul Krichell looked at me, and finally Frank Lane signed me shortly after that.

"I worked out with the Reds. The Reds even let me play in an exhibition game. They did things funny back in those days. I played in an exhibition game and got three for five, and I wasn't even a signed prospect, just a guy trying out. They wouldn't think about doing that today."

Mick had been with Amsterdam in 1946 and promoted to the Norfolk Tars at the beginning of 1947. The Rugmakers found themselves in need of an outfielder, and the Yankees said Bunny was available but had a sore arm.

"Send Mick, sore arm and all," wired the Ruggies.

Bunny swore he'd hurt his wing in a 19–3 exhibition pasting administered by the parent Yankees: "I ran 50 miles in centerfield chasing the hits and flies. I threw almost as many balls from centerfield to the infield as our pitchers did from the mound to the plate. The next day I could barely lift my arm."

"I recall that story," says Bob McCullough, with whose family Mick boarded on Amsterdam's Brookside Avenue, "but I also remember Bunny told us he had hurt his arm playing basketball for the University of Florida at Tampa. That's why he couldn't make the throws from the outfield to home plate. He told me if I ever went to college to stick to one sport...

"I could hit well enough to play in the big leagues," contends Mick, "I just couldn't throw."

The fans showered Mick with cash for one great play after another. One time, according to the *Leader-Republican,* he was the recipient of $65. His landlord had just broken his leg in a fall. Bunny told his teammates: "I'm going to take this to the hospital and give it to my landlord. My landlord needs it more than I do."

Bob McCullough remembers it slightly differently: "My father broke his ankle with a bowling ball. He never bowled. But he went out for the first time — maybe with Bunny — and as he went to throw the bowling ball, it broke his ankle."

"Bunny was very likable. He would always talk to the people," recalls fan Grace Bergen. "He was very good to our young daughter, who would get up and cheer for him when he came to bat. He even brought her back a teddy bear from one road trip."

"Everybody in town was wonderful to me," says Mick. "I got free haircuts and free meals and free sodas in the soda shoppe and everything you can imagine. In fact, all next winter I was still collecting from it long after the baseball season was over because I stayed up there and worked for the newspaper....

"They picked the Most Popular Player for 25 years up there, and I won that after I left. They sent me a plaque. In fact, Dizzy Dean presented it to my father-in-law when I was managing ball clubs for the Yankees.

"I didn't expect that kind of a reception in a cold northern town, because usually the people in like New York City are cold as hell, you know. They're not very friendly with you. I was very surprised at this upstate New York town being warm and friendly just like the deep South. They were outstanding, couldn't do enough for you. I can't say enough for Amsterdam, greatest bunch of people. Treated me better than any other place I've been in my life."

But why the name "Bunny?" "Everybody asks me that," says Mick. "My mother, when I was born, apparently I wiggled my nose like a rabbit when I was in the crib, and she named me that and it stuck like glue."

While roundball was Bunny Mick's downfall, it was the salvation of one of his teammates. Dark-haired, 6′ 5″ Carl Braun hurled for Amsterdam in 1947. "My best recollection," says Brownie Blaszak with marvelous understatement, "is he didn't get too many people out." Braun, a 19-year-old Colgate University dropout, burst onto the NBA scene in the 1947–48 season, with a then-record 47 points in a single game. He went on to play guard for the New York Knicks in the off-season and continued on to over a decade of successful playmaking.

"Funny thing about Carl Braun," says Bunny, "was, as great a basketball player as he was, usually a guy that has that kind of ability is a great competitor.

"Boy, he could find a way to lose a game! He'd get out there and he had good enough stuff to be a major league pitcher, but he was waiting for you to take him out of the game.

"If he was winning two to one in the seventh inning you could pretty well figure he was planning on losing. Unbelievable. I used to get mad at him. I remember hollering at him in the dugout, saying 'C'mon, Man! Suck 'em up!' I could hear him talking like he was giving up."

Former Amsterdam Deputy Mayor Joe Pepe's father owned a restaurant during the Rugmaker era, and Joe recalls 1947 Amsterdam shortstop Carl Lombardi:

"My [big] sister had a thrill for Carl Lombardi. He used to buy me off with baseballs to get rid of me. But my father, he was old-fashioned. He wouldn't let her talk to anyone. So when she was working in the kitchen she put a note in his club sandwich.

"He ate it. He thought it was lettuce."

History records that Lombardi batted just .259 and had 52 errors in 1947.

It just wasn't his year.

In 1942 Joseph Morjoseph patrolled the outfield for the Glovers. The previous year, playing for St. Joseph's, he led the Michigan State League with 30 homers. That abundance of "Josephs" got him featured in *Ripley's Believe It or Not.*

How he arrived in G'ville was equally off-beat, as he'd originally been assigned to Springfield of the Three I League. However, he refused to play for anyone but the new Glovers manager "Mickey" Hornsby and went home to California. Desperately short of talent, Hornsby wired him the $107 in carfare. The investment paid off when the slugger led the loop in homers with 20 and became All-Star centerfielder.

"We had a fellow who lived in Gloversville," says Harry Dunkel, "a baseball nut, his name was Joe Joseph, dead now, of course. . . . Joe Joseph decided to give this ball player, Joseph Morjoseph, $2 for every home run he hit. That didn't last too long. . . ."

Postwar pitcher Al Barkus was also a popular Glover, hurling for them in 1947, 1949, 1950, and 1951. "He was at least ten years older than any of my other players," says Harry Dunkel. "He just came back every year. He liked Gloversville and he liked baseball. He used to coach third base when he was wasn't at bat or running the bases."

So he wasn't exactly a prospect. "We had to let him go one time," says manager Ben Huffman, "but we ran out of pitchers, and we had to take him back."

"One time my family went down to Schenectady to that beautiful McNearney Stadium for a doubleheader," remembers fan Eber Davis. "The Glovers were short of pitchers, as minor league teams often were, and, well, my father used to say that Al didn't put enough energy into a pitch to get tired. Anyway they followed his thinking, and Barkus pitched both games, going all the way in the first, and then starting the second, although I think they relieved him in the fifth. It saved another arm on the staff.

"He threw a ball that was so slow, it's a wonder that gravity didn't pull it down."

But Al was an exceedingly popular Glover. A decent (twice winning 16 games) if somewhat geriatric pitcher who hit well, he was rewarded with an off-season job in Bob Rothschild's leather mill (if you can call working in a leather mill a plum), and on August 11, 1950, was feted with "Al Barkus Night" at Glovers Park. Al was given a variety of prizes including $217 in cash, of which $117 came from fellow employees at G. Levor & Co., and $20 from his fellow Glovers. "With which," the *Leader-Republican* revealed, "the righthander is supposed to purchase smokes so he won't have to 'bum' them from members of the club."

One Opening Day in Amsterdam, the Rugmakers had a capacity

crowd, but were short a third baseman. Paul Krichell and Herb Shuttleworth conferred and signed a local prospect who was in the park and had been to spring training with the club. In the course of negotiations in Herb's car he got his monthly salary raised from $80 to $100 a month.

"Oh, God," wailed Shuttleworth, "have we got a holdout, and he's got us."

The first two batters walloped impossible "sizzlers" that the rookie fielded flawlessly, and on the first pitch thrown to him. . . "Right out of the ballpark. Home run."

Krichell and Shuttleworth were feeling pretty savvy.

But the next chance hit at him went right through the wickets, and that was the norm. "His first three moments were perfect," says Shuttleworth, "but after that, nothing."

Now that's what I call a bush leaguer!

Then there was the strange case of pitcher William J. Sisler, no relative of George Sisler or any other Sisler you ever heard of. The 5' 6" southpaw played with little effectiveness for Ogdensburg in 1936 (eight games), Oneonta in 1940 (one game), and Quebec in 1942 (two games).

Now a record like that is hardly worth mentioning except that the Rochester native somehow conned not only these three teams into signing him but suckered nearly 50 other teams into doing so from 1923 to 1948. The pattern was this: Sisler would talk his way on to the roster. He would pitch, and in just a handful of games would play himself off the squad. He even tried his hand at managing — in the Border and Eastern Shore leagues. Again he failed to finish out the season anywhere.

He was the most travelled player in baseball history. So here's to you, Bill Sisler, wherever you are. What you lacked in talent you made up in perserverence.

But I'd like to conclude this chapter with a story about Carl DeRose, a 19-year-old 1942 Rugmakers hurler, because of what Cookie Lavagetto said about guts on page 94.

Fast. Carl was fast, and then some. While still at Amsterdam, *Life* magazine wrote him up as the next Feller as he struck out 204 batters in 227 innings. Then came the war and the Army Air Corps. DeRose almost made the Yanks in 1946 and 1947 but instead spent both seasons with their Kansas City farmclub. He worked construction in the winter of 1946–47 and became musclebound. When he opened the 1947 season in frigid Denver he felt something pop in his arm.

The pain increased. "I went to the doctor," DeRose once related to author Jack Etkin. "He said, 'You've got calcium deposits in your shoulder such that you can't probably finish the season.'

"I said, 'Why don't you phone them instead of me telling the ball club? I'd rather have you do it—a doctor.' So when I got to the ball game that night, [manager] Billy Meyer asked me if I wanted to start tomorrow night. I said, 'Yeah, fine.'"

DeRose threw the first perfect game in American Association history on that evening of June 26, 1947. Only two balls were hit hard, yet it was virtually the end of his career. Amazed fans, knowing the story, raised $4,000 for DeRose—including a buck from General Dwight Eisenhower.

"There's no doubt about it in my mind I would have been a good pitcher in the big leagues," says DeRose. "I'm not bitter. Kind of disappointed. I mean, you look forward to the major leagues, because at one time you could care less who was at bat. You could figure you could blow it by them...

"I felt bad about it. But the arm goes; it's one of those things, the way I figured. You're disappointed but not angry. Just like the service. That was prime time. But that's life, the way I figure it."

Big league attitude, Carl. Big league, and don't let anyone tell you different.

Chapter 6

Take Me Out to the Ballpark

"Is there anything that can tell more about an American summer than, say, the smell of the wooden bleachers in a small town baseball park, that resinous, sultry, and exciting smell of old dry wood."
Thomas Wolfe, 1939

Welcome to the world of baseball parks. You see, unlike any other arena, the diamond can be as much a part of the game as the teams themselves. Where the game is played is often as important as how it is played, as each ballpark plays a vital role in creating the atmosphere and mystique of baseball. It can have a short right or a deep left, be domed or decrepit, possess a pebbly dirt infield or antiseptic, modern Astroturf.

And if you think the major league variety is bewildering, just wait until you get to the minors.

Oh, how these emporiums may vary! A current Texas League park has a drive-in section; an ancient one had a giant venetian blind, shading patrons from the sun. Nashville's odiferous Sulphur Dell (aromatic not from sulphur, but due to a nearby garbage dump) featured a right field that rose 25 feet above the infield. Pennington Gap, Virginia's, Leeman Field in the Appalachian League featured a 900 foot shot to left, a gargantuan 1,200 feet to center and a more conservative 600 feet to right, while the Milwaukee Brewers' archaic Borchert Field was measured at just 268 feet down either line. Even supposedly sacred dimensions could be tampered with. First base at San Diego's termite-ridden Lane Field measured a mere 87 feet from home.

Different cities, different times, different parks. Each has a personality of its own, its unique sounds and shapes, its own definite impact on the score and on our hearts.

The Canadian-American League offered a span of facilities, ball yards ranging from rough and ready high school diamonds to parks that would go on to serve in higher classifications. Some were rickity (no shortage of "old, dry wood" at all) and some were spanking new. Some are long gone, and barely remembered by anyone. Several still serve today.

Lighting for night ball was an important design element. The Can-Am

League wasn't among the leaders in the field. Yes, Oswego had lights as early as 1936 but eventually sold them off, and their absence contributed to the franchise's demise. Cornwall was only the second team to install a system, putting in a very decent operation in 1938.

All this was pretty unusual, for by 1938 the Can-Am was the only one of five Class C circuits to be largely unlit. In fact only two other darkened fields existed in all of Class C, and every higher classification minor league had most (if not all) of its diamonds illuminated.

Utica put in lights in 1939, pacing league attendance despite a last place finish, and finally, their cohorts saw the necessity for arclights. Utica's success caused Gloversville-Johnstown, Amsterdam, Oneonta and Auburn to turn on the juice the next season. Ironically enough, the Can-Am's last unlit diamond was that of the 1942 Pittsfield Electrics.

A capsule history of the parks in each league city follows.

Watertown

The fairgrounds are old, real old, dating back to 1829 and the oldest county fair in the United States. The grandstand Bill Buckley eyed in 1936 had been built in 1851! Baseball had been played there since 1873, pro football since 1896.

In 1903 Watertown's "Red & Black" football team had quite a reputation, travelling to New York by train to play Philadelphia for the national championship, with a military band and 250 rooters accompanying the team. The city's mayor, who was in charge of the squad, bet $10,000 on the outcome. However, the locals, betraying some overconfidence, spent the night in Manhattan's saloons and whorehouses, and were minus six starters when the whistle blew.

They lost 12–0.

"We had a state league in the 1900s," recalls Alex Duffy, who is a veritable "Mr. Watertown" ("St. Lawrence University gave me a degree, a Doctorate of Humanities, in October [1987]. That will look nice in my obituary."). "We were in the Empire League in 1910. We had several semipro teams. . . . We had a white team and a black team, which was the Havana Red Sox, a very fine outfit. It was coached by a man named 'Pop' Watkins, John Watkins. He was a teacher, a professor of something in a black college, and 'Pop' was here five or six years and played out of Watertown as a base and played the whole eastern part of the country."

Major league barnstorming teams featuring the likes of Babe Ruth, Lou Gehrig, Grover Cleveland Alexander, Satchel Paige, and Connie Mack visited in the late '20s and early '30s.

All of which was precious little comfort to Bill Buckley when he chose

Mohawk Mills Park, Amsterdam, N.Y., late 1930s. (Courtesy of Richard Karabin.)

the fairgrounds as home. As the season approached nary a spade had been turned to accommodate him.

There was no place for the team's practices, and no fence in the outfield. "I have the word of Bob Quinn," fumed Buckley, "president of the Boston Bees, that he would aid the local team if the fence was provided around the fair grounds ballpark. If I cannot make the necessary arrangements, I may have to play somewhere else."

Quinn actually visited on April 28, 1936, to aid Buckley. First, he visited the Knickerbocker Grounds, but lost enthusiasm on learning its grandstand was condemned.

A barrier was erected, and a public address system installed (actually a fairly progressive measure; Sportsman's Park in St. Louis didn't receive one until that same season and Wrigley Field had added one only in 1934). But soon the annual Watertown Horse Show forced the Bucks to vacate the Fairgrounds for nearby Carthage. When they returned their newly laid-out infield was ruined.

Oddly enough, the Bucks were no longer there in 1937.

Now, what becomes of a jilted ballpark? Does it die of a broken heart? Not usually. The Watertown Collegians filled the fairgrounds void under manager Hank Hodge (Alex Duffy's brother-in-law) in the late '30s and early '40s and featured such promising semipros as "Spec" Shea.

The Border League then occupied the park from 1946 to 1950.

Following a playoff tilt in September 1947, the grandstand was destroyed by a fire of undetermined origin ("the unwritten law that all minor-league ballparks at one time or another burn down," as Charles Einstein once wrote). This was just after 4,000 fans had filed out. Alex Duffy contends, "It was a case of arson.... One big woosh and it was gone."

But of course it was rebuilt, and even after the Border League folded, it saw action with the New York–Penn League from 1983 to the present.

Massena

Alex Duffy was also a semipro ball player in the 1920s and he remembers playing at Alco Field, the Can-Am's shortest lived park: "It was a pretty good ball field. At that time they had a regulation field up there with a mound. A lot of these fields up North didn't have mounds. Massena had one and with the backing of the Aluminum Company of America spent a lot of money on the place. They had a big grandstand. Covered."

Ottawa

Lack of a fence was a pretty common condition in those days. This malady also plagued Ottawa, as it started 1936 without a proper barrier. Lansdowne Park, on the Rideau Canal, was a 10,000-seat football stadium built in 1909 for $100,000. "A fence is being erected," reported the Oswego *Palladium-Times* on June 3, 1936. "It will be placed about 300 feet from home plate and give the batters something to shoot at."

As noted earlier, the park was employed by the Canadian Army in World War II as a troop training site. On other occasions the team was forced to vacate the premises to make way for the Central Canada Exposition.

"It was a rough park. The field wasn't kept up," says Spencer Fitzgerald. "The stands were really long and the troops lived under them."

"No one ever hit a ball out of that park. It was over 400 feet to left. I think they had a standing offer of $1,000, from Jack Dempsey or someone who had been up there, if anyone hit one out. Nobody ever collected," says "Dutch" Howlan, who pitched for the Border League's Ottawa Nationals.

Lansdowne Stadium was also used for the International League's Ottawa Athletics in the mid-1950s, and was expanded to 17,301 seats in 1961. In 1966 the old grandstand was demolished to make room for the city's Centennial project, the Civic Centre, a multipurpose facility consisting of a 33,000 square foot exhibition hall, a 9,355 seat arena, offices, meeting rooms, and dressing rooms. All of this was incorporated into a new 14,842 seat stadium grandstand.

Lansdowne Stadium now features Astroturf and hosts the Canadian Football League's Ottawa Rough Riders.

Brockville

Fulford Field was donated to the City of Brockville by George Taylor Fulford in 1908, near the Fulford Home for Retired Ladies (despite rumors, it was *not* at the corner of Fulford and Fulford). A fence and the clubhouse were erected in the late 1920s. When the Pirates played there in 1936–37 its infield was still skinned.

The Oswego *Palladium-Times* reported on some rather haphazard conditions: "The Brockville playing field was far different from the spacious [Oswego] local ball yard. The outfield range was restricted, with balls hit over the left field fence counting for two bases. The sun also bothered the Oswego fielders, two or three flies going for extra bases when the gardeners lost the ball in the glare."

Left field was a mere 275 feet down the line. Left center was but 300 feet, and anything hit over the fence to First Avenue was two bases.

The park has also been used since for football, cricket, soccer, and Little League baseball. It is now the home of the fearsomely named Brockville Bunnies of the Ontario Baseball Association, who having reached the finals seven times (and won them four times) in the 1970s are a lot tougher than they sound.

Perth

The Perth Board of Education built Perth Collegiate Institute (P.C.I.). Park before the turn of the century as the local high school field, and it still stands today. The Perth franchise was allowed to use it and erected bleachers. The Rome *Sentinel* termed it "a diamond far from ideal," and Gloversville's *Leader-Republican* noted that only one ball had been hit out of it in 1936.

Despite the field's huge dimensions, it had the smallest seating capacity in league history with less than 1,500 seats.

"The infield," recalls Ronald White, "had no grass — clay — and you can imagine the speed of ground balls.... In the outfield the ground was very hard, you had to go like a hound to catch up to the balls....

"Left field had a row of beautiful maples perhaps 335 feet out. There was no fence. You couldn't knock it out, but it might roll out. Beyond the trees was a street. Center field was wide open to at least 420 feet out. Right field had a snow fence about four feet up about 320 feet out...."

Oswego

Oswego's previous pro teams played at Richardson Field, but that had long been torn down and replaced by the county's public works garage.

Otis Field, named after Depression-era mayor John Otis, was built circa 1931–32 on the site of a city dump. It served as a park for a semipro squad and for youth teams in general, seeing some improvements on the Netherlands' arrival in 1936, such as stands and fences, but did not receive a grass infield. "A grass infield," it was noted, "has long been advocated by players to counteract the uncertain hops encountered on a dirt infield...."

Oswego's Mike Naymick agrees: "That field we played on, it would look like a rock pile. It wasn't well taken care of. Conditions really weren't good at all."

Former Nets fan Bob O'Brien recalls the dimensions as being about 340 feet to both left and right field, and "very, very deep, at least 450 feet to center. I think Josh Gibson once hit a ball over it." Raymond Haynes, who helped build the park, estimates even steeper figures — 550 to left, 585 to the center field flagpole, 600 to deepest center, and 428 to right. He contended that only two fair balls were ever hit out.

Of the lights that were installed in 1936, Francis Regan wrote, "they were nothing to become excited about," and were sold in 1939. Their removal played a part in the Nets demise.

"During the 1940s," recalls O'Brien, "the kids pulled the grandstand apart, and some people were said to have removed boards to stoke their stoves and furnaces."

Otis Field was torn down in the mid-1950s to make way for the Leighton Elementary School. "That was a mistake," asserts O'Brien, "because of the former dump, there were problems of sinkage."

Smiths Falls

The Smiths Falls ballpark had been built in 1916–17 by the Canadian Pacific Railroad Recreation Association. Its salient feature was a 20-foot-high tin fence guarding its short left field barrier.

Francis Regan wrote that the town boasts "one of the finest baseball parks in minor league baseball. Operated by the Canadian-Pacific Recreation Club, the park has a grandstand extending down the first and third base lines with a seating capacity of 2,200. There is a grass infield, smooth and fast, and a fine outfield. A short left field fence is the only drawback but at that the distance is 270 feet. Center is 410 feet and right field 400 feet. There are pennants with the names of each of the eight teams in the league flying at different points from the roof of the grandstand. There is a scoreboard in center field, a board with the names, numbers and positions of visiting players in left field...."

Can-Am ball returned briefly in July 1938 when Ottawa, displaced from Lansdowne Stadium by an Exposition, played three tilts there.

The tin fence is now gone, but the park is still recognizable. Soccer is now sometimes played there and two ice rinks and a lawn bowling pitch are adjacent.

Ogdensburg

Winter Park began as an ice skating rink run by Father Martin and St. Mary's Church and quickly evolved into a full-fledged ballpark under Knotty Lee. The park opened in spring 1936 with work on the grandstand uncompleted but was finished, including a very, very small roof, by June.

There were problems. "I know," recalls Perth's Norman Hibbs, "one game we were playing, and the grandstand roof collapsed. Nobody was seriously hurt, but a few people were hurt a little bit."

"Left field was awful short," says Spencer Fitzgerald. "They had balls that used to bounce off the roofs of the house. It wasn't much of a ballpark." Right field, however, was fairly deep.

"You could urinate over that left field fence," Barney Hearn sums up succinctly.

Lights were installed only after the Can-Am League departed. In 1946, the Border League arrived, and Bradley & Williams of Syracuse installed a system for $17,500. In the early 1950s, after the loop folded, the lights were sold and reinstalled in Valley Field, Quebec.

Winter Park presently stands as just a ball diamond, devoid of lights and stands, and is now called Father Martin Park.

Cornwall

The Cornwall Athletic Grounds were built in 1908 and purchased by the city of Cornwall for $3,000. It was described by the *Sporting News* as "one of the finest in Ontario."

"Cornwall," contends Emil Graff, "had one of the best ball fields you could play on. It was all tiled, drained, and you could play doubleheaders down there, and your feet weren't sore. It was a beautiful ballpark."

They installed lights on July 6, 1937, with Father Martin tossing out the first ball. "The lighting plant," reported the local paper, "is one of the most powerful installed in Canada so far with 56 huge reflectors illuminating every corner of the field to daylight brilliance. The plant has a capacity of 168,000 watts and required 112 carefully focused 1,500 watt lamps. There are five field towers and two reflector stands mounted on the grandstand." Sixteen-hundred fans attended that contest, including those from Ogdensburg, Massena and other New York communities.

It's also been used for field lacrosse, wrestling, boxing, track and field, and football, and is still used for baseball. Into the 1950s and '60s the field was still used by local semipro squads.

Amsterdam

In Amsterdam, Mohawk Mills Park began life in a slightly different fashion as a Progressive-era version of Baseball City, that is, as part of an amusement emporium called Crescent Park. It opened on Memorial Day, 1914, featuring a dance hall, shooting gallery, motion picture theater, miniature railroad, and boating and bathing on "Lake Crescent."

"Spend Decoration Day at Home," read the ad, " – in the Shade of the Forest Primeval – Every Charm and Every Feature of the Big Summer Resorts Available, All Within a 5¢ Car Ride of the City of Amsterdam."

From the beginning there was a ballpark, and admission to games was free with admission to the grounds. The opening contest was between the local Empires and the Philadelphia Colored Giants, described as "one of the best colored professional teams in the country."

And they were, at one time featuring pitcher Rube Foster, second baseman Charlie Grant (whom John McGraw attempted to sign), and even heavyweight champ Jack Johnson. The locals, however, took both ends of a doubleheader, and within a month played squads like the Schenectady Mohawk Giants, with such great black stars as pitcher Frank "the Red Ant" Wickware and catcher Chappie Johnson, along with a contingent called the Chinese Students Team from the University of Hawaii.

The park eventually changed its name to "Jollyland." In the early 1930s it was sold to the Mohawk Carpet Mills, which closed the midway. When the Can-Am arrived, it was run down, with a skin infield and a fence supported by braces that intruded onto the playing surface. "You'd see the ball hit back there and rattle around," remembers one fan, "and the players would have to dodge around to field it."

Soon the infield was finished off and a new, higher, 16 foot, more professional fence was installed. As were lights in 1940.

"We got to the point where we let the people out from the offices at four so they could go to the ballpark," recalls John Pollard, "but that was just Mohawk Mills. I wanted the whole city to be able to go to the games.

"I used to drive Herb Shuttleworth's father. They had a Lincoln. When he had to catch a train out of Schenectady, I had to drive him. One day he asked how the team was drawing. Now, he was tickled that Herb was taking an interest in the ball club, doing something for the community. Herb was just out of college, and was very backward and timid in getting up and talking before a group.

"I said we needed lights. He said, 'If Herb wants the lights, he'll get the lights.' They cost $10,000."

"We went to General Electric," continues Herb Shuttleworth. "Lights were a novel thing, and we had the state of the art.

"When we turned them on for the first time, there in the back of the park was a little shed with the controls for the lighting. It looked like the machinery for the Queen Mary.

"Wally McQuatters and I go down to throw the first lights. There's a huge handle with an arm on it. We're ready to throw the lights, and we realize how much power is in this thing.

"'Wally, after you,' I say.

"He says, 'After you,' but I just stared at him, and he realized he wasn't going to win this one, so he looked around for a rubber mat to stand on. He was just rubbing his hands, looking at the switch.

"He threw it, but we were both pretty nervous."

"You have to give Herb Shuttleworth a lot of credit," says John Shuler. "If there was a nail out of place, he'd send some carpenters down from the mill to fix it."

The park featured an extremely short left field barrier — 279 feet. That dimension was tempered, however, by the fence's great height, at least 26 feet. The park also possessed one of the league's deeper center fields — 409 feet. And in center field, in play, on the field, in fair territory, was the park's flagpole.

In July 1942 the New York Yankees, with DiMaggio, Henrich, Keller, Rizzuto, Gordon, Selkirk, and Rolfe in their lineup, struggled to a 9–5 ten-inning victory over the Rugmakers, but that wasn't the unusual part of the story.

Let's back up a little.

"We was in Three Rivers," recalls Rugmakers road secretary Spencer Fitzgerald, "[manager] Tom Kain and I, in '42. Morel, he was a sportswriter for Three Rivers, he come down the street. I hollered at him, 'Paul. C'mon over!' I said, 'He's talking about 'Stadium de Baseball pfoof!'"

"And they talked in French, and, that's when our ball park burned down...."

Mohawk Mills Park had been incinerated. It was a small fire when the groundkeeper's wife first saw it, and her husband rushed out to battle it with a garden hose, but just as he completed the run from his home, the sputtering blaze became a conflagration. The fire department was called in

Amsterdam Rugmakers business manager Wally McQuatters. (Courtesy of Bill Tuman.)

but soon discovered there wasn't enough water pressure to fight the rapidly growing inferno. Four hours later, the entire 900-seat grandstand, the adjoining fences, and the concession areas were a sodden pile of charred wood. Luckily, the first and third base bleachers were saved.

"I was called on a Sunday morning in the middle of the night," says John Pollard, "that the park had been set on fire. It was arson."

That should have been the end of the story. It was only the beginning.

"We went to the hotel," continued Fitzgerald, "and called up [business manager] Wally [McQuatters], and he told us. Tom Kain said, 'Are we gonna play the Yankees?'"

"'Oh yeah. We're going to play the Yankees.'"

It was hard to see why McQuatters should be so sanguine. With just eight days to go before the Yankees' arrival, disaster was staring them in the face. Insurance would not even cover all of the $15,000 loss. Archrival Gloversville offered the use of its park for the game, but the Rugmakers replied, "No, thanks," and rolled up their sleeves.

Before the weekend ended, the club's directors awarded a contract to rebuild the ruined grandstand. Favoring them was the fact that the team was on the road the next week. Debris was hauled away. Hammers and saws replaced bats and balls at the site, and a miracle happened. By the time the Yankees arrived, not only had every barbequed seat been replaced, but the park's total capacity had been increased by 200 seats.

Not that everything was restored to its former "grandeur." No roof had yet been installed over the new grandstand. That would have to wait. Part of the delay was due to the wartime shortage of supplies. Otherwise, there's no telling what wonders the contractor might have accomplished. Also missing was a coat of paint—no use risking several hundred pairs of freshly painted trousers.

The town was in a mood to celebrate when the world champions made a special stop from the State Express at 12:35 PM on a beautifully sunny Monday, July 20, 1942.

It went wild.

Thousands of ecstatic fans met the Yankees at the station. Hordes of autograph seekers hemmed their heros in. Even Joe McCarthy, notorious for his aversion to signing, caught the spirit. Bands played and brightly colored crepe paper rained down on the motorcade to the luncheon at the ornate local Elks Club. Businesses were shuttered, and signs proclaiming, "Welcome Yankees—Closed for the Afternoon" sprouted on each storefront. A seven-year-old heart patient, little Johnny Martuscello, got to meet his idol, Joe DiMaggio. Miniature commemorative carpets marking the afternoon's contest (one of which, by the way, can now be found in the Baseball Hall of Fame) were bestowed on the visitors. Even normally hard-bitten New York scribes were impressed.

"I felt like a red corpuscle the other day," wrote an amazed Jack Smith of the New York *Daily News,* "or perhaps it was a white one. My travels with the Yanks carried me through the bloodstream of baseball and finally into the City of Amsterdam, N.Y. (pop. 35,000), pumped me into the heart of the game itself. Rising industriously on the banks of the Mohawk River, the city is deep in the Class C minors. But for sheer love of baseball, enthusiasm and support it outstrips major league owners, officials and fans. It reflects the pure, wholesome attachment of American people for the game and contrasts with the blase 'give us a winner' attitude of the big cities."

When the Yankee bus left the Hotel Thayer, two players were missing: Joe DiMaggio and Lefty Gomez. Both were left wandering on Division Street. Fan George Sandy pulled up in his 1937 Buick, and gave the two a ride to the park. "The first thing DiMaggio said when he got in the car," recalls Sandy, "was, 'Where in hell are all the girls in this town?'"

A question male Amsterdamians have been asking ever since.

The game itself, played before 4,034 delirious fans, was a beauty. The

Joe DiMaggio at Mohawk Mills Park to play the Amsterdam Rugmakers, July 20, 1942.

Rugmakers pulled ahead 2–0 in the third; then New York came back to tie it in the top of the fourth on a two-run homer to right by DiMaggio ("Thanks, George!"). The Ruggies promptly went up again by one in the bottom of the frame, then added one more in the fifth to pull ahead 4–2.

The Yanks chipped away with runs in the seventh and eighth (that one on a four-bagger by Joe Gordon), and then finally exploded for four tallies in the tenth to put it away.

And now for a bit of "Believe It or Not."

"When the stands burned, with the heat from the fire and the weight of the lights, the poles bent over to the ground," recalls Herb Shuttleworth, "just like the snow on the branches of a tree.

"We put everyone we knew to work on the stands. They were back in a few days, but what do we do with the lights? That was the biggest problem.

"Absolutely miraculous, but as those poles cooled, they went right back, straight, and we never had to touch 'em. I never saw anything like it."

And the Yankees had never seen anything like their welcome to Amsterdam, either.

Carpet made to commemorate visit of the New York Yankees to Amsterdam, N.Y., in July 1942.

Well, that was the glory. After the Rugmakers left, the park had to scramble for excitement. Semipro teams such as the Rugmakers and Stars continued to be play there, but it slowly deteriorated, finally being deeded over to the City in September 1964. The City had planned on buying it, but instead the Mills turned it over to the municipality for one dollar. From August 1, 1955, to June 12, 1980, there were no night games at the field. By this time it had been renamed Shuttleworth Park, honoring Herb Shuttleworth.

It was rebuilt with federal Community Development Agency funds in the mid-1970s, but in the process its dimensions were altered, its grandstand butchered, its high wooden fences removed, and much, if not all, of its charm lost. Even its restrooms and concession areas were stupidly removed to an area a hundred yards from the ballpark itself. It was a pathetic rehab, with little concern for tradition or utility. New lights were added only later, paid for by private subscription. Currently, Bishop Scully High School and Legion ball are played there, but if you are seeking the glory that was Mohawk Mills Park, look at a photograph, don't visit its depressing current state.

Glovers Field, Gloversville, N.Y., 1940s. (Courtesy Bill Tuman.)

Gloversville

The Fair Grounds, later known as Berkshire or Glovers Park, must have been fine for auto races, boxing, wrestling, standardbred and greyhound racing, and even for shows and circuses, but it was just not very suitable for baseball when the Can-Am League first laid eyes upon it in 1937.

"The outfield was a hayfield in those days," recalls Harry Dunkel. "Terrible. The ballpark wasn't any good. It didn't have good fences around it. They were the kind they put along the roads in the wintertime, snow fences."

That wasn't all. On the Beavers' first visit to the place in 1937, the Smiths Falls *Record News* reported: "The mud was so deep that hard-hit balls plopped into the mud and were frequently turned into double plays."

Actually, baseball had been played at the site for some time. On May 31, 1898, the local McKeevers and Adelphis played to a tie; the game ended after three and a half innings when the only available ball was hit into some weeds on the edge of the outfield and was lost!

In 1940 installation of lights was financed via the sale of stock. Guy Barbieri remembers the park as "kind of dilapidated" in 1947. In 1948 the park was thoroughly overhauled again, and in 1950 a new orange and black color scheme was added to the scoreboard.

But that was at the very end of its useful life. We next come across the park as a mouldering shadow of itself.

In 1960 *Leader-Herald* sports columnist "Jigger" Thompson wrote about Glovers Park as it stood in decay, and the picture he drew was all too true of so many of the old parks.

> It's no longer Glovers Park. It's Lovers Park. Someone painted out the "G" on the grandstand.
>
> It no longer bustles with activity as it did ten years ago. Even nine years ago, the last year there was Canadian-American League baseball....
>
> There's no outfield fence to skid homers over. The grass and weeds are high.
>
> The last reminder of Can-Am ball is the scoreboard, weather-beaten but still readable.
>
> The grandstand still is there. So is the press box and what's left of the locker rooms.
>
> You can almost hear shouts of "Play Ball!"
>
> You can almost hear shouts of "Let's go, Glovers!"
>
> Almost.
>
> It took local fans several years to convince themselves that Can-Am baseball never would return.
>
> Like street cars, home brew and Stutz Bearcats — it's gone.
>
> But drive past Glovers Park. Drive past the grandstand and the open outfield and the scoreboard. And if you're a Glovers fan — a dyed in-the-wool Glovers fan — it may be gone but it's not forgotten.

The park was demolished in the mid-1960s for the Nichols Plaza Shopping Center, and only the light towers remained as brooding, silent witnesses to what had been, until they too were finally removed in the mid-1970s.

Pittsfield

Talk about Wahconah Park, and everyone says one thing: It's built backwards. Since it was designed before night ball came to pass, no provision was made to take into account the setting sun. Surprisingly, this flaw was never really corrected. Only in 1989 did management finally install a mesh screen in center field to help shield batters' eyes from sunset's blinding rays. Nonetheless, somewhat unique "sun delays" are still common at the scene.

Wahconah Park has been the scene of ball games since at least 1892. Two seasons later it hosted the city's first pro entry, a New York State League team. That experiment ended in just a month.

The year 1919 saw significant changes for old Wahconah. First, the 50-acre site was donated to the city. Secondly, the Eastern League's "Hillies" took up occupancy, remaining until the circuit folded in mid-1930.

The park has undergone renovation after renovation. In 1927, the even-then badly deteriorated grandstand was repaired. A dyke was installed on the nearby Housatonic River in an attempt to prevent recurrent flooding. In 1931, to provide jobs for the unemployed, 1,300 men were hired to regrade the field. They were given work in three day stints, at a cost of $25,000.

But that was long before the Can-Am League arrived, and actually the Electrics never meant to use Wahconah, instead planning on a new park on Dalton Avenue. While construction was still going on, owner William Connely petitioned the Pittsfield Parks Commission for use of the Common, downtown.

Despite idle threats from the league that it would pull up stakes if permission wasn't granted, the Parks Commission just said "No." Instead they provided rather primitive Dorothy Deming Field on Elm Street. Aside from its generally poor facilities and lack of lighting, that "park" was plagued by massive dust swirls à la Candlestick Park.

"They had no place to play," rues John Pollard. "They played in an open field with just one of those wire fences."

The Electrics arrived at Wahconah late in 1942. Night baseball followed in 1946, as eight 80-foot light towers were shipped in by train from Boston. Erected too was a new $1,800 scoreboard, courtesy of the Sports Service Corporation, a concessionaire. That year's rental agreement with the city was one cent per admission with a maximum season payment of $500.

It still needed work. "It was just a lousy ballpark," recalls Spencer Fitzgerald, "it was old, run down." In the fall of 1949 work began on major renovations. Heavy pilings were driven into the soggy soil to provide a firm foundation for the new grandstand. Recurrent rumors held that Wahconah was built over a city dump, but excavations revealed nothing of the sort. New fences, toilets, concession areas, and lockers were among the improvements. The field was again regraded. Total cost was $114,000.

The dimensions were uniform, in fact a bit too uniform: 352 to left, 362 to center, and 333 to right. From 1965 to 1988 the Eastern League located franchises several times in the park, and in 1989 the New York Mets relocated the Little Falls team of the New York–Penn League there. In 1976 it was again renovated, this time with $700,000 in federal funds. Once more, the major emphasis was on halting floods from the Housatonic.

You might ask why in 1949 or 1976, with massive renovations afoot, the field was never reversed to properly align with the sun. So have a lot of other people over the years.

That point aside, though, Wahconah is a good place to watch a ball game from, cozy, comfortable and with excellent sightlines. It's no pillar of luxury and still looks Class C in a domed stadium world, but maybe that's part of its charm.

Three Rivers

Municipal Stadium in Three Rivers, according to author Bob Ryan, was "built in 1938, as part of Exposition Park, a large recreational complex within the city limits. Reminiscent in some respects of the American WPA projects, it has a feel all its own."

"It was up on a fairgrounds," says Guy Barbieri, "it was up on a hill, and we used to stay at a hotel across the street from the Market Square."

"It was kept up," recalls Three Rivers hurler Ed Yasinski. "It wasn't a cow pasture."

The stadium was, of course, used by the Provincial League until it folded on April 27, 1956, and from 1971 to 1977 by the "Aigles" ("Eagles") of the Eastern League.

Quebec

Located in Parc Victoria, Quebec's Municipal Stadium was largely a carbon copy of the Three Rivers field, not only in name, dimensions, and exterior facade, but also in that it was also used again in the Provincial and Eastern leagues. There was one significant difference, however: Quebec had a larger seating capacity—7,500 to just 6,000 in Three Rivers.

"Outside of the Quebec City ballpark," recalls Guy Barbieri, "was a convent, and we could see nuns watching the ball game from way out there. The Quebec City ballpark was enclosed all the way around. It was a nice stadium."

"The Prime Minister of Quebec," adds Spencer Fitzgerald, "he built Sorel, Quebec, and Three Rivers, all about the same time. The three would be identical."

"It was all concrete stands," adds Quebec Braves hurler "Moose" Erickson. "It was built like most good ballparks were built, like a stadium. The field was down a little lower, and the fans were kind of up and as far as the ballpark was concerned it was a fine ballpark to play in especially for that type of league."

Schenectady

The McNearney brothers went all out to give Schenectady a first-class facility, operating from the beginning with an Eastern League franchise in mind. McNearney Stadium was a concrete and steel park as opposed to the wooden grandstands that dominated the circuit, save for the two Quebec stadiums. Architecturally, it was similar to their nearby beer distributorship.

Two views of Trois Rivieres Stadium.

Among its innovations were a coin-operated turnstile (which took silver dollars—I'm sure everyone was carrying silver dollars in 1947) and a new electric scoreboard. It also was reputed to be the only minor league park with a real restaurant on the grounds.

It was lit by the newest of General Electric floodlights, the same as were just being installed at Yankee Stadium. A hundred and sixty of the new bulbs, providing 278,000 watts, made McNearney the best-illuminated field in the league.

Management and General Electric were so proud they arranged an exhibition for the press, emphasizing not only the brightness of the new product, but also its durability.

"The system," noted the Schenectady *Gazette,* "was subjected to a test worse than the Yankees probably will ever give it, when a playground full of teenage ball players at Oneida School batted, pegged, and generally rained balls at the floodlights for a half-hour period. The boys stood only 20 feet distant and put all the steam they had on the ball, but the new flood-light treated the entire procedure as a tin roof treats rain."

In addition to that a local danseuse, Shirley Yaker, was called on to perform a few routines on one of the new floodlights. "The lights' special glass lens designed to resist baseballs," attested the *Gazette,* "can hold the weight of a 200-pound man and thus had no trouble supporting 118-pound Shirley..."

While the park had those fine lights from the beginning, it did not have a covered grandstand, as its roof did not arrive until 1948.

The locker rooms were another drawback. "They were tiny," says Wally Habel, "terrible. And they were so hot and humid, after you'd shower and change, you would still be a mess."

Other events could occasionally be booked, as in 1947 when an outfit called M-M-P Enterprises carded a lengthy series of boxing matches at the stadium.

After the Can-Am League was deserted in 1950, the stadium, sometime called Schenectady Stadium, was home to an Eastern League franchise from 1951 to 1957.

During that last season, fans could actually see work being done on the golf course that was to spell the park's doom. The "Stadium Golf Course" was opened by Pete McNearney on July 10, 1958, incorporating the grand-stand's shell into the clubhouse's design. The grandstand seats, bleachers and lights were sold. A "pitch and put" par-three course was even estab-lished on the former playing field itself.

Sacrilige!

Rome

The Colonels played their first year in West Rome's League Park, formerly Murray's Park. The structure had served industrial league teams and needed a lot of fixing up to raise it to minimal standards. Additional fill was added to the outfield. Management installed a cinder warning track, a grandstand roof, a new scoreboard and concession stand, and additional bleachers. A high wire fence was erected in right to cut down on homers. The outside of the fence was painted, and a sign, "League Park, Fort of the Rome Colonels," was hoisted.

Despite these improvements (Hal White terms it "an old, rundown place near the railroad tracks"), in 1938 the new management built Colonels Park on Black River Boulevard and Pine Street for $15,000. Closer to downtown, it featured all sorts of plusses such as 80 box seats, a press box,

McNearney Stadium, Schenectady, N.Y., now "The Stadium Golf Course."

dressing rooms, showers, and public restrooms. It seated 2,500, and would boast "an imposing front entrance with two main gates and aisles. The ticket office and concession booth will be set in the fence which will be decorated with lattice work and painted. Shrubbery will be planted near the fence to increase the general attractiveness."

Interest ran high. An estimated 10,000 Romans came to view construction, but the new park wasn't ready for Opening Day, and the site was ironically moved from Rome to Carthage. That proved no solution, either, as the next two contests were called due to bitter cold.

"It had a skin diamond, hard as a rock, clay," recalls Cornwall's Joe Gunn. "Boy, was that hard. Just like artificial turf today."

"It was a hitter's park," contends Blue Jays and Colonels hurler Lynn Lovenguth—"short left, short right. I think I hit three or four homers there myself."

"I loved Rome, that was my favorite park," adds 1947 Oneonta backstop Steve Salata. "It was built like Boston, okay, but if you were a right-center field hitter, it was a piece of cake, because that was the shortest park.... You did everything you could to keep the ball away from a left-hand hitter who could pull it." But in his eyes the park had one drawback: "The lights were terrible. They were so low, if the ball went over them it was an adventure to go and get it."

Night ball was not played there until August 1941, when a portable system was installed for five contests. Attendance averaged 1,581, and a fixed system was installed the following year.

Rumors of the park's sale had preceded the league's demise, and it was torn down in 1952 to make way for a housing tract. The Rome *Sentinel* gave a sorry report of its end:

> Where outfielders once roamed, smooth green turf is now overgrown with high patches of weeds and marked by low depressions filled with water.
> The infield ... no longer presents its well-groomed appearance. Tire tracks from vehicles moving around inside the fences to remove the lights have made large grooves in the clay loam surface.
> Underground conduit pipe, running from the south end of the grandstand to the scoreboard, has been dug up. Fixtures in the concession stand have been ripped out with no thought given to possible restoration. Doors to the rest rooms have been taken off and the floors in the players' showers have been pulled up.
> The overall scene presents concrete evidence that professional baseball is through in Rome....

The developer built a home for himself in what was left field. Also on the site is a senior citizens center and an armory. A plaque from the park honoring three Colonels who died in the World War was moved to a local veterans' post.

Auburn

Auburn's Falcon Park is a fairly standard, classic minor league wood grandstand structure, and survived (and even improved) after the departure of the Canadian-American League.

It's infield was rock hard. "Oh boy! The balls would come at you up there like on a concrete sidewalk," says Cornwall's Joe Gunn. "If it wasn't hit right at you, give it up, that's a hit!"

Falcon Park would be used by the Border League (1946–50) and by several New York–Penn League teams. It was unlit for the Boulies, but on at least one occasion portable lights from Syracuse were used. Fixed lighting was installed in 1940.

"It was owned by the Polish Falcons and it's not in a great section of town, but it's much better now," observed Barney Hearn. "When I got [the Falcons] interested in baseball [in 1946] I had them move that grandstand which was down below town, down in Schaffer Park, which was ruined, and they moved it to Falcon Park and had it rearranged there. And they worked on the infield. It was a lousy park. It dipped off about four feet from home plate to center field. A guy had to be six foot five to play center field or he'd miss 'em. So they filled it in.

"It was a tough park to play in. The infield? It was right better to play in a garage."

Oneonta

Baseball had originally been played at the Fairgrounds (now the Belmont Circle), but that changed in 1905 when a ball field was built on Neahwa Park's site. In October 1908 Dr. Lewis Rutherford Morris, a descendant of Governor Morris, a framer of the United States Constitution, bequeathed 75 acres of land, including the field, to the city. The area was known as Morris Park until 1911 (gratitude evidently didn't last very long even then) when it was renamed Neahwa (meaning "Gift") Park.

Collegiate players from Brown, Holy Cross, Syracuse, and Williams College played ball there in the summers of circa 1910-12. The New York–Penn League's Oneonta Giants, under "Big Ed" Walsh, briefly had Neahwa as their home in 1921.

Many major league barnstorming teams visited the site, including Babe Ruth's and Christy Matthewson's. Ruth walloped a number of gargantuan blasts at the park, but the longest homer ever was hit by shortstop Austin Knickerbocker.

In 1930 a grocer left $5,000 in his will to fix the place up. In 1939 another five grand (this time in WPA funds) was expended, replacing the 1908 wooden grandstand with a steel supported structure (although if you look at it today, it sure looks like it's been there since 1908). Lights were installed in 1940, just in time for the Can-Am League.

"It was a tremendous ball field," adds Knickerbocker. "Down the line it was about 337 on each line and then it went out to about 400 real quickly and continued that way all around the ballpark. There were only two balls hit out all year. I hit one, and Leon Riley of Rome hit the other."

The ballpark itself was renamed Damaschke Field in 1968, after "Dutch" Damaschke, vice president of the old Can-Am team and chairman for over 35 years of the Parks and Recreation Commission.

In 1966, the Oneonta Red Sox returned in the guise of a New York–Penn League franchise, but the next year the working agreement switched to the Yankees and remains so today.

But even now the park is sort of run down, its low bleachers appearing to have come from some defunct Southern Class D circuit. The operation refuses to sell beer. Promotions are relatively few and far between. Varmints occasionally scurry in from the woods to either the stands or onto the field. (If you've never witnessed a bullpen full of players attacking a marauding rabbit with their bats, I can assure you, it's quite a sight.) And yet the team draws amazingly well. Oneonta is a town that loves its baseball, and as the smell of hot dogs and popcorn and sausages wafts through the crowded stands, you can almost see Austin Knickerbocker over at short...

Utica

Purchased by Amby McConnell when he returned to Utica in 1937, Braves Field was near the Mohawk River. Often fog from the waterway made outfield play difficult. Of dubious comfort, its bleachers were known locally as "splinters haven." It was one of the largest-dimensioned fields in all of baseball, with distances of 389 to left, 503 to center, and 400 to right.

When lights were installed in 1939, eight towers with 100 bulbs per pole were erected at a total cost of $10,000. The park was renamed McConnell Field on August 12, 1942, after the late owner (a plaque was placed there in his honor) and from 1943 to 1950 served the Eastern League's Utica Blue Sox. It was torn down in the mid-1950s to make way for an access ramp to the New York State Thruway.

"It was a pretty good ballpark," remembers Austin Knickerbocker. "It was an older park, but it wasn't run down. It had one of the larger seating capacities in the League. Seats went even beyond the left field fence which was very unusual."

"You could probably compare it to the Rugmakers' field over there," says the Blue Jays' Charley Baker, who played for Utica in the Eastern League. "It wasn't modernized like McNearney Stadium, but it was a decent ballpark. You know, it was never really brought up to date."

Kingston

Before the advent of Dietz Stadium baseball was played at the wooden fairgrounds, which burned to the ground in the 1930s. On its site Dietz Stadium was built, named after Staff Sgt. Robert Dietz, a Kingstonian killed in the Second World War who was a Medal of Honor winner. A WPA project that still stands, it was really designed for football (basically it's a single row of concrete bleachers along the first base side), and its dimensions made it difficult to hit one out, featuring a very deep right field.

Nonetheless many fine black teams (the Kansas City Monarchs, Philadelphia Stars, Homestead Grays, Cleveland Buckeyes and Baltimore Elite Giants) played there as well as several barnstorming major league squads (the Cardinals, Brooklyn Dodgers, Pittsburgh, Boston Braves, and

Phils). From 1951 to 1988 it was used for high school football and semipro ball, but in 1989 the park was transferred to the Kingston Board of Education in exchange for another site and will now be used exclusively for football and track.

"We traded tradition for money," commented one Kingston councilman.

Chapter 7

Man in Black, Men in Blue

"Something like four thousand bottles have been thrown
at me in my day, but only about twenty ever hit me. That
does not speak well for the accuracy of the fans' throwing."
Veteran minor league umpire Harry "Steamboat" Johnson

In a field somewhere—anywhere—baseball can just happen. Walk
over to some deserted sandlot diamond, with a bat, ball, and glove, and
from out of nowhere some shy fat kid will appear with a silent, balefully
eager look on his grimy mug.

"Want a catch?" is all you have to say.

Instant smile. Instant baseball.

It doesn't operate that way in organized ball. That requires planning,
money, time, work, work, work, and more work. And, yes, as corny as it
may sound, it takes a lot of love for the game.

When we talk about the organization of the Can-Am League—and
about love of the game—we must start with Father Harold J. Martin.

Father Martin, league president from 1937 to 1944, was a major force
in its history. Beyond that, he was the only Catholic prelate serving as a
league president and the only one selflessly serving without remuneration.
His story is a fascinating one, to say the least.

Born in South Boston on November 10, 1895, Martin excelled in sports
at Boston College High School, Boston College, and Fordham University.
Adding to his prowess was the fact that he was ambidextrous as a pitcher.
"He used two toe plates," recalls one scribe.

"The scouts of other teams were kind of interested in Martin," adds
Daniel McConville, "particularly for John McGraw. But once they found
out he wanted to be a priest, they wouldn't touch him."

At Fordham he roomed with Frankie Frisch and in 1920 signed with
the Eastern League's New Haven and Albany clubs. Martin's record was
hardly overpowering (2–4 with a 4.58 ERA), but he used his earnings to
help pay for studies at Baltimore's St. Mary's Seminary and Christ the King
Seminary at St. Bonaventure's University, where he coached baseball for
two seasons.

Ordained in 1923, he was assigned to the Ogdensburg Cathedral for the next 12 years. While there he organized the Northern New York Semi-Pro League and starred for its Ogdensburg squad, hurling for seven seasons under the alias "Doc O'Reilly."

"It was a poor parish and I felt that if I could get $100 for pitching a ball game for two hours, it would help the exchequer," Martin explained. "I thought I was being cute about it, pitching under an assumed name, but those things get around and eventually the pastor heard about it and called me in for an explanation.

"I told him I was using the money to start a recreation center for the children of the parish. When I got through, the old pastor looked at me, smiled benignly and said, 'See if they need a $50 first baseman.'"

In 1932 the cleric retired from the mound. Ammonia fumes damaged his eyesight when he rushed into a burning building to minister to a trapped fireman.

Martin never mentioned the incident nor would he boast of his bravery.

"In 1935 he imported a colored semipro team under Chappie Johnson," recalls Dan McConville. "They didn't have a nickel; he was hitting people up for five dollars and ten dollars to keep them eating. . . . They had it rough. They couldn't even get a barber to cut their hair. . . ."

Johnson was one of those legendary Bingo Long–type black barnstormers. He purportedly trained his squads to win by exactly two runs. "Any less," wrote William Humber, "and Chappie got nervous, probably because he had a bet riding on the outcome, and no more because white crowds would get restless."

"They were betting all the time," recollects one former semipro. "They were going around the stands with handfuls of money, and they acted as if they didn't know it was illegal. This was right out in the open. They'd walk right along the grandstand and bet ten bucks or whatever you wanted to bet. . . ."

"It did prove one thing to Martin, that pro baseball might prove viable in the area," contended McConville.

Father Martin became a vice-president of the Ogdensburg Colts in 1936. He also supervised the construction of Winter Park in Ogdensburg. ("He was good at getting things donated, lumber, etc. . . . He was trying to get kids interested in hockey.") Later he became part owner of the Utica Braves (he'd known Amby McConnell since 1908), selling his share of the team (then in the Eastern League) in 1943 and selflessly pouring the profits into a new youth center at Winter Park.

One of his continuing goals was the free admission of children to all league contests, a policy he insisted on with the Colts. "There is nothing more pathetic," he contended, "than the sight of a boy trying to sneak his way over a fence into ball game because he is without funds to purchase a ticket."

"I occasionally get letters," Martin once said, "from young fellows who ask me if baseball would interfere with a vocation for the priesthood. I tell them by no means. So far as baseball is concerned, I tell them there isn't a cleaner or more honorable way of making a living on God's earth.

"I contend there is no better solution to the juvenile problem than baseball. Just give the boys a few bats, some baseballs and gloves and you won't have to worry about their future."

The influence Martin exerted on those around him was seen in an item in the 1939 *Sporting News* noting that 16 Colts plus Knotty Lee had received corporate Holy Communion with the St. Peter's Holy Name Society in Ogdensburg. Which leads to the only slightly facetious question: Did Martin only recruit Catholic players?

Martin's clerical background was also evidenced in the rules ("Instructions to Managers, Players and Umpires") he prepared for the league.

One stated: "A coach may address words of assistance and direction to the baserunner or batsman. He shall not, nor shall any player or manager, by words or signs, incite or try to incite the spectators to demonstrations, nor use language which will in any manner refer to or reflect upon a player of the opposite club, the umpire or the spectators."

Another read: "Attention of the managers, coaches and players is specifically directed to the heavy penalties which are to be imposed for assaults or indignities imposed upon umpires. A suspension of 90 playing days is automatic for assaulting an umpire, and this may be increased if the occasion warrants."

The instructions ended with the ringing words: "Play for God, country and baseball. America should thank God for baseball."

End of sermon. Pass the basket. Play ball!

Despite tough words about abusing arbiters, Martin could sympathize with a young ball player. Francis Mason, who met Martin when he pitched for Albany, tells this story: "Down in Amsterdam, when Eddie Sawyer was managing, they had a big shortstop [Armand Sergiacomi], about six feet, who could go into the hole. Well, one evening he lost his poise, and hit an umpire.

"The next morning, down in the rectory in Huevelton, the good padre gets a call from Ed Barrow of the Yanks, who wanted to know what happened.

"He tried to protect the youngster, and Barrow barks at him, 'Leave your stole in the confessional, act like a league president now, and tell me just what happened!'

Father Harold Martin, Canadian-American League president, 1937–1944

"Well, he told him, and they transferred the kid right out of Amsterdam. And at the time he was thought of as a better prospect than Rizzuto. Never heard from him again."

"The thing was overblown to start with," declares Sawyer. "There was certainly no slugging. He touched his mask. That was all he did. There was a lot of pressure in the newspapers because we were doing well to suspend him. Because Father Martin was there they almost forced him to suspend this kid."

"He was a priest who should have been an athletic director," added Sawyer. "He was crazy about baseball. He couldn't make up his mind whether he wanted to be Commissioner of Baseball or Pope!"

"He'd fine me for something and the next day the same umpires would bring the check back to me at home plate.

"Or he would suspend somebody. You see we only had 16 on the roster at the time, and we couldn't afford to have anybody suspended because we didn't have that many players and we had to play pitchers at other positions, but he'd suspend somebody and then go on retreat, and he'd be a little hard to find.

"But he was very colorful and did a good job holding the league together."

"He'd give you the shirt off his back," contends Carrol Belgard. "Once he went to a millionaire's house to ask for money, probably for the ball club. It was a cold day, and the millionaire gave him a fur coat.

"He wore it out of the house, and the next time I saw him he didn't have it.

"I asked him what happened to it. He said he had given it to Tommy Needle, the town drunk. He let him live with him, he had two or three bedrooms in the rectory, trying to rehabilitate him, rather than have him in the jail.

"That's the way he was. He was a really great guy."

His life wasn't all baseball and benedictions. At isolated Heuvelton the St. Raphael's rectory was sometimes freezing cold, and he'd have to drive to Ogdensburg's Hepburn Hospital to sleep in whatever empty bed was available. It was then that he gave away his warm coat to Tommy Needle because, as he put it, "I found someone who needed it more than I."

"He was really the backbone of the league," remembers another league veteran. "I know one time from one of his parishioners, a woman, he got $10,000 personally, a gift. He put it all in the league. He didn't take a dime out. He did everything for baseball."

He was once asked why he spent so much time on the game. "I am trying to repay baseball," he replied, "in a small measure for what the game has done for me."

Unfortunately, Martin's association with the league ended rather sadly. In Buffalo at the 1944 annual league session, Al Houghton succeeded Martin as president. The transition, termed a "surprise" by the usually knowledgeable Rome *Sentinel,* may not have been the very model of grace.

"It was said," the *Sporting News* cryptically reported, "that Rev. Harold Martin ... was unable to be on hand and his name was not presented for re-election."

"We got rid of him," says the Glovers Harry Dunkel bluntly, "and got an active president."

Actually, before the war Martin was extremely active, and the daily press of almost every league city reveals numerous visits by the peripatetic prelate. It makes one wonder how the bishop allowed such activity.

"I think there was a little feeling there between Houghton and Martin," says Jack Minnoch. "I don't know what it was. He used to be Martin's secretary at Utica in the Eastern League."

"He was drinking a lot," reveals Barney Hearn, "during the baseball season, probably after the war too. But he was a nice man. I suppose they drove him to drink, a lot of those people."

"Duke" Farrington, who pitched in the league from 1936 to 1940, offers this on the subject: "He was quite a drinker, a good natured guy — you know — an Irishman that would drink, not a drunkard by any means."

But in 1946 Martin (along with Knotty Lee) was still able to help found and become honorary chairman of the board of another Class C circuit, the Border League. Once again he was a part owner of the Ogdensburg franchise. That loop would be a veritable Can-Am alumni association, with former league cities Ottawa, Auburn, Ogdensburg, Cornwall, and Watertown among its members. Barney Hearn and Charlie Small served as managers there. Eddie Sawyer even dropped in to help get the Geneva franchise off the ground. A former treasurer of the Can-Am was John G. Ward, president of the Ogdensburg Trust Bank, who later became Border loop president, and Martin served as his advisor. "They were kind of Amos and Andy up there," says Barney Hearn. In 1948 National Association prexy George Trautman paid the "Baseball Priest" the honor of journeying to Ogdensburg to attend the silver jubilee of his ordination.

In failing health ("he had an extended illness in January or February of 1957 and rarely said mass after that," says Monsignor Griffith Billmyer who cared for him from 1955 on), Father Harold J. Martin died of a heart attack at 11:55 AM on Thursday, May 8, 1958, at Canton, New York.

Eulogized the Ogdensburg *Journal,*

> he thought only of others, never of himself. He completely lived the religion he professed. His greatest happiness and satisfaction was in helping the poor, the sick, the lonely, the defeated, the unfortunate. He had a host of prominent friends who gave him money, clothing, food, automobiles, all sorts of things for his own comfort. He never kept any of them any longer than it took him to give them away to those who had what he considered a greater need.

Succeeding Father Martin in December 1944 was Albert E. "Ned" Houghton, one-time proprietor of the Gloversville Business School. Houghton wasn't the colorful figure Martin was, but he too loved his baseball. He worked mightily to keep Lou Gorski's Glovers from leaving town and in 1938 served briefly as business manager and secretary of the team's new version. Ned then became league secretary and statistician.

As league secretary in 1940, Houghton instituted the league's "Orange Book." Modeled after the major leagues' Green and Red books, it was a yearly guide to the circuit's history and status. Starting out at just ten pages, it grew to a publication that was the equal or better of many larger circuits' logs. The *Sporting News* termed it "one of the most comprehensive brochures on league-records and histories ever put out by a smaller circuit." It was.

Albert E. "Ned" Houghton, Martin's successor as league president, 1944–1951.

In 1943–44 Houghton served as business manager of Utica's Eastern League team, but gave that up to take a post with Schenectady's U.S. Army Depot.

"He held that league together," recalls former Gloversville newspaperman Bill Evans. Harry Dunkel adds: "He was a great worker. I don't know when he slept." In the late 1940s he moved to Schenectady. By 1954 he picked up stakes again, heading for Williamsport, Pennsylvania, where he became associated with the national Little League organization, first as Eastern Regional Director, then as International Tournament head. Even in old age, he was a ramblin' guy, moving in 1969 to San Bernadino, California, to become the Little League's Western Regional Director. There he spearheaded the development of their regional center, which in his honor was renamed Al Houghton Park in 1981.

He died at San Bernadino on October 4, 1984, at the age of 83.

Publicizing the league was the Can-Am League Writers Association. Founded in May 1938 by Oswego *Palladium-Times* sports editor J. Russell

Gill, it was comprised of representatives of papers from around the circuit, and eventually from radio stations as well. It worked to promote the league, to improve facilities for the press at parks, and to elect an MVP each year who would receive a "Baseball Writers' Trophy."

Bill Evans served as official scorer at Glovers Park. "They gave us $2 a game," he recalls, "if there was a doubleheader $3. They said we were at the park anyway. But when they instituted split day-night doubleheaders, they still gave us $3!"

The first league All-Star Game was played on July 7, 1939, at Utica in front of a mediocre crowd of 1,568 paying customers, although considering the downpour that occurred just before game time perhaps that wasn't too bad. The Northern Division — Quebec, Three Rivers, Rome, and Utica, managed by Rome's Lee Riley — was pitted against the Southern — Amsterdam, Gloversville-Johnstown, Oneonta, and Pittsfield, piloted by Pittsfield's Art Funk. Sportswriters selected the participating stars. The purpose of the game was to establish a $1,000 fund to be divided among players of the first division teams at season's end — which sounds great but averaged less than $20 per player!

The league employed a playoff system by which all first division clubs qualified, the so-called Shaughnessy Playoffs. In 1936 Bill Buckley tried to cajole the New York State Kiwanis organization into donating an award for the winner, but nothing much came of the idea. In 1938, though, A.W. Shuttleworth, president of Amsterdam's Mohawk Carpet Mills, provided a suitable trophy, a huge silver bowl, adorned with the figure of a ball player. Permanent possession was to go to whichever club first took the playoffs three times, an honor that went to Oneonta for winning in 1941, 1942, and 1948.

To replace the Shuttleworth prize, Harold Ford, president of the Oneonta Red Sox, donated a trophy in memory of his father, the late Arthur E. Ford. It was topped by the likeness of a catcher. A few months after donating the award, Ford himself died in Ocala, Florida, preparing for spring training.

In the spring of 1948 the Can-Am brain trust realized that pennant winners were being slighted by all this playoff hoopla, and authorized a golden trophy on a walnut base to be awarded to the first place club. The initial recipients were the Rome Colonels, whose bad luck couldn't be shaken even in normally joyous circumstances. Magnate Dan Mellen couldn't receive this handsome bauble personally from Al Houghton, recuperating as he was from a broken leg.

In 1938 President A.D. Campbell of the Class D Cape Breton Colliery League proposed a postseason playoff with the Can-Am teams, but nothing resulted from the idea of playing the Nova Scotia–based circuit.

That same year was the only time the playoffs weren't completed.

Schenectady Blue Jays manager Lee Riley receiving the 1947 Can-Am League Championship Trophy. (Courtesy of Guy Barbieri.)

Miserable rain and cold kept delaying the final round between Amsterdam and Cornwall. Enthusiasm ran high—over 20 Bison partisans made the long trek down to Mohawk Mills Park and stayed over for several days awaiting play to begin. Valiant efforts were made to get the contests in. Over 50 gallons of gas were burned on the infield one day. In the end, it was all for naught. Players had to return to off-season jobs or school, and Father Martin called a halt to the proceedings.

Until 1947, there was no substantial reward for players who finished first or made the playoffs, although the gates were certainly lucrative enough for management. That year, a $6,000 "player pool" was established, with $250 apiece coming from each of the eight ball clubs and the remainder from playoff revenues (postseason attendance of 40,000 was anticipated—56,000 was achieved). The regular season winners were to divvy up $2,000, playoff champs were to divide $1,700, with the other two first-division teams to split the rest.

Some front-office personnel were especially noteworthy. Amsterdam business manager Bruce Henry climbed up the Yankee chain and served as business manager of the big club for ten seasons as well as stadium manager for one. "I did it all," professed Henry, the originator of major league "Bat Day," of his Amsterdam tour of duty, "I sold tickets, helped fix the field, did the promotions, made speeches, arranged travel and the rest."

"Dizzy Dean spent an awful lot of time here," says Harold McMullen, who ran the Mohawk Mills Park concessions in 1950. "He was the pitching scout. Bruce Henry would be the one to tell 'em if they had made it. Dean would make the decision. He'd [Henry] tell 'em: 'I hope you didn't unpack your bags.' Just like cattle!"

"I had a good offer from . . . the East Palm Beach club in the Florida International League," Henry once said. "I called Mr. Weiss and asked him for more money, so he told me I had done a fine job and he wouldn't stand in my way."

Not exactly a raise, Bruce.

There were jobs for everyone, even kids. "I was thrilled," says Don Decker of his stint as Rugmakers batboy. "God. My first paycheck was from the New York Yankees — the first paycheck I ever received in my life. I think it was $3.50 a week, 50 cents a game. That was fantastic, to get the checks from Yankee Stadium."

And there were plenty of jobs for umpires. Minor league umpiring featured abysmal pay, infinitesimal salaries and physical danger. If you think calling balls and strikes in the majors is a controversial post, try it in the bushes. Umpires have been clubbed to death at home plate by bat-wielding fans, had sand poured in their crankcases, had their teeth knocked out, been tear-gassed, and chased through town by howling mobs.

Aside from that, it was swell.

As you would expect turnover was rather high. In June of 1952, for example, the entire Western Carolinas League staff handed in their resignations *en masse.*

Umpiring in the Can-Am circuit started out haphazardly. The circuit's first arbiters were usually local boys. Retired players could be offered posts. Eventually, to eliminate any hint of hometown favoritism, a geographical limit was imposed, and no one residing within the Can-Am's boundaries was considered for a berth. Toward its end, a plan was put forward which would systematize advancement to higher classifications.

Sometimes, however, the arbiters never even showed up, as in August 1936 when Brockville visited Oswego. Umps Knight and Farrand were nowhere to be seen. To fill in, Watertown's Admiral Martin went behind the plate, and Ogdensburg team captain Bernie Fasullo umpired the bases.

Both were given high marks, but neither considered it their real calling. Why they just happened to be hanging around Oswego at the time is unknown. On another prewar occasion, Auburn sportswriter Leo Pinckney was pressed into service. And in May 1947 the arbiters were AWOL at an Electrics–Blue Jays contest at McNearney Stadium.

As we said before, shouting "Kill the Ump" (and more than occasionally really meaning it) is a time-honored American tradition, and the Canadian-American circuit made it an international one as well.

In July 1937 the Cornwall *Freeholder* reported: "Fearless Fido Murphy was at the game [in Cornwall], not as umpire but as a spectator. He is taking a two week rest at the suggestion of League President Martin who thinks Murphy has been 'overworked.' The fact that Murphy tossed aside his mask after the Cornwall-Ogdensburg game the other evening and challenged anyone in the crowd to a bout of fisticuffs may have something to do with the mid-season vacation."

"He was a whackeroo," adds outfielder Barney Hearn, "I knew him pretty well. He was umpiring one day in Ottawa, and in Ottawa they had the horses out in the outfield, circus days, you know. They had the circus out there a couple of days before. So Murphy called me out at the plate. Lousy pitch. So I said, 'You're horseshit, Mr. Murphy.' He said, 'You pop off once again, and you're gone!' So I didn't do anything more. I went out in the outfield, and I grabbed hold of a dry horse ball. When I came in, a couple of innings later, I dropped it on home plate, and I said, 'That's what I think of you!' He ran me out of the ball game. People didn't know why I was being run. That was it!

"That was terrible. Real corny."

Sometimes the humor turned to outright violence, as Smiths Falls Beavers pilot John Haddock struck an umpire named Arthur on August 5, 1937, during a game at Perth. He was fined $100 and suspended for ten days by Father Martin.

Cornwall seemed particularly sensitive about umpiring. The Cornwall *Freeholder* in 1939 was vehement in regard to arbiter Gene Oppel: "While ordinarily we refrain from comment on the grounds that the men in blue are out there doing their best and are entitled to make an odd mistake, we must admit we've never seen the like of Oppel in organized ball. His work is lousy behind the bat and on the bases. We hope Father Martin will keep Oppel away from the Cornwall ballpark from now on. Cornwall fans are by no means umpire baiters. Most of the arbiters agree 'it's a pleasure to work in Cornwall.' But one of these days our mild ball fans will land on Oppel with both feet."

Thanks to such barely disguised incitement to riot Father Martin changed the umpiring rotation to spare Oppel any further trips to Cornwall for some time.

But that wasn't enough for the howling Bison fans. Later that year umpires Wally Evans and Pat Padden were working a Bisons-Nets game there, and a close Padden decision gave Oswego a 5-3 win.

The fans were outraged. At game's end they surrounded the clubhouse, and only a police cordon could get Padden and Evans into their dressing room. Once there, they were "virtually under siege" and though the mob was cleared, that didn't solve the problem. When the two umps finally departed, both arbiters and police were roughly jostled before they could speed away.

"You know," observes Barney Hearn, "those babies up there wanted to smash somebody. An umpire kicked one or didn't call a strike or ball right, they'd charge the plate. You know, hockey stuff and lacrosse. Christ, everybody had a welt on their face!"

Yet things were worse at Utica on July 6th of that year. It all started when star Utica hurler Emil Hemenway beaned "G-ville" centerfielder Alex Clowson ("He was a troublemaker," observed Utica pitcher Art Horsington) in the eighth inning of a close contest.

"The ball glanced off Clowson's head," noted one journalist, "and he trotted off to first without a complaint." Umpire Bob "Frankenstein" Crouch ejected Hemenway, charging he'd intentionally thrown at Clowson. The game was held up a quarter hour as Utica players wrangled on the field and as bottles and other debris rained down from the stands. "After the ninth," reported the Cornwall *Freeholder,* "Crouch was taken to the park office, and a police patrol was summoned to escort him out of the park as fans stormed around the office. During the melee several pop bottles were thrown. One struck a policeman [Patrolman John R. Jones — obviously an alias] on the head inflicting a painful but not serious injury."

A few weeks later the colorful Crouch was canned after calling a game on account of darkness in Gloversville — a decision that cost Utica a win over the Mittens. The Braves had gone ahead by three runs in extra frames, but when Crouch called off the contest, the score reverted to the top of the frame. The dismissal actually led to over 1,000 Rome fans petitioning for his reinstatement — but to no avail.

Father Martin granted Crouch a hearing, but contended that the controversial Glovers-Braves call had nothing to do with "Frankenstein's" exit. What actually did him in was that after the fracas in Utica, Martin ordered Crouch to avoid that city. Soon afterward ump Enos Vaughan called on Crouch to help him officiate there. Crouch did, and when Martin found out, both were history.

That Martin was part-owner of the Braves didn't seem to upset anyone.

Crouch came to the league in 1938 with a somewhat mixed reputation.

He had umped the 1935 season in the Class D Pennsylvania State Association, and in one contest at Butler erroneously called a ball hit by a Charleroi batter that bounced over the right field barrier a home run.

The next Sunday, he was again in Butler, and before the game a small boy, carrying a very large sign, marched on to the field. His placard read: "Rule 49 of the baseball rules states that a ball that bounces over the fence is a two base hit."

As luck would have it, in the seventh frame the visiting shortstop hit a ball which caromed over the left field barrier.

Crouch bowed low to the howling fans and intoned formally: "That, ladies and gentlemen is a two base hit."

The crowd went wild.

Also in 1939 Amsterdam shortstop Armand Sergiacomi and Oswego first baseman Joe Zagami each received 90-day suspensions from National Association president Bramham for assaulting umpires. Sergiacomi had ripped the mask off umpire Fred Melton at Amsterdam on July 20. Bramham (who hated any such behavior and in 1943 suspended Richmond Colts pilot Ben Chapman for a whole season for such an altercation) warned that any further incidents would automatically merit the same punishment.

Ah, the good old days!

A number of big league umps served in Can-Am ranks. American League arbiter Joe Paparella called balls and strikes in 1938–39. "My real break came in 1937...," he once told author Don Honig. "A Catholic priest named Gallagher came over to me after the game. He said he liked my style and asked if I had ever thought of turning professional. I told him that was my dream. He said he would recommend me to a friend of his [Father Martin].... Three days later I got the call to report to Ogdensburg for an interview. I drove up and came back with a contract for the next season. I got $180 a month, which wasn't much money when you figure I had to send money home to support my family and also pay all my expenses on the road. I made the playoffs that first year, and guess what my salary was the second year? A hundred and eighty a month. I never even got a five cent raise."

Ump Shag Crawford worked the loop in 1950, his first pro stint. Things hadn't changed much. "The money was horrendous,' confirmed the 20-year National League vet. "When I broke into the Canadian-American League, I got $250 a month. I had to send that home to my wife and kids. I lived on $100 a month expense money, which meant I was paying $1 or $1.25 a day for a room. There was always a lot of company in those rooms — bedbugs and what have you. I used to look for restaurants that served a lot of bread. That's the truth. If they served lots of bread they had me for a regular customer."

Yet it gave him a real chance. "I never went to umpiring school," he

Herbert Shuttleworth, Wallace McQuatters and American League umpire Art Papparella meet in Amsterdam, 1948. (Photo courtesy of Amsterdam *Recorder*—Val Webb photo.)

admitted, "I was plucked right off the sandlots.... I was very fortunate because if I had been required to go to umpiring school, I never would have made it. I would never have been able to go because it cost too much money. I was married and had three kids, so it would have been impossible to attend the school."

Paparella and Crawford weren't the only ones to advance. American League umpires Ed Hurley (Can-Am League 1942) and Nestor Chylak (1948) and National League arbiters Artie Gore (1937–38), Frank Dascoli (1946) and Tom ("anytime I got one of those 'bang-bang' plays at first base, I called 'em out. It made the game shorter") Gorman (1948) also made the grade.

"We had another thing," recalls Spencer Fitzgerald, "maybe they weren't supposed to do it, but Hurley and Joe Papparella, they would always find us after a game out of town, and they would talk over the calls, what Eddie's [Sawyer] views were as manager and me as a spectator. Hurley, he became pretty good."

One ump who didn't advance was William O. Haynes, but then again he didn't exactly need the cash. Haynes, who officiated in the league in 1939, was a 32-year-old Rochester, New Hampshire, millionaire sportsman who had inherited his fortune just the year before. Prior to umping for Father Martin, he'd scouted for the Bees and Yankees and wore blue for the Class B Piedmont League, which he abandoned because he preferred a less southern clime. When he quit the Can-Am it was to go back to Boston as their New England scout.

His dry cleaning bill was probably higher than the contents of the league treasury.

Chapter 8

War Is Hell

"Our people don't mind being rationed on sugar and shoes, but these men in Washington will have to leave our baseball alone!"
Fiorello LaGuardia, 1942

The Second World War altered every American's life and affected baseball as part of the bargain. Thousands of ball players entered the service, and a labor shortage resulted. Millions of fans went into uniform or into defense work, and attendance dropped.

Teams nationwide held a series of promotions to aid the war effort, including "Smokes for Servicemen Night," "Aluminum Night," and the unfortunately named "Waste Fat Night" in Louisville, where patriots donated 2,587 pounds of grease.

Life changed in many ways. With most menfolk gone a women's pro league sprang up. In 1943 Phil Wrigley put together the All-American Girls Professional Baseball League, with teams like the Racine Belles, Grand Rapids Chicks and Fort Wayne Daisies.

Minor league ball was a particular casualty.

It was no sure bet that baseball would survive the war. World War I was an almost total disaster. In 1917, 20 minor leagues began the season, but only nine started 1918, and only one, the International, finished out the year. The *Sporting News'* circulation sank to a mere 5,000. By Armistice Day 144 National Leaguers and 103 American Leaguers were in uniform. Major league attendance dropped by over two million in 1918 to just 3,080,126, the century's lowest total. The season ended on Labor Day. The World Series itself nearly was cancelled. Only the Kaiser's surrender saved the game for the 1919 season.

Baseball was not about to go down that road again. Commissioner Landis would not approach Franklin Delano Roosevelt directly, but in his stead had Washington owner Clark Griffith contact him. FDR gave baseball a "green light" to operate during wartime.

"I honestly feel," Roosevelt wrote, "that it would be best for the country to keep baseball going. There will be fewer people unemployed and everybody will work longer hours than ever before. And that means that they ought to have a chance for recreation and for taking their minds off their work than ever before."

Baseball was back in business.

The military draft actually preceded Pearl Harbor, starting in November 1940. Former Rome Colonel Billy Southworth, Jr., now with Toronto, was the first player to enlist. By August of 1941, 153 minor leaguers (out of a possible 5,000) had been drafted. Eventually 4,000 would serve.

The majors were deluged with players boasting one 4-F qualifying malady after another: Jack Kramer (asthma), George Binks (deaf in one ear), Frank Mancuso (bad back), Dick Sipek (totally deaf), Tom Sunkel and Jack Franklin (each blind in one eye), Mike Garbak (hernia), Vern Stephens and Lou Boudreau (bad knees), Hal Newhouser (bad heart), Dizzy Trout (poor eyesight), Tommy Holmes (sinuses), and Leo Durocher (punctured eardrum).

Calling Doctor Kildare!

Then there were the kids: Cincinnati's 15-year-old southpaw Joey Nuxhall, the A's 16-year-old hurler Carl Scheib, and Brooklyn's 16-year-old shortstop Tommy Brown. And the old timers: the Cards' 40-year-old Pepper ("the Wild Hoss of the Osage," himself) Martin; Yankees catcher Bill Steinecke (who'd played for 21 minor league teams); Cubs pitcher John Miklos (back from a beat on the Chicago Police Department); and Reds righthander Hod Lisenbee (tosser of the Babe's 58th dinger in '27).

With players like that in the majors, one can imagine what was in Class D. After the 1941 campaign, 10 of 41 bush leagues folded. The Can-Am struggled on, but accommodations were made.

Ironically, it was on its best footing. For the first time in its short history there were no franchise shifts. Every team except Three Rivers had some sort of tie-in with a higher classification club, and every park save Pittsfield's now had permanent lights. Rome had just installed a new $10,000 system, which proved a necessity, when due to defense-work overtime the club shifted all its Saturday games to evenings.

Travel restrictions made southern spring training impossible, even for big leaguers. The Dodgers trained at Bear Mountain, New York, and the Yankees at a high school gym in Asbury Park, New Jersey. So 1942 saw the Quebec Athletics become the first professional team ever to hold camp at Cooperstown's Doubleday Field, the game's reputed "birthplace."

Hotel accommodations were tight. Teams visiting Rome had to lodge in nearby Utica. Then on June 1, 1942, the government banned charter bus travel. Since only Amsterdam and Gloversville-Johnstown owned buses at the time, that spelled trouble, as train travel was prohibitively expensive.

Father Martin saw the bright side: "As far as the Canadian-American League players are concerned, having learned how to ride in every conceivable posture in buses, they'll welcome riding trains or regular bus lines."

"The first year [1941]," observed Amsterdam's travelling secretary Spencer Fitzgerald of roadtrips to Quebec and Three Rivers, "we went up the whole way by bus. The second year, the gas rations got so we'd only drive to Montreal, park the bus there, and then take the train to Three Rivers and then to Quebec and then back to pick up the bus...

"You had to manifest everything for customs. Put down if you had two fog lights and one spare tire, and you'd better have two fogs and one spare tire when you went back across the border. They'd only let you take one dozen new baseballs across. You could take as many beat up balls as you wanted, but only a dozen of the new ones. They were rough....

"I used to bring a carton of cigarettes each trip for Morel, the sportswriter in Three Rivers. They only had Player's cigarettes. They were like smoking hay!"

"You couldn't trade anybody or make any deals or get rid of anybody before you left Canada," adds Eddie Sawyer, "because whatever you had on your manifest going up, you had to have on your manifest coming back. And they counted heads. So you had to wait until you got back to make any trades and so forth."

While visiting clubs could bring a few baseballs across the border, the two Canadian clubs themselves were barred from importing any horsehide spheres. The *Sporting News* reported that hitters complained the Canadian balls' stitches were pronounced, that the "rabbit" had been extracted, and that only the hardest hit balls really carried. Utica's Jodie Phipps noted that "on every pitch the ball does something. The fast ball really takes off — sort of shoots away from the batter. And when you want to throw, that apple sure bends."

"I loved it there," exclaims 1942 Quebec outfielder Barney Hearn, "but I didn't like the baseballs they were using. Canadian balls, Christ! You'd hit 'em through the infield, and the infielders would catch up to them and throw you out. They were dead balls. They were accepted in the league, but they were deader than hell. It was a ball just like the Rawlings ball or the Wilson ball, whatever, but it was deader than hell!"

Immigration problems surfaced. Three Rivers hired their 1941 catcher, Tuck McWilliams, as their manager for 1942, but he fell afoul of immigration and was dropped. Besides McWilliams, other managers were lost due to the war. Utica's 1941 pilot Frank Zubic went into the Army. Outfielder Henry Block, Lee Riley's scheduled replacement at Rome, instead chose to enter defense work. Considering how the team fared with their new Phils working agreement, he made the right choice.

Players were equally vulnerable to immigration's snares. The Rugmakers' Winnipeg-born catcher Eddie Gibb was nearly stranded across the border in 1941, but manager Eddie Sawyer pulled strings to get him back to the States. On one road trip Utica's third baseman Jorge Torres and pitcher George Comellas, both Cubans (Comellas fled after the 1934 revolution), were almost denied access to Canada, although for Havana-born first baseman Regie Otero it was no problem. For Opening Day, two Three Rivers players were unable to travel to Pittsfield. Once Pittsfield left behind seven at the border, which must have meant a pretty small squad made it through.

Canadian-born Joe Krakauskas was with Washington in 1939. Even though the Dominion hadn't resorted to conscription in World War I, Joe was taking no chances, and promptly announced plans to seek U.S. citizenship. "Ever since I have been in organized baseball, I have intended to become an American citizen," revealed Krakauskas. Going on, he bluntly stated, "I may be drafted by Canada, but I do not plan to enlist."

Nice try Joe, but you went anyway.

From the majors to the worst Class D league, talent was in short supply. Cornwall's Phil Marchildon was hurling for the 1942 Philadelphia Athletics and did quite well (17–14), but the team behind him was no prize, featuring the era's usual 4-Fs and retreads.

"They couldn't make the double play if you hit a line drive," Phil told author William Mead. "Dick Siebert he had a brace on his knee, and the other guy on third base, Buddy Blair, he had a brace on his knee. They couldn't move very far, either of them. There was a fellow playing shortstop by the name of Davis; he wasn't much of a player either. Oh boy. There was a challenge. You got quite a kick out of being able to win."

And there were financial problems. Due to the war, the bulk of Phil's big league salary went to a Canadian bank for deposit. For a while he lived on $25 a week. "I squawked about trying to get by on 25 bucks," Phil told the Cleveland *Press,* "so they upped me $10. I try to get by on $35 now, but it isn't easy, the way we have to live."

Many of the Can-Am's better players were no longer available, but Father Martin again viewed the silver lining: "Undoubtedly we shall have many more young and inexperienced players than in former years. This may even be a benefit to the game, for the opportunities for the youngsters may bring to light another Maurice Van Robays or Mel Queen or Hal White."

To entice players, on May 26, 1941, the league raised its monthly salary limit from $1,600 to $1,800 (the Class C limit). "Defense pay," commented the *Sporting News,* "was making minor league berths less attractive."

Especially hard hit was Rome, which began the season having just one pitcher with pro experience. Nine of the 19 players in camp had no pro background. Defending champion Oneonta opened its camp with not one holdover from the 1941 squad.

When Mel Simons gave up the Quebec managing post, veteran bush league skipper Guy Lacy was given the job—on one condition, that he deliver five new players. He couldn't, wiring the Athletics: "All ball players I know have jobs and I'm sorry." Ex–Three Rivers manager Charlie Small got the call at that point.

"My ball players were afraid of being drafted during those years," reveals Glovers prexy Harry Dunkel, "they were all in good health. They were all the right age for the service to grab, and my manager, Bill Hornsby, couldn't stay for the playoffs. He got two postponements to report to his home in California, and he left us during the playoffs. . . .

"The recruiting officers wanted all my ball players. I had to pull all kinds of tricks. One fellow, Gene somebody, he was a centerfielder, came from down around Boston. [His father was a naval officer], and he wasn't about to be drafted. I had to send him to the dentist to get his teeth fixed and tell the dentist not to fix them but to give him an appointment three months from now when the season was over. So we saved him.

"I made deals with the recruiting officers that so-and-so signed up, but he didn't have to report until some time in September.

"When the war came on I had three ball players that Gloversville owned. The rest of them were all Browns players, and I went to some kind of a meeting, and the business manager of the New York Yankees, he said: 'I'll give you $300 apiece for any ball players you got, if they got two arms and two legs.' I said: 'All right. I'll transfer to you three players, three local boys.' They weren't regulars. So I got $900, and that took care of the club's expenses for taxes and incidentals for when we had no ball games during the war."

Obviously, the Yankees hadn't heard of Pete Gray. For if they had, they'd have shown more interest in any one armed ball players the Can-Am had.

Gray was the fabled one-armed outfielder for the St. Louis Browns in the war-year of 1945. He was also one of the more spectacular players ever produced by the Can-Am loop—before, during, or after the war.

At age six, Pete fell off a horse-drawn delivery truck, catching his right arm in the spokes. It was amputated at the elbow. He learned to do everything lefthanded, including playing baseball.

He had a special glove constructed, enabling him to play the outfield. "You know," Gray once revealed, "I had a shoemaker make that glove for me special. He'd take out most of the padding, and I'd use it like a first baseman's glove, keeping my pinky inside. It helped me get rid of the glove quicker. I'd catch the ball, stick the glove under my stump, roll the ball across my chest, and throw it back in. No big deal. It was just grounders that gave me some trouble."

In the late 1930s he played semipro ball (including a stint at Three Rivers, hitting .283 in 60 games), and when in 1942 Three Rivers finally gave him a chance to play in organized ball, he didn't think twice.

"They signed me by telephone," recalled Gray. "When I got up to Montreal, the manager met my train. I had a coat draped over my stump, and when I took it off, the guy almost passed out. But I figured I already had a contract, and he might as well give me a chance."

His debut was pure story-book stuff. Word spread about him, and the unusually large crowd was chanting "We want Gray," but he didn't get into the game until the ninth, as Three Rivers was being shut out one to nothing.

"It was like in the movies," Gray says, "the bases were loaded with two out, and they sent me up to hit. The crowd went crazy. I was swinging two bats around my arm, and they kept screaming my name in French. The count went to two and one, and I lined the next pitch down the rightfield line. The next thing I remember, everyone was throwing money at me. By the time I finished stooping, I'd collected over $700. Hey, I figured this game was made for me."

He continued hot, going five for his first eight at-bats, but in late May he fell after catching a fly ball, fracturing his collarbone. He went home to Pennsylvania but came back to hit .381 in 42 games.

"I was amazed to see him out there," says Barney Hearn, who was then with Quebec. "He could run like hell, but he couldn't hit [for distance]. We'd shade him in left field. He couldn't hit the ball over your head, but he could beat out a lot of bunts, but he lost a lot of runners by putting the glove under his arm. He couldn't [hit a change-up], but he did a pretty good job for what he had. He could *bunt* .350 anywhere! He'd drag down first base. Christ! The pitcher would scoot over there, and he'd bunt up the middle. He was a cutter!"

Eventually Gray made his way to the Browns in 1945 where he hit .218 in 77 games. Amazingly, his bat control was so proficient, he fanned only 11 times in 234 A.L. at-bats.

One thing to remember about Gray is that he was not *just* a war-time phenomenon. He continued playing minor league ball until 1949 and hit .290 in the Eastern League in 1948.

In 1942 special games were held in each league city to aid the war effort. Special uniforms were worn, with home teams clad in white with red and blue trim. The league's name was on the front and a large "V"—for victory—was on the back. (One can be seen today in Cooperstown). Visitors were adorned in blue with red and white trim and lettering. The circuit seemed defensive about all this sartorial splendor, however, going out of its way to note that this was all part of the national program and not something they had dreamed up on their own.

They must have sensed disaster. Two games were washed out entirely, and three were nearly cancelled by rain. In Quebec $240.30 was turned over to the local chapter of "Les Voltiguers de Quebec" after a game with Rome.

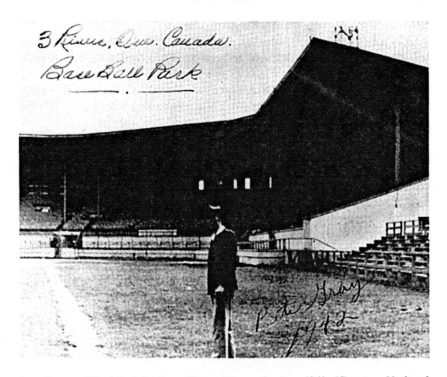

Pete Gray at Municipal Stadium, Three Rivers, Quebec, 1942. (Courtesy National Baseball Library, Cooperstown, N.Y.)

Oneonta at Utica netted $530 on June 5, but after those two contests pickings were slim. Utica at Gloversville returned only $68.98. The Glovers at Pittsfield and Rome at Amsterdam both lost money, but the Rugmakers kicked in $25, anyway. Three Rivers at Rome returned just $7.02, for a not very grand total of $871.30.

Careers were short circuited. The New York *Times* in spring 1945 estimated that of 5,800 professional ball players, 5,400 were in the armed services. "A lot of these players were hurt by the war," contends Eddie Sawyer. "They were drafted after they were with me, and a lot never came back to play. Of course, some of them were hurt in the service too. A lot of the fellows in Class C were just coming into their own when they had to go into the service."

Dozens and dozens of Can-Am players were drafted or enlisted and lost prime years—like Vic Raschi, Kenny Sears, Torby MacDonald, Roland Gladu, Bob Lemon, Allie Clark, Joe Collins, Hal White, Bill Kennedy, Al Rosen, Jim Cullinane, Bunny Mick, Brownie Blaszak, Joe Lutz, Gene Hasson, Clyde Smoll, Whitey Platt, Frank Shea, Pete Elko, Eddie McGah, Chuck Harmon, John Wright, Ben Huffman, Stan Partenheimer,

Dick Fowler, Bob Crues, Conklyn Meriwether, Joe Krakauskas, Herb Karpel, Mel Queen, Duke Markell, and Maurice Van Robays. Even "front office" personnel like the Rugmakers' Herb Shuttleworth and Spencer Fitzgerald left civilian life.

Phil Marchildon, as noted earlier, ended up in a German POW·camp. Yale-educated Cornwall catcher Walt Klimczak (who advanced to the A's 1942 spring roster) was shot up badly in the Pacific theater.

"I got drafted by Jersey City in the International League after 1941," recalls Oneonta's Austin Knickerbocker. "I was there a month, and I went into the service and didn't play ball again for four years. In other words, from 23 to 27, I was out of baseball entirely. I came back, and I got bought by Toronto, played there, went to the Philadelphia A's. They were allowed to buy two guys—Hank Biassatti and myself—for ten grand. Well, neither of us blossomed. By the time I got there I was 29. I was too old. If you don't show outstanding ability at 29, they won't fool around with you. They sell you the first chance they get, which happened to me."

Not all the players went into combat. Many ended up on powerful service clubs, such as Cornwall's Whitey Platt or future black Can-Am players John Wright and Chuck Harmon at Great Lakes Naval Training Center in Illinois, future Gloversville pilot Ben Huffman at Norfolk's Naval training station, or 1941 Rugmakers catcher Tony Ravish at Sampson Naval Training Center in upstate New York. "I was in the service for four and a half years," says Ravish. "I caught for Sampson Naval base for three years. We had Johnny VanDermeer. Konstanty was there. Hal White from Utica. We had a great pitching staff. We beat the Red Sox. We beat the Cleveland club. We had all the good fellows in the service, you know."

He wasn't exaggerating. Sampson beat Boston 20–7 and walloped the Indians 15–2. They were good.

Packy Rogers also played for Sampson in 1944 and 1945, then went over to the Pearl Harbor Submarine Base (along with Kenny Sears) when he won All-Star status in the tough Fourteenth Naval District League.

Several other Can-Amers wound up playing in that very same circuit. Bob Lemon and Whitey Platt were on the Aiea Barracks team on Oahu. Catcher Eddie McGah was with the squad from Base 8 Hospital.

It was in Hawaii that Bob Lemon became a pitcher. Before entering the Navy Lem had twice failed to dislodge Kenny Keltner from the Cleveland hot corner, but was still a third sacker—and an All-Star one—in Hawaii. When pitchers Fred Hutchinson and Lou Ciola came down with injuries, Aiea manager Billy Herman, hearing his hard throwing infielder also possessed a sharp curve ball, pressed Bob into mound service. The experiment was a success, good enough for Lemon to pitch in an American versus National League All-Star Series on the islands.

A sidelight. Late in the war, Keltner was drafted and sent to Hawaii.

Jim Cullinane, Gloversville-Johnstown manager and MVP in 1949.

He wasn't too crazy about sleeping in the regular three-tiered bunks, and thought he'd be better off with the ball players. He got his way, and went about looking for a suitable berth. Checking out the area, he came upon none other than a snoozing Bob Lemon. Pulling back the mosquito netting, he shook Bob awake. "Oh, no," moaned the groggy Lemon to his perpetual nemesis, "not you again!"

While Lemon found a career in the service, some players had their careers ruined before they commenced. Postwar Quebec hurler Bill Fennhahn had served in Europe. "I got hurt pretty bad," he explained. "Both legs were broken. A nerve injury in my right leg, and I got 90 percent disability eventually...." He returned home and was signed by the North Atlantic League's Peekskill Highlanders. He found his way to Quebec in 1947. "A lot of guts," says his manager in both places, Tony Ravish, "I always pitched him in seven-inning ball games because he had shrapnel in the back of his legs ... then his legs would get tired naturally. But for seven innings, boy, he could fire that ball for me!"

Billy Southworth, Jr., the 1939 League MVP, got an even rougher deal. Southworth was the finest player Rome ever produced. His stats were impressive — 15 homers, 20 stolen bases, and a .342 average.

"Billy was a fabulous talent," says Red Ermisch, "what a great guy. He was the only son of Billy Southworth, Sr., I believe. He was the apple of his father's eye. He could run, throw, and hit. He was Major League talent. He could do everything very well.

"Sort of a spoiled big kid. Course, I guess he was spoiled by his father.

I'll never forget one incident. His father gave him a Plymouth, two-door, hard-top sedan, and we rigged one of those spark plug bombs to go off when you turned the ignition key on, and nobody would sit in the front seat. He was taking guys from the ballpark back to our rooms, and he turned the key on, and a huge cloud of smoke came out of his engine, and he broke out of that door, and we followed him. We took off from that car when that bomb went off — it was a firecracker — and he charged us. He chased us all around the parking lot of the ballpark, hollering, he was going to break our backs and everything. Just roaring, but he took it not too bad after that. But I'll never forget that. He really came after us. He thought the engine had blown up!"

Billy took his car — and his patriotism — seriously. The six foot, 175-pound Southworth had been the first pro ball player to enlist, when he joined the Army Air Corps in September 1940. He rose to the rank of Lt. Colonel, piloting 25 bombing missions in Europe, wearing the Cardinals cap his dad had given him for good luck. Billy, who dubbed his B-17 Flying Fortress the "Winning Run," won the Air Medal and Distinguished Service Cross. A genuine hero, he was given a ten-year movie contract (to take effect at war's end) by Hollywood producer Hunt Stromberg.

But in February 1945 disaster struck. He took off from Mitchell Field near present day Shea Stadium. One of his engines gave out. Attempting an emergency landing, he overshot the runway and crashed into Flushing Bay. Months later his body washed ashore in the Bronx. He was 27.

"He was a very tall, handsome boy," recalls Isadore Kaplan, a Rome dentist who later owned the Colonels, "and Wally Schang, who was playing with the Ottawa team, picked him off first base, knocked out four front teeth. I was his dentist, so I took care of Billy. His dad came to Rome to see him, that's how I got to meet his dad.

"He was an excellent prospect. In fact he started the baseball cap for pilots. He was a helluva nice guy. It's just too bad. He was a helluva handsome looking guy. I know that all the girls liked him. So he didn't have any trouble drawing female attention.

"Billy finished his series over in England, and he was going to the Far East with the B-29's, and he was training pilots out of New York to land the big planes and one of them, their plane, overran the runway and blew up, and all the bodies were shattered. I had to go down to New York and identify his mouth, his head, because I could tell by the dental chart whose head belonged to who. It's like fingerprints. So that was the end of Billy Southworth."

Other Can-Am alumni besides Southworth made the supreme sacrifice. Perhaps they weren't as glamorous or as talented, but their deaths were just as tragic and as meaningful. They were:

Keith F. Bissonette, Utica's 1941 second baseman, died in Burma.

Lieutenant Ordway Harold Cisgen, a pitcher with Amsterdam in 1941 and Utica in 1942, was killed in action in France on June 11, 1944. Age 23.

Lieutenant George E. Gamble, Jr., outfielder with Rome for 14 games in 1938, was killed in action over French Indochina on December 4, 1944. It was his 29th mission as a Mustang fighter pilot. Age 28.

Technical Sergeant Frank Janik, a fixture with the Colonels as a catcher and outfielder from 1937 to 1940, was killed in action at Okinawa at the very close of the war, April 29, 1945. He had won the Bronze Star at Saipan. Age 28.

Marion P. Young, a Rome second baseman in 1942, was killed in action with the Marines in the Southwest Pacific area on December 13, 1944. Age 22.

William Sarver, outfielder with the Rugmakers in 1940 and 1941, killed in action in Germany on April 6, 1945.

Arthur Chester Vivian, Jr., pitcher with Amsterdam in 1942, killed in action in France on August 20, 1944.

Walter G. Loos, shortstop with the Glovers in 1939, was killed when his air transport flight crashed in Dutch Guiana on January 16, 1944. Age 27.

Glenn Sanford, Pittsfield pitcher in 1942, was killed in a plane crash at Nichols, California, in November 1944.

On February 22, 1943, at Albany's Ten Eyck Hotel, the Can-Am voted to curtail operations until war's end. All told, the minors dropped from 41 loops in 1941 to 31 in 1942 (five of which called it quits in mid-season) to just ten in 1943, and one of those survivors was the unique Class E Twin Ports League, the so-called "shipyards circuit" that folded in June 1943.

Nonetheless, packing it in wasn't easy. Father Martin argued passionately to continue. The Yankees' George Weiss was there to support a halt. The vote was razor thin: Pittsfield, Oneonta, Amsterdam, Gloversville-Johnstown, and Rome for suspension; Three Rivers, Quebec, and Utica against.

The Can-Am went into mothballs.

During the interregnum, the circuit's officers continued to hold annual meetings, although very little business was transacted. One such quiet session was held at Quebec, but at Buffalo in December 1944 Father Martin was unceremoniously canned and replaced by Al Houghton.

As Allied armies advanced, baseball not only stabilized but gradually recovered. The Ohio State, the Carolina and the North Carolina State Leagues actually resumed operations before V-J Day. As talk circulated in Canada of resuscitating baseball, the Can-Am League almost lost the two Quebec teams. In 1944, the possibility of a new 8-team "Quebec-Ontario League" was bandied about, and both Quebec and Three Rivers were interested. Quebec even had assurances of a Cubs working agreement, and the Can-Am voted to "lend" the two franchises to this circuit, but nothing came of the plan.

It was just as well, because prosperity was just around the corner, and Quebec and Three Rivers were to be an integral part of it.

Chapter 9

Postwar Prosperity

> "The fact that the [owners] produce baseball games
> at a profit, large or small, cannot change the
> character of the games. They are still sport, not trade.
> *District of Columbia Court of Appeals, 1921*

America's pent-up craving for baseball was a force to be reckoned with following V-J Day. In 1946, with servicemen home and quality lineups reestablished, 11 of the 16 big league teams set new attendance records. The majors drew 18,534,444, smashing the previous high of 10,951,502. The American League doubled its previous best season. The Yankees broke their 26-year-old record of 1,289,422 fans by drawing a remarkable 2,265,512.

And the minors weren't to be outdone as they enticed a record 32,704,315 customers in 1946 (the old record had been 1940s 20 million), and soon outdid that with 40,505,310 in 1947. In New York State, the rise in interest was dramatic. In 1946, 27 Empire State cities operated in organized ball, the previous mark being just 19 in 1942.

Happy days were here again.

The Can-Am League was part of the trend, seeing attendance soar. Before going into mothballs, their best regular season draw was 337,391 in 1942. President Al Houghton predicted 1946 would "be the greatest year in our history" and that "no club will be more than ten games out of first place at any time during the season."

He was half right — and it was the important half. While the balanced pennant chase Houghton prophesized was nowhere to be seen, as last place Quebec finished 30½ games back of rival Three Rivers, the circuit drew a record 494,893 regular season fans.

Baseball fever ran high that year, as witnessed by events in Rome during the playoffs. The *Sentinel* (as it had in 1939 and 1941) had Western Union wire scores from games at Three Rivers to their newsroom where a telegrapher decoded the action. Then the "play by play" was broadcast via loudspeaker to excited fans thronging North James Street.

The league saw great things ahead for 1947 and brashly expanded from a 126 to a 140 game schedule. Houghton forecast a gate increase of 100,000.

He was pleasantly wrong. For 1947 the circuit drew much more—a total of 635,030 regular season patrons, and new National Association president George Trautman was calling it "one of the best" of his circuits. And it got better. In 1948, attendance was 703,143, and in 1949, held steady at 696,726.

Records were set for single contests. On September 15, 1947, a playoff game, Amsterdam at Schenectady, drew 6,209. On May 7, 1947, a regular season tilt at Quebec's Municipal Stadium against Rome attracted a phenomenal 7,881 fans.

Everyone, everywhere was baseball crazy. Rugmakers batboy and later P.A. announcer Don Decker recalls: "The whole thing was the Rugmakers. God! That ballpark would let out, and the traffic coming out on Crescent Street, down Locust Avenue was just unbelievable, the way the traffic emptied out of that ballpark at 10:30, 11 o'clock at night when the game would end. Everybody went to the games, you know. That was it."

Resumption of play saw problems as well as opportunities. In 1946 transportation was still iffy, and teams scrambled to secure buses. Only Pittsfield still owned one, and charters continued at a premium. Hotel rooms weren't easy to corral. Arriving in Quebec one afternoon in August 1946 the Glovers discovered themselves without lodging, as hordes of tourists scoffed up every room in sight. Manager Ben Huffman found himself at a pay phone with a fistful of Canadian nickels trying to correct the situation. "We couldn't do anything about it," says Huffman, "even though we had reservations."

Housing too was in short supply, and Schenectady's *Dorp Sporting News* reported that promising Blue Jays hurler Lynn Lovenguth might have to leave town simply because he couldn't find a place for his family to stay.

Roster spaces had to be reserved for returning servicemen. In May 1946 the Can-Am voted to carry three extra ex-servicemen per club, bringing the roster limit up to 18. (Rosters were crammed with ex-servicemen, anyway. For example, Rome's 1946 preseason 21-man squad contained 16 veterans — 5 Army, 1 Coast Guard, 3 Marines, and 6 Navy.)

"That was an experience," comments Ben Huffman. "See, after World War II, a lot of the kids [who had been] in the service, they didn't want to take orders from nobody. It was difficult; '46 was a tough year breaking in as a playing manager."

Yet it was no piece of cake for new players either. Competition was fierce. "The first year out of the service I faced about seven shortstops," recounts Amsterdam infielder Brownie Blaszak. "They were all eliminated,

The Glovers' Henry Williams crosses home after his winning home run in the last game of the semifinal playoffs versus the Oneonta Red Sox on September 14, 1947.

but everytime I thought I had the team made, somebody from Kansas City or Newark or someplace like that would come down. It was tough."

Oneonta catcher Steve Salata was another of those returning vets, getting out of the service in December 1945 and soon hooked on with the Red Sox chain. "It was tough baseball because everybody was back from the service," he contends. "You couldn't jump up a league or two. You had to advance like you were going to college, you know, learning each step of the way, and I think it was good for baseball. . . .

"I played for $200 a month, that was $50 a week. It was $800 to $1,000 just for the summer. I did very well. Of course, prices were wonderful. We used to get two dollars and fifty cents for meal money, and it lasted, which is hard to believe, but you could have breakfast, lunch, and supper on it. Breakfast was maybe 60 cents. Lunch was maybe 90 cents. A dollar for supper, which was ample. Of course, in those days you only tipped a dime. . . ."

But the big news was the addition of the Schenectady franchise. At a league meeting at Quebec's Chateau Frontenac on November 11, 1945, Utica permanently bowed out, and despite bids from Ottawa and Sherbrooke, the Electric City was installed in its place. Nearby Albany of the Eastern League (just 20 miles away) could have blocked the new Blue Jays but didn't, and in return the Can-Am schedule was juggled to avoid conflicting dates between the two cities.

To celebrate organized ball's return after 43 years, Schenectady's Old

Time Baseball Players Association and the Chamber of Commerce threw a banquet at the swank Van Curler Hotel, with Commissioner "Happy" Chandler as featured speaker. Tickets were $3 apiece; 250 attended, and radio station WSNY broadcast the proceedings live.

Chandler effusively praised the McNearneys and asserted that the Phils organization was one of the finest around. He concluded: "I ask the boys to play baseball in memory of those fine kids who are not coming back and for those boys in hospitals who are unable to play the game anymore.... America has 150 years of glorious history behind it and with God's help and with baseball's help, it must not and shall not perish from the earth."

Baseball's return was moving people to poetry. Blue Jays employee Dan O'Connor published a series of rhymes in the local *Union-Star*. His first effort was called appropriately (if not originally) "Play Ball":

PLAY BALL!
The baseball lid is off today
Once more we hear the call
    The smiling pans
    Of happy fans
Will greet the cry "PLAY BALL!"

For weeks we've seen the photographs
Of stars and future greats
    They'll start today
    To earn their pay
Inside the local gates.

The peanut vendors come to life
And hawk their tasty wares
    The hot dog scent
    Makes every gent
Forget his daily cares.

Gay Bleacherites will call the strikes
And keep things on the jump
    Once more they'll shout
    "The guy is out
"We ought to kill the ump."

The Blue Jays have a lot of class
With lads you'll want to know
    "We'll take Quebec"
    Sez Stan Wnek
"Like bellhops take your dough."

Sawatski packs a vicious clout
(You'll see him swat a few)
   He earns his cokes
   By lengthy pokes.
And drives 'em out o' view.

The pitching staff looks extra sound
And though it's early May
   The boys will prove
   They're in the groove
at Central Park ... today.

Bill Cronin's lads intend to win
With just a bit to spare
   So park your frame
   And see the game
The gang will all be there!!

With new-found prosperity and a raft of big league tie-ups, spring training was no longer the "Show Up at the Home Park Two Weeks Before the Opener" operation of prewar days.

Teams could journey south, if not always to Florida, then at least sort of south.

Quebec still headed to Cooperstown in April 1946. In 1947 Rome worked out at Nazareth, Pennsylvania; Amsterdam at Chambersburg, Maryland. The Glovers went down to Charleston, West Virginia, to an old Army base. Rome trained at Easton, Maryland, in 1951.

By 1948, though, the trend was much farther south. Rome was still at Green Castle, Pennsylvania, and Quebec only inched down to Peekskill, but the Glovers made it to Pine Bluff, Arkansas, the Ruggies to Windsor, North Carolina, Oneonta to Melbourne, Florida, Three Rivers to the newly founded Dodgertown in Vero Beach, and Pittsfield to Suffolk, Virginia.

Peekskill really wasn't as dismal as it sounded. "We trained at an old armory," says Quebec pilot Tony Ravish, "where they used to keep the cavalry, and they had a dirt floor where I used to work out my kids on the infield. That's where I had the jump on everybody."

Schenectady had their 1946–47 spring sessions at Dover, Delaware, 1948 at Darlington, South Carolina (where they dueled a young Robin Roberts), 1949 at Milford, Delaware, and 1950 at Laurinburg, North Carolina.

Not exactly impressive burgs. "We'd have to flip a coin," wrote the Schenectady *Gazette*'s John "Bonny" Bonifacio from Darlington in 1948, "to decide which was worse, this town or Dover...

"They've got one theater here and it'd take you about five minutes to walk around the business district. The hotel is a little better than the one at Dover. This at least has one elevator....

"It is a good place for a training camp, though, 'cause there just isn't any place for the boys to go. Midnight is a curfew for the players and you don't have to worry about them not keeping it....

"We brought our golf clubs along, thinking maybe we'd get a game in some morning, but they have a little thing called snakes down here, so we just kept the clubs right in the car. Particularly after the other morning when the boys got out of their bus at Williamson Field and wriggling there in the middle of the road was a nice long one, about four feet. The boys killed it in nothing flat and when we saw it that convinced us. No golf, particularly for a guy like me who is bothered by a slice.

"As we said before give us home."

Far more significant than these sojourns was the matter of racial integration.

In the nineteenth century, over 70 blacks played in the minors, over half performing for all–Negro teams in otherwise white leagues, the last such squad being the 1898 Acme Colored Giants (with an abysmal 8–41 record) representing tiny Celeron, New York, of the Oil and Iron League. Except for light skinned Jimmy Claxton, who posed as an Indian to hurl briefly for Oakland of the PCL in 1916, there were no blacks in organized ball from 1899 to 1946.

Contact with blacks was limited to exhibitions. The Can-Am had several such encounters, including those in 1937 when the Glovers took on the Albany Black Sox ("one of the best colored semipro organizations in the country.... Their record to date has been excellent, and they are certain of not being a soft touch") and Schenectady's Mohawk Colored Giants. The Glovers took both games.

Similar exhibitions took place in 1942 between both Rome and Utica against those same Mohawk Colored Giants.

In any case, most fans are well aware of Branch Rickey's Great Experiment involving Jackie Robinson and the opening of baseball to blacks, but are unaware that three other leagues—the International, the New England and the Canadian-American, were integrated before Jackie ever set foot in Ebbets Field. Roy Campanella and Don Newcombe worked for Walter Alston's Nashua Dodgers of the Class B New England League. Robinson and two pitchers—John Wright and Roy Partlow—toiled for Clay Hopper's Montreal Royals in the International League.

In fact, recently discovered papers of Rickey reveal that the Mahatma's original idea was to sign not just Robinson but instead to ink five prominent blacks—and Partlow was to be one of the pioneering quintet.

The 27-year-old Wright and the 30-year-old Partlow (he may actually have been 34) were both talented Negro League veterans, but weren't nearly as poised as Robinson, and both were optioned to Three Rivers. Wright went down first (after just two games with the Royals) and struggled. The 5' 11", 168-pound Wright was a legitimate star. In 1943 he was 30–5 with the Homestead Grays and hurled two shutouts in the Negro League World Series. He'd also pitched in the Negro League All-Star Game that year before 51,723 fans in Comiskey Park but in the Can-Am could muster only a mediocre 12–8 record.

"Wright, he was a bachelor," recalls Negro League outfielder Gene Benson. "Robinson had Rachel to go home to. He was from Louisiana, from the Deep South.... He was just nervous."

"Wright was just so-so," says Three Rivers pilot Frenchie Bordagaray. "He was light. He was a little too light. He didn't have enough meat on him, you know. But he was a knuckleball pitcher too. I hit against him when we used to play games against the services when I was with the Brooklyn club, and I hit against him then. Then I run into him again in Three Rivers."

Partlow, a Georgia native, had played in the Negro Leagues since 1934, hurling for the Cincinnati White Sox and Tigers, the Memphis Red Sox, the Philadelphia Stars, and the Grays. In 1945 he led the Negro National League in strikeouts but had a rocky 5.59 ERA with Montreal. His progress at Three Rivers, however, was far greater than Wright's, as he won his first nine games and rolled to a 10–1 record, being named All-Star Left Handed Pitcher and Playoffs MVP. Roy even impressed at bat, hitting .404 (not too surprisingly, since he'd paced the Cuban Winter League with a .441 mark in 1941). "He was an excellent lefthander," recalls Gene Benson. "He could really pitch. They said he had earned a right to go up with Jackie Robinson. But he was kind of mean, kind of tough to get along with. He had fights with his own teammates."

"Not with me he wasn't," Bordagaray responds when asked if Partlow was trouble. "I didn't have any problems at all with the blacks.... He was a good hitter and a good pitcher and everything, and if it weren't for him we wouldn't have won the thing. We won it that year.

"My God, he was a big league ball player playing in C League. I was a big league ball player in a C League too."

The Dodgers didn't consult Bordaragay before sending Wright down. "We had all nationalities," Frenchie recalled to author Jules Tygiel, "blacks, whites, dagoes, Frenchmen, Jewish boys. We had the whole works. The funny thing about it was I never thought of him as black. I just thought of him as another ball player."

The two blacks' presence stirred little controversy. Tension erupted but once. Late in the season, a veteran hurler, a Southerner, was removed in favor of Wright. He griped: "Why did you have to take me out for that jigger?" Bordagaray calmed the situation down, and that was it.

"We dressed together. We were all in the same place together. We took showers together," noted Bordagaray to Tygiel. In Three Rivers the two pitchers were popular with the fans and even dated French-Canadian women. On the road they stayed in the same hotels as their white teammates, with one exception. "When we got to Schenectady," says Bordagaray, "they put us in a hotel and they wouldn't let the black boys go in there. So I had to take them and put them in another hotel."

Both were gone the next year. Wright barnstormed with the Jackie Robinson All-Stars, but was released in January. He returned to the Homestead Grays, but his career soon ended. "His arm was bad," says Negro League pitcher Larry Kimbrough, "he couldn't break a pane of glass."

Partlow arrived late for spring training, and rumors floated that he wanted more money. Jackie Robinson contended he was "one of the greatest lefthanded pitchers in the game . . . [but] unless he gets the feeling that he wants to play he may as well forget about the game from the standpoint of organized ball." Don Newcombe once observed that "Roy was the kind of man who had his own attitude, and his attitude was he'd pitch like he wanted to pitch, not like he had to pitch."

He hurled poorly that spring and was released when the Dodgers travelled to Panama for a series of exhibitions. The Pittsburgh *Courier,* a black paper, noted that Wright and Partlow "seemed to have a tendency to choke up while laboring among caucasians."

"He walked off the team," recalls Gene Benson. "[Manager] Clyde Sukeforth didn't know what happened. Partlow was the best hitter on the team, the best pitcher, the fastest baserunner. He just got tired cause they weren't going to use him, just use him as a draw."

He rejoined the Philadelphia Stars, making the 1947 Negro National League All-Star team, and hurling until 1950.

Partlow was hardly a role model for anybody. He died in April 1987 and was described by one source as a "wino" and even startlingly as "evil."

A sad chapter in baseball history.

Generally very few other blacks were coming into the minors (although six played for the player-hungry 1947 Stamford Bombers of the Colonial League), but two more joined Can-Am ranks in 1947. First, Brooklyn signed 18-year-old Detroit shortstop Sammy Gee for Three Rivers. Gee's ragged work at short soon got him a transfer to the outfield, and before the season was out his batting average sunk down to .184. All in all, he was a 34 game flop.

The St. Louis Browns signed four blacks in July 1947—Hank Thompson and Willard Brown of the Kansas City Monarchs, Piper Davis of the Birmingham Black Barons, and former University of Toledo basketball star Chuck Harmon. Brown and Thompson were sent immediately to the big club. Davis stayed with Birmingham although he was an option to the

The 1951 Gloversville Glovers. *Front row:* Jesse Baro (pitcher), Guy Coleman (pitcher), Walter Slovenski (centerfielder), Barney Vogt (catcher), Sal Stampiglio (outfield). *Seated:* Dick Hoey (business manager), Bill McMillan (rightfielder), Al Barillari (playing manager), Pedro Arroyo (shortstop), Bill Long (second baseman), Ernie Desperito (third baseman). *Standing:* Al Barkus (pitcher), Jacques Jeaneau (pitcher), Pete Caniglia (leftfielder), Lawson Williams (first baseman), Walter James (pitcher), Oakie Henderson (pitcher), Paul Wargo (pitcher).

Browns. Harmon was actually signed by their Toledo farm and assigned to the Glovers.

"The Browns," reported the *Leader-Republican,* "wired if the club would accept a Negro. The telegraphic answer was in the affirmative, provided the ball player was good enough to really help the team.

"Then Bob Barton, center gardener, jumped the squad . . . and since a catcher has been working the outfield. The Browns were apprised of the situation and hurried up the signing of Harmon for the local outfit."

"We used to knock him down," says Blue Jays hurler Charlie Baker, "and he'd get a little pale, and we'd never have any trouble with him, but he learned, too, along the way. We used to knock him down every time up. He'd back off."

"I didn't feel any different from anything else," says Harmon, "just playing every day. It wasn't like college ball playing two or three times a week. Travelling around you get experience, but as far as feeling any different, doing anything else, as far as I can remember now, it was no different. . . .

"You know I was just there to play ball, and you just enjoy playing. I always got along good with the umpires. I never squawked. I figured if you got to three strikes they could make a mistake too, and if you let them call you on the third one, that's your fault. I was a free swinger.

"The fans, I never paid attention to the fans, 'cause I played in college there in West Virginia in some of them places — you know even in high school in Indiana — you'd get called a lot of names, but that never bothered me. Made me play harder. It didn't upset me. . . . As far as the players were concerned, I never heard anything out of any player.

"I was out to do a job. If I was there to fight I would have joined the boxing team."

Harmon hit a fairly respectable .270, even married a local girl in December of 1947 and moved to Gloversville for awhile. In 1954 became the first black to play for the Cincinnati Reds.

"Well, Harmon was a good boy," recalls his Glovers manager, Pack Rogers. "He minded well. He was late one time, and I jumped on him good. He reminded me of it ten years later when he saw me in spring camp."

Harmon's pro transition was eased by Rogers. "He was a great, great teacher," says Harmon. "Really, he was some type of character too, but he was fair and a really good manager. I really enjoyed playing for him. He was one of the best of the probably fifteen I had. He was a great manager. I really enjoyed playing for him."

Amsterdam, Oneonta, and Schenectady never integrated as they followed their parent clubs' lead. But the Glovers continued to employ blacks. Outfielder Harry Wilson and an outfielder named Daniels played in 1950. Shortstop Pedro Arroyo and pitcher Walter James carried on the "tradition" in 1951.

"Wilson was a big, lumbering lefthander," recalls Glovers pitcher John Coakley, "[but as for Daniels] I can't remember that name. They invited a lot of fellows here to work out. He may have been one of those, and he may have started the season, but to be honest with you, I don't even remember him."

"I don't think they had any problems," says fellow Glovers pitcher Loren Stewart. "This Wilson fellow was kind of quiet, but, no, I'd say there wasn't any trouble."

The 1949 Pittsfield Electrics boasted a black pioneer of a different sort — Harlem Globetrotter, New York Knick and Detroit Piston Nate "Sweetwater" Clifton. Clifton, who played first base, got into 24 games, hitting a respectable .275 despite 31 strikeouts in just 80 at-bats. In 1951 Clifton became the first black to ever play in an NBA contest.

Pitcher Brooks Lawrence came to Pittsfield in 1950, going 11–13 with a 3.74 ERA. At 25, he was a little long in the tooth for Class C, but in June 1954 he became the initial black pitcher in Cards history. He just missed,

Robert Rothschild, president of the Gloversville-Johnstown Glovers.

in fact, the honor of integrating the club to first baseman Tom Alston, who made the team earlier that year.

The 1951 Rome Colonels had two blacks in spring camp—the first signed by the A's organization—19-year-old pitcher Marion Scott and 18-year-old shortstop Clarence Williford. Both were inked by Hall of Fame Judy Johnson. Neither, however, actually made it to the Colonels roster.

Exhibitions with higher classification rivals continued in the postwar era. In July 1948 the Glovers humiliated Packy Rogers' Elmira Pioneers (including many 1947 Glovers) 14–6 before 2,434. An odd feature was that Al Barkus, then with Port Chester of the Colonial League, came over to pitch for the G-J's. In 1951 the new Kingston Colonials squeaked by Fargo-Moorhead of the Northern League 4–3 in 11 innings while the Pittsfield Phillies were taking on Quebec's new Provincial League entry.

Schenectady hosted the Eastern League's Utica Blue Sox in July 1949 and was walloped 16–4 before 3,215 fans. The next year they bested the Uticans before 1,213 customers.

"In fact," says the Blue Jays' Charlie Baker, "in '47 McNearney tried to make a deal with Utica after the Can-Am Playoffs to play a series here between Utica and Schenectady, and Eddie Sawyer [then manager of the Blue Sox] refused because he said, 'We'd get our hind end walloped with that team you've got there!' The saying was that the team that came to Schenectady in '47 was supposed to be the '47 Blue Sox. Whether that was true or not, I don't know. Sawyer wouldn't play us because he was afraid of getting embarrassed.... He was here with [George] Earnshaw and [Herb] Pennock, but he wouldn't agree to a series because McNearney said he'd give the entire gate receipts to the winner!"

The Boston Braves visited Rome on July 9, 1946. Their visit had a poignant touch as the Braves were managed by Billy Southworth, father of former Rome Colonel Billy Southworth, Jr. As noted earlier, young Southworth was quite a prospect, but died in the last days of the war. Southworth, Sr. and shortstop Alvin Dark flew into the Rome Army Air Field (now Griffis Air Force Base) in Lou Perini's private Beechcraft monoplane immediately after the 1946 All-Star Game, meeting up with the rest of the team.

A bronze plaque at the third base entrance to Colonels Park in memory of Billy and the two other Colonels, Frank Janik and George Gamble, who had also given their lives in the war, was duly and properly dedicated.

"The Boston manager," noted the Rome *Sentinel,* "found it difficult to control his emotion when called to the microphone during the brief but impressive dedication ceremony preceding the game. With tears in his eyes he said he was deeply grateful for the memorial tribute...."

The Colonels kept pace with Boston in the early going, chasing knuckleballer John Niggeling, but rookie Warren Spahn relieved and slammed the door as the Braves triumphed 15 to 7 before 2,844 fans. The visit was not all sentiment. The Braves exercised their option to take 60 percent of the gate, coming away with $1,741.54. They had been guaranteed a minimum of $1,500.

Major leaguers returned to Glovers Park on July 13, 1948, when Zack Taylor's St. Louis Browns, fresh from a 7–5 victory over the Phillies in the annual Hall of Fame Game, dropped in. Despite fielding a team of second stringers (and the thought of second-string Browns is not a pleasant one), St. Louis rapped out 26 hits, triumphing 24–11 before a crowd of almost 3,600. Ex–Cornwall Maple Leaf Whitey Platt was in the Browns line-up, but the real star was St. Louis utility man Andy Anderson. Anderson, who homered twice at Cooperstown, slammed three more round-trippers versus G-ville. In his Major league career Andy would homer exactly twice.

Before the game Glovers prexy Bob Rothschild presented each visiting Major leaguer a pair of locally produced gloves. (Big spender!)

"They towered over our players, they were just so much bigger," recalls fan Eber Davis, "and the balls that were hit went over the light towers. We'd never seen anything like it."

In May of 1949 the Yankees' George Weiss called Rugmakers business manager Wally McQuatters angling to get a playing date at Mohawk Mills Park, one of only three mid-season New York exhibitions that campaign. The league schedule was promptly juggled, and Casey Stengel was there to address the throng at the Elks Club (like Lincoln's Cooper Union Address there is no record of the oration). A crowd of 4,564 witnessed the Yanks triumph 9-2 in just an hour and fifty minutes. The home team committed seven miscues. Ruggie alumni Spec Shea and Dick Kryhoski toiled for the visitors, and Yogi Berra for some inexplicable reason played centerfield.

"God! The people were sitting on the field," exclaimed Rugmakers play-by-play announcer Don Decker. "They couldn't hold enough people in the stands. The people actually sat on the first base line and on the third base line."

"They were kidding Yogi Berra," says one fan. "He couldn't get them out in the creek over there in right field, and he finally zeroed in. He was hitting everything foul, you know. He was hitting everything to the parking lot. And then, boy, he got them! You ought to see him whacking the balls. They must have been going over the creek for Christ's sake!"

A few months later, on September 7, 1949, the Phillies, featuring Richie Ashburn, Granny Hamner and Robin Roberts, visited their Blue Jay farm. The third-place Philadelphians were giving up an off day, having just played three straight road doubleheaders. Attendance was disappointing — only 3,028 — as the two teams battled to a 5-5 tie through eight frames, but the weary big leaguers broke through with one run in the ninth to take it. After that it was on to Brooklyn on the 12:48 southbound.

The Phillies were scheduled to play Schenectady again in August 1950, but as Eddie Sawyer's "Whiz Kids" had the matter of a pennant race to consider, the trip never materialized.

Quebec started the postwar years with a poor squad, finishing dead last in 1946-47 and advancing only to seventh after obtaining a Giants working agreement in 1948. "The first year I was there [1947] it was a pretty horrible team," recalls Alouettes hurler Bill Fennhahn. "We had better players here in town, semipros, than some of the guys that played there."

"The Giants didn't give us [any good players]," added 1947-48 Quebec pilot Tony Ravish, "because that [Quebec] was sort of an extra ball club. Their regular ball clubs, they supplied the better players to. The Giants would fill in a player here and there. The rest of the players were left over from the previous year when they were independent."

The club reverted to independent status in 1949-50 and turned it to its

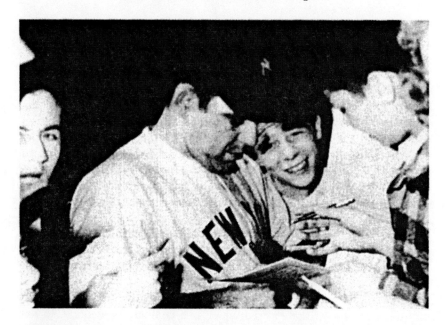

Yogi Berra signs autographs as the Yankees visit Amsterdam in 1949. (Photo by Val Webb—courtesy of *Amsterdam Recorder*.)

advantage, becoming the Can-Am's powerhouse. Stung by last place finishes, construction magnate Ulyses Ste. Marie shelled out big money to turn things around. "He was a real nice person," says 1949–50 Quebec pitcher "Moose" Erickson, "and he wanted to give the people of Quebec a winner, and they went out and bought a few fellows who had played in the high minors, who had had good years. They got Frank McCormick who was a great star at Cincinnati for years to manage, and they bought various players like myself who had experience in the International League and so forth, and just put together a ball club they thought would win. They wanted to have a winner."

Not that Ste. Marie had been cheap prior to that. "He gave me $5,000 even before I started managing," says Tony Ravish. "That was a lot of money in those days, and I had to fly up, sign a contract, and go home. We had a little trouble because I wanted American money.... He was generous, one of the best paying jobs I had, so I can't complain."

Under managers Frank McCormick in 1949 and George McQuinn in 1950, Quebec used veterans who easily overwhelmed the often green opposition. The Braves won by 14½ games in 1949. Then in 1950, they won 97 contests for a second pennant and a .708 won-lost percentage. "One of the things that happened that second year," adds "Moose" Erickson, "they got an agreement with the Boston Braves. You remember the old Braves?

New York Yankees at Amsterdam, May 1949. *Left to right:* **Bill Dickey, Casey Stengel, Mayo Smith and Jim Turner. (Courtesy** *Amsterdam-Recorder* — **Val Webb photo.)**

We got a couple of players on option and stuff. It might have been a little agreement with Boston, and the next year they were going to be a farm club....

"They kind of cut expenses a little bit [in 1950] and let a couple of the players go. They let Shetler go during the year. They cut down a little. That's when George McQuinn had to start playing, but all in all there was no problems."

"Those guys got big money," grumbles Glovers pitcher John "Lefty" Coakley. "They were a veteran professional baseball team playing against a bunch of young, up and coming, prospects. They completely dominated the league.

"Those guys, their salaries were well above the average young player in the league. They made three to four to five times the salary the other players were making.

"I remember pitching against them in Quebec in '50, and I beat them one night, five to one. I wasn't especially pleased because I beat Quebec, but I was pleased because I beat a veteran ball club. That was a thrill for me."

Quebec led the league in most significant categories. First baseman Vernon "Moose" Shetler had paced the Piedmont League in homers with

Sam Piacentino, Amsterdam outfielder, nipped at the plate in 1949 at Amsterdam by Quebec catcher Jim Parker as catcher John Rankin and teammate Mike Morrongiello look on. (Photo courtesy *Amsterdam Recorder* — Val Webb photo.)

Portsmouth in 1947 and set the all-time Virginia League mark for RBIs with Franklin in 1948 with 150. The investment in Shetler paid off as he led the Can-Am in RBIs with 133 in 1949.

Third sacker Pete Elko, a former Cubs prospect and Southern Association batting king, paced the Can-Am in average that same year. Bill Sinram, who had played with Amsterdam in 1941 and had gotten as far as Jersey City, pushed "Moose" Shetler off third base and into the outfield.

Outfielder Garland "Butch" Lawing had a cup of coffee with the Giants and Reds in 1946. "He played right field for us because he had such a great

**Quebec second baseman Mike Fandozzi getting ready to slide under Oneonta Red
Sox catcher Steve Salata at Quebec's Municipal Stadium in 1949.**

throwing arm," says Moose Erickson. "He had a tremendous arm and was
a good hitter who knew the strike zone. He got a lot of walks and could
hit the ball out of the park." With Ogdensburg in the Border League in 1948
he crushed a monster 525-foot four-bagger at Winter Park. Only "Bomber"
Van Robays had tagged one farther there. Lawing won the Can-Am Triple
Crown in 1950 with 19 round-trippers, 141 RBIs, and a .346 average.

The pitching wasn't shabby either. Bespectacled Harold "Moose"
Erickson led the circuit with 21 victories and a .778 won-lost percentage in
1949 and a 2.40 ERA in 1950. Sidearming Fred Belinsky had the most victories, with 22, in 1950, while John Ambrose had a league-leading .818
percentage. Erickson led the loop both seasons in strikeouts.

It was the league's last hurrah.

Chapter 10

Kukla, Fran & Dunkle

*"I'm going to write a book, How to Make a Small Fortune
in Baseball. First you start out with a large fortune...."*
Ruly Carpenter

The golden summer of postwar attendance was all too short-lived, and
the Can-Am's slide was irreversible. There was to be no quiet autumn, only
a quick, chilling snap of winter for the Can-Am League. Survival was not
in the cards.

Modern communications did in the Can-Am League and minor league
ball in general. They were a godsend on one hand but absolute destruction
otherwise. Local radio stations such as Gloversville's WENT, Rome's
WKAL, Schenectady's WSNY and Amsterdam's WCSS broadcast Can-Am
games and created greater interest, but fans could also tune in to big league
contests such as Brooklyn on Albany's WPTR or both the Red Sox and
Braves on Pittsfield's new WBEC-FM.

And that competition was the rub.

The very first sports "broadcast" dates back to 1899 when accounts of
the Kingtown Regatta went over the wireless to the offices of the Dublin
Daily Express, which proceeded to scoop everyone around. The first
baseball heard on the etherwaves was on Pittsburgh's KDKA from Forbes
Field on August 5, 1921. Newark's WJZ and Schenectady's WGY aired the
Yankees-Giants World Series that fall. Some clubs, such as William
Wrigley's Chicago Cubs, were all in favor of radio. At one time seven
different Windy City stations broadcast Cubs games—for free.

Recreated games, such as the Cubs' on Des Moines' WHO, featuring
a young Ronald Reagan, were also in vogue. Such dramatizations long pre-
dated radio. We read of games being sent over the telegraph to ballrooms
where a telegrapher would translate the dots and dashes with appropriate
drama, and eager fans would hang on every pitch. In Greenville, South
Carolina, in 1908, for example, baseball bugs could gather around the
Grand Opera House and pay 15 cents for the privilege of getting the dope
on the road games of the Greenville Spinners—and of their new centerfielder, a promising fellow called Shoeless Joe Jackson.

With such fan devotion, radio broadcasts of minor league games, such as those of the Birmingham Barons as early as 1931, were hardly surprising. The announcer at Rickwood Field: a future southern sheriff named T.E. "Bull" Connor.

On the other hand, many clubs feared the airwaves from the start. In 1932 baseball came very close to banning radio altogether, but sidestepped the issue by allowing each club the authority to broadcast or not to broadcast (and that included banning any play-by-play from your park — including that of the visitors). The three New York teams were downright hostile, signing a five-year pact in 1934 against radio (Gothamites had to settle for the Newark Bears on WINS). It took Brooklyn's brash newcomer, Larry MacPhail, to scrap the agreement and allow broadcasts in 1939 in return for $70,000.

But by 1950 all such reticence was ancient history, and 850 radio stations carried league ball, including 350 Mutual Broadcasting System affiliates (eventually CBS would grow to 431 affiliates — all largely on re-created games, sound effects, and bluff). The Schenectady Royals even had to face the added competition of Albany Senators broadcasts on nearby WABY, which was airing all the home and away games of their Eastern League neighbor.

And then there was the little magic box called television.

The first televised game was Princeton at Columbia in the spring of 1939, with Bill Stern doing the honors for NBC. On August 26, 1939, Larry MacPhail pioneered again. Red Barber drawled away for NBC's New York station W2XBS as the Reds took on the Dodgers at Ebbets Field. The New York *Times* reported viewers "as far away as fifty miles viewed the action and heard the roar of the crowd." Now, not only was this the first major league telecast, it gave us the first TV commercials ever — for Ivory Soap, Wheaties, and Mobil gas (this was before the invention of Bud Light).

In 1940–41 Brooklyn was televising a game a week. World War II interrupted the march of the tube, but the postwar years saw rapid expansion. The number of stations grew from 12 in 1946 to 46 in 1948, with 78 new ones under construction and 300 applications flooding the FCC.

Baseball was a natural part of any programming schedule. In 1946 Larry MacPhail — who else? — signed the first TV contract with the fledgling two-station Dumont Network for $75,000. Not a bad price considering metropolitan New York had but 500 sets. By 1948 every major league club save Pittsburgh was telecasting part — if not all — of its schedule. Plus, the Philco TV Network was getting into the act. That season also saw the first world series telecast. In 1949 even some minor league games were aired (for instance, Fort Worth's WBAP was doing Texas League contests, and WFBM in Indianapolis was featuring American Association games).

The New York Yankees take over operation of the Amsterdam Rugmakers on January 5, 1950. *Seated:* **Eugene J. Martin (Yankee farm director), Judge Felix J. Aulisi (outgoing Rugmaker president).** *Standing:* **John Pollard (outgoing Rugmaker director), Herbert L. Shuttleworth II, (outgoing Rugmakers vice president) and Paul Krichell (Yankee scout).** (Photo courtesy of *Amsterdam Recorder* – Val Webb photo.)

By 1949 the effects of this novelty were being seen all along the East Coast, but particularly in New England and New Jersey. The fabled Newark Bears could no longer withstand Big Apple telecasts and were sold by the Yankees and transferred to Springfield, Massachusetts, for the 1950 season (one rumor had them fleeing all the way to Quebec). In 1950 additional clubs bit the dust, and the New England–based Colonial League collapsed in mid-campaign. By 1951 Jersey City followed Newark's lead, transferring to Ottawa.

The onslaught was just beginning. On August 11, 1951, CBS telecast the first game in color, the Braves at Ebbets Field. Soon afterward American Telephone and Telegraph completed installation of a $40 million television microwave system to the West Coast, and fans there were able to witness the Miracle of Coogan's Bluff and the world series that followed. There was no turning back.

Minor league attendance sank like a rock, from 49,982,335 in 1949 to 34,735,967 in 1950, and 27,518,837 in 1951.

"It was profitable when I was president," says the Glovers' Harry Dunkle. "After the war, television came in. There was no television before that, but after the war people began buying television sets, and our attendance started dropping right off. Kukla, Fran and Ollie was the only thing on television, but people had television sets, and they had to stay home and watch Kukla, Fran and Ollie. [Louise Kukla, by the way, was the first secretary of the Glovers back in 1937. Honest.] I attempted to get my Board of Directors to quit baseball. We had $25,000 in the bank. No debts. I did a good financial job, paying all the bills, accumulating that money, and the directors wouldn't go along with me. I said, 'All right. Then you do it,' and I turned $25,000 over to them, and after only two years they had to quit, owing everybody again."

After the still-prosperous 1949 season, there was a flurry of activity in the Can-Am League. There was even talk of advancing to Class B status, but that was tabled. Three franchises changed hands. First, the parent Yankees bought the Amsterdam club from local interests.

Dr. Dan Mellen tired of being Rome's financial angel. The Colonels' 1949 attendance was only 40,323 — less than half of the 1948 total — and operating losses were pegged at $20,000. Mellen sold out to a syndicate of 15 local business and professional people, headed by dentist Dr. Isadore Kaplan.

The price was $5,000, and the new group agreed to rent Colonels Park for $3,500 annually.

And from Quebec came news that the Braves were passing from J. Ulysses Ste. Marie's ownership to that of Dr. J.L. Bellefort.

Beyond that, Albany owner Thomas F. McCaffrey bellowed about not renewing permission for the nearby Blue Jays to continue operating within their territorial limits when the existing agreement expired on February 1, 1950. "No request has been made of me by any Schenectady club official for any meeting," McCaffrey noted.

He demanded five percent of the Jays' gross grandstand receipts after taxes. Al Houghton negotiated with him, and the league passed an obsequious resolution thanking him for past permission. Houghton even travelled to Colombus, Ohio, to confer with National Association president George Trautman on the issue, but the latter was unsympathetic. So was Commissioner "Happy" Chandler, but he, nonetheless, allowed Schenectady to play the 1950 season.

So that problem was sidestepped, but another one was not.

Going into 1950, Houghton generated his usual optimism. "At Pittsfield," he noted, "a new and completely modern grandstand and at Rome, park improvements and new ownership will mean greatly increased attendance at both places. Indications are that all other clubs can count on at least the same attendance as last year. If this holds true attendance for the year may exceed 1949. At any rate, we expect a great year for clubs, players, and owners."

National Association president George Trautman visiting Three Rivers in 1948. *Left to right:* Dr. Jean Rochefort, president of Three Rivers; René Phaneuf, club treasurer; Albert Houghton, league president; Trautman; Marcel Dufresne, club general manager.

Not quite.

Regular season attendance plummetted 35 percent to 453,132. The same scenario greeted all of minor league baseball. As teams, and even whole leagues, folded in midseason, observers saw the same fate facing the Can-Am. "There should be no doubt," warned Bill Evans in the *Leader-Republican,* "in the minds of Canadian-American game patrons that their own baseball loop is in jeopardy. No one in Gloversville or Johnstown should be sure that professional baseball will continue here."

The Glovers, Indians, and Colonels all suffered significant losses. Problems in Rome were typical. Dr. Kaplan's new group lost even more money than Dr. Mellen. "Toward the end of the [1950] season," Francis Regan wrote, "the club was playing to almost deserted stands as patrons remained away in droves despite numerous promotional events." To prevent the fall of Rome, fresh money was poured in, a new Athletics working agreement was obtained, and even the lighting at Colonels Park was significantly upgraded.

Aside from television, continuing dominance by the Quebec Braves was blamed for the league's woes. The Oneonta *Star*'s 6' 7" sports editor, Steve Shields, suggested restrictions on the number of veteran players a team could carry. In order to generate enthusiasm among the also-rans, Glovers president Bob Rothschild proposed a complicated scheme to expand the playoffs to six teams. It enjoyed initial support, but went nowhere.

"They were always taking shots at us for some reason," contends Quebec pitcher "Moose" Erickson. "You know, when you're winning like we were, it's like the old Yankees when they were winning the World Series and pennants every year. Everybody was trying to shoot them down."

In 1951, three of the stronger franchises abandoned ship.

Schenectady's territorial issue flared again, and this time the National Association ruled in favor of Albany. The Blue Jays cut a deal, confirming rumors that had floated since July, switching in December 1950 to the Eastern League, paying McCaffrey $4,000 annually for the honor.

Owner McNearney displayed little class as he left. "Our efforts toward this goal extend back over three years," he sniffed. "In the meantime it was necessary to go along with Class C baseball until such a change could be made."

Then Quebec and Three Rivers transferred to the revived Provincial League, which was returning to the National Association after yet another fling as an "outlaw" loop. Most Mexican League "jumpers" had played in the Provincial. Sal Maglie, Max Lanier, Roland Gladu, Fred Martin, Bobby Estalella, Harry Feldman, Roy Zimmerman, Adrian Zabala, and Al and Danny Gardella all sought refuge up North.

But peace once again reigned between the Provincial League and organized baseball, and by 1951 Quebec and Three Rivers were ready to rejoin their countrymen. Al Houghton and his Quebecqois counterpart, Albert Molini, made the joint announcement. The gruelling travel between Quebec and the States was now eliminated with an estimated 26,000 miles saved each year, 14,000 by the league's American teams. National Association president Trautman expressed approval of the realignment.

For awhile, the transfer was in jeopardy. Other Provincial members insisted Quebec should guarantee $300 per game to visitors, while itself being assured of only $150 while abroad. "This," reported the Associated Press, "was based on Quebec's greater population."

The Can-Am almost took them back. "We've operated that way for seven years," noted Al Houghton with resignation, although he termed the realignment "the only sensible thing to do."

But the shift did take place, and the Can-Am announced plans to operate with six teams for the first time since 1936. Rumors floated in regard to Schenectady's replacement. Rutland and Burlington, Vermont; Portland, Maine; and Glens Falls and Kingston, New York, were immediately named. Generally, it was a pretty weak and/or distant selection to choose from. But soon Utica was offered the honor.

The prodigal franchise did not return. A Korean War ban on new construction for amusement purposes killed Utica's plans to build a new stadium on the site of the Rhoads military hospital, and Mayor Boyd Golder reluctantly announced that his city was out of the running.

Kingston, formerly of the defunct Class B Colonial and Class D North Atlantic leagues, signed up, paying the $500 franchise fee. Considering the city's uncertain history in organized ball, it was a danger signal of the league's accelerating decline.

As the Can-Am now had no Canadian teams, talk circulated about renaming it. Only four major league working agreements continued (reflecting a national trend, from 62 percent of all teams in 1946 to just 47 percent in 1951). Remaining were the Yankees in Amsterdam, the Red Sox in Oneonta, a new Athletics farm team in Rome, and a shift of the Phillies tie-in from Schenectady to Pittsfield. The Glovers got a few players on loan from the American Association's Milwaukee Brewers. The Kingston Colonials were totally on their own.

Amsterdam virtually had to beg for their Yankee pact to continue. A 34-man committee formed to cajole the Bronx Bombers to remain, and they met with assistant GM Roy Hamey and farm director Lee MacPhail. When the Amsterdamians promised a 20,000 ticket advance sale, the deal was made.

League attendance still faltered, dropping to a just 180,382. The playoffs drew a pathetic 11,800. Every club lost money.

"I went to a few games the last season," recalls one Rugmakers fan. "They didn't even have enough baseballs to finish the games. They had to throw the balls back from the stands."

The Glovers trained in Mayfield, New York — *north* of Gloversville. "We never stayed over on the road, except in Kingston," recalled Glovers hurler Francis "Dutch" Howlan. "We always went back on the bus."

Cost-cutting measures weren't always appreciated. "In 1951," says Glovers hurler John "Lefty" Coakley, "I had a four and one record, and Al Barillari was the manager at that time. At this particular low level of minor league ball, they wanted you both to start and relieve.

"Barillari came up to me one day, and he said, 'John, we would like you to relieve when you're not starting.' I'd injured my arm that spring. I pulled a muscle, and I could pitch on a Monday night, and I would need four full days of complete rest. I just couldn't relieve in between.

"He says, 'If you can't relieve in between, we're going to put you on the disabled list,' and I said, 'If I'm on the disabled list, does that mean I will be paid?'

"He says, "No, we won't be able to pay you.' I said, 'No way. I gotta have money to eat, for room and board, and if you can't pay me I gotta go someplace and find a job.'

Judge Felix Aulisi, president of the Amsterdam Rugmakers.

"So that was the end of my minor league baseball career.

"And you know, ironically, the following year he was managing a club up in Drummondsville [of the Provincial League], and he sent a messenger down to Gloversville, and they approached me and asked me if I would like to go to Canada and pitch with Al Barillari. I said, 'No. You can go up there and tell that Italian that I wouldn't pitch for him ever again, even if he paid me $10,000 a month!'

"I hated the guy."

The new Kingston club was a disaster, drawing just 16,961, as it got off to a horrendous 11–47 start and finished dead last overall. By late May, the franchise was about to fold, and a transfer to Utica was bandied about.

At about the same time the Border League collapsed. The Geneva Robins withdrew on June 26. Cornwall was reduced to playing only road games, and a merger with the Can-Am was discussed. But the Can-Am would only take on two Border franchises. The Border League decided instead to muddle on with only four teams. The strategy didn't work, as it disbanded on July 15.

Pitcher Robert J. Sise, now the Deputy Chief Administrative Judge of the New York State Office of Court Administration, was one of the last of the Can-Am players.

He'd had previous trials as a third baseman in the Border and North Atlantic leagues, some semipro mound experience, and was already a practicing attorney when the pitching-starved Glovers turned to him for help, signing him to a $250 a month contract.

"Attendance was down at the beginning of the season," he recalls, "television was really hurting the league, and we were down to six to seven hundred fans a game. There was talk we wouldn't finish out the season.

"I was scheduled to start against Rome, when the Gloversville management placed a full page ad in the *Leader-Republican*. 'This is it,' it read. 'Its do or die for Glovers baseball. If you want baseball to survive in Gloversville, come out to the park tonight. Admission free!'

"Anyway, 2,500 to 3,000 people showed up, and if you were ever pumped up to pitch a big game this was it. At the time MacArthur has addressed the Congress, and 'Old Soldiers Never Die' was very popular, and the fans in the third base stands were singing 'Old Glovers Never Die.'

"A very popular old Gloversville pitcher, 'Duke' Farrington, got on the public address system and made the announcement that people were coming through the stands selling books of tickets, six for the price of five.

"Hundreds of the books were sold. Attendance picked up in June and July—a thousand, eleven hundred a game. It saved the franchise."

But only until season's end. In November came a flurry of activity. Addison Jones announced Kingston was dropping out. Conflicting rumors abounded. The Can-Am would fold. It would expand. Watertown and Auburn, former Border League franchises, were reportedly interested in joining up. Ellsworth Haver, ex–Border loop prexy, met with Can-Am officials to discuss Watertown's entry.

Dr. J.L. Rochefort of Three Rivers suggested that his city and also Quebec might return to the Can-Am fold, and posed the possibility of a strong eight-team circuit with membership equally divided between both nations.

The Yankees dumped Rugmakers ownership back on local interests, and dropped their working agreement. Club prexy Felix Aulisi doubted the club could continue even with one. Directors of the Glovers voted to stay on only if the league expanded to eight clubs. Pittsfield backed them up.

The entire minor league system was heaving and shaking. In 1950 there had been 58 leagues. In 1951 only 50. That went to one less when the Border League collapsed. Other circuits wobbled. Five individual Class D clubs had folded in mid-campaign, and having a winning team was no longer a guarantee of survival. The Pittsburg (California) Diamonds of the Far West League died on June 13 while in first place. The Ohio-Indiana

League's Newark Yankees (piloted by Bunny Mick) expired after copping the first half championship. The military draft was causing a manpower shortage. Whole leagues were now starting to slide. In December the Class D Alabama State League was the first to fold. Then came the Class B Southeastern.

"At least ten more will go," prophesized an anonymous minor league official, "I'm afraid it will be more. There just won't be enough ball players to go around."

The Canadian-American continued on in limbo until January 1952. "It was a surprise to me the league finished last season," Al Houghton confessed.

He blamed the tube for its woes: "What else can it be? Television is the only new element in the picture. With the large increase in the sale of sets in the past two years, baseball attendance has dropped off tremendously. We bucked such things as poor weather, increased cost of materials, labor, etc., and still operated successfully in the past. Television therefore seems to be the only reason."

On January 26, 1952, at Schenectady's Hotel Van Curler, Rugmakers' secretary Archie McKee made a momentous proposal. He had Houghton's backing.

"I got the reputation," says McKee, "of having killed professional baseball in Amsterdam. At the annual meeting, I made the recommendation that we suspend operations for a year.... None of the teams except for Oneonta with the Red Sox had working agreements. The Yankees pulled the rug out from under us."

Pittsfield and Oneonta talked of retreating to the semipros. Amsterdam gave it some consideration as well. Kingston returned to the loop at the end and went into suspended status with the rest. A decision was to be made by November 15, 1952, as to whether play would ever be resumed.

It never was.

So that was how the Can-Am League ended, in a Schenectady hotel room. You can kill a league, but you can't kill baseball. Slowly, imperceptibly, the game returned to its member cities—to Ottawa, to Quebec, to Three Rivers, to Oneonta, to Auburn, to Utica, to Pittsfield, to Watertown.

Old ballparks were torn down. New ballparks were built. Teams shifted from coast to coast. Browns became Orioles. Senators became Rangers. Pilots became Brewers. Designated hitters gamboled on chemically green artificial turf. Baseball went on. It will go on forever...

The dream continues, but in thousands of aging hearts there are thoughts of Bunny Mick and Billy Southworth, Jr., and Al Barkus, of warm summer nights and stands full of friends and neighbors. The memories are etched in stone, carved in the maleability of youth. All across the country there are similar visions, of misty outfields and dreamlike scoreboards, reminicenses of the Kitty League.

The Southern Association
The Evangeline League
The Kansas-Oklahoma-Missouri League
The Far West League
The Provincial League
The Border League
The Georgia-Florida League
The Cape Breton Colliery League
The Big State League
The Sunset League
Etcetera. Etcetera. All too unfortunately, Etcetera.
Goodbye Can-Am League. Goodbye.

Appendices

Teams of the Canadian-American League, 1936-1951

City	Years	Nickname	Ballpark	Affiliation
Amsterdam	1938–42, 1946–51	Rugmakers	Mohawk Mills Pk.	Yankees
Auburn	1938	Bouleys	Falcon Park	None
	1940	Falcons	Falcon Park	None
Brockville	1936–37	Pirates	Fulford Field	Red Sox
Cornwall	1938	Bisons	Corn. Ath. Grds.	Buffalo
	1939	Maple Leafs	Corn. Ath. Grds.	Toronto
Gloversville	1937	Glovers	Glovers Field	None
Gloversville-	1938	Glovers	Glovers Field	None
Johnstown	1939	Glovers	Glovers Field	Dodgers
	1940–41	Glovers	Glovers Field	Albany
	1942, 1946–49	Glovers	Glovers Field	Browns
	1950–51	Glovers	Glovers Field	None
Kingston	1951	Colonials	Dietz Stadium	None
Ogdensburg	1936–39	Colts	Winter Park	None
Oneonta	1940	Indians	Neahwa Park	None
	1941–42	Indians	Neahwa Park	Red Sox
	1946–51	Red Sox	Neahwa Park	Red Sox
Oswego	1936	Netherlands	Otis Field	Buffalo
	1937–38	Netherlands	Otis Field	Indians
	1939	Netherlands	Otis Field	Senators
	1940	Netherlands	Otis Field	None
Ottawa	1936	Senators	Lansdowne Park	None
	1937–38	Braves	Lansdowne Park	'37 Bees
	1939	Senators	Lansdowne Park	None
Ottawa- Ogdensburg	1940	Senators	Lansdowne Park	Phillies
Perth	1936	Blue Cats/ Royals	P.C.I. Park	Buffalo
Perth-Cornwall	1937	Grays	P.C.I. Park/ Fulford Field	Buffalo

City	Years	Nickname	Ballpark	Affiliation
Pittsfield	1941	Electrics	Deming Field	None
	1942	Electrics	Wahconah Park	Buffalo
	1946–49	Electrics	Wahconah Park	Indians
	1950	Indians	Wahconah Park	Indians
	1951	Phillies	Wahconah Park	Phillies
Quebec	1941	Athletics	Municipal Stad.	Dodgers
	1942	Athletics	Municipal Stad.	Rochester
	1946	Alouettes	Municipal Stad.	Cubs
	1947	Alouettes	Municipal Stad.	None
	1948	Alouettes	Municipal Stad.	Giants
	1949–50	Braves	Municipal Stad.	None
Rome	1937	Colonels	League Park	None
	1938–41	Colonels	Colonels Park	None
	1942	Colonels	Colonels Park	None
	1946–50	Colonels	Colonels Park	Tigers
	1951	Colonels	Colonels Park	Athletics
Schenectady	1946	Blue Jays	Central Park/ McNearney Stad.	Phillies
	1947–50	Blue Jays	McNearney Stad.	Phillies
Smiths Falls	1937	Beavers	Can. Pac. Rec. Fd.	Yankees
Three Rivers	1941	Foxes	Municipal Stad.	
	1942	Foxes	Municipal Stad.	None
	1946–50	Royals	Municipal Stad.	Dodgers
Utica	1939–40	Braves	Braves Field	None
	1941	Braves	Braves Field	Buffalo
	1942	Braves	Braves Field	Springfield
Watertown	1936	Bucks, Grays	Fair Grds. Park	Bees

Canadian-American League Pennant Winners and Playoff Champions

Year	City	W	L	Pct.	Mgr.	Playoffs	Mgr.
1936	Perth	50	30	.625	Yerkes	Perth	Yerkes
1937	Perth-Cornw	69	37	.651	Yerkes	Ogdensburg	Lee
1938	Amsterdam	79	40	.664	Martin	None	---------
1939	Amsterdam	81	41	.664	Sawyer	Rome	Martin
1940	Ottawa-Ogdens	84	39	.683	Morgan	Amsterdam	Kain
1941	Oneonta	78	46	.629	Barnes	Oneonta	Barnes
1942	Amsterdam	77	46	.626	Kain	Oneonta	Barnes
1946	Three Rivers	72	49	.595	Bordagaray	Three Rivers	Bordagaray
1947	Schenectady	86	51	.628	Riley	Schenectady	Riley
1948	Rome	79	57	.581	Smoll	Oneonta	Marion
1949	Quebec	90	48	.652	McCormick	Quebec	McCormick
1950	Quebec	97	40	.708	McQuinn	Quebec	McQuinn
1951	Oneonta	83	34	.709	Scheetz	Oneonta	Scheetz

Canadian-American League Batting Leaders

Home Runs

1936	James Stevenson, Ottawa	15
1937	Maurice Van Robays, Ogdensburg	43
1938	Anthony Gridaitis, Ogdensburg	34
1939	John H. "Pappy" Lehman, G-J'town	22
1940	Paul Badgett, Amsterdam	31
1941	Leon F. Riley, Rome	32
1942	Joseph Morjoseph, Gloversville-J'town	20
1946	Albert Rosen, Pittsfield	15
1947	Benjamin Gregg, Schenectady	15
1948	Eugene Hasson, Pittsfield	27
1949	Donald Marshall, Schenectady	27
1950	Garland "Butch" Lawing, Quebec	19
1951	John Jones, Amsterdam	18

Runs Batted In

1936	Frank "Lefty" Marinette, Perth	80
1937	Maurice Van Robays, Ogdensburg	150
1938	Anthony Gridaitis, Ogdensburg	130
1939	Edwin Sawyer, Amsterdam	103
1940	Paul Badgett, Amsterdam	119
1941	Austin Knickerbocker, Oneonta	135
1942	Costic "Jerry" Navrocki, Pittsfield	104
1946	Albert Rosen, Pittsfield	86
1947	Benjamin Gregg, Schenectady	117
1948	Eugene Hasson, Pittsfield	106
1949	Vernon "Moose" Shetler, Quebec	133
1950	Garland "Butch" Lawing, Quebec	141
1951	John Jones, Amsterdam	127

Batting

	G	AB	R	H	2B	3B	HR	RBI	SB	AVG.
1936 Michael Sperrick, Perth	73	286	58	103	20	6	2	62	19	.360
1937 M. Van Robays, Ogdensbg.	105	432	135	159	28	9	43	150	14	.368
1938 Charles Harig, Auburn	109	421	95	162	33	9	20	109	12	.385
1939 Edwin Sawyer, Amsterdam	122	458	96	169	53	3	16	103	4	.369
1940 John Lehman, Glov.-Johns.	113	417	75	147	27	10	10	89	12	.353
1941 A. Knickerbocker, Oneon.	120	498	113	202	45	10	12	135	18	.406
1942 Regie Otero, Utica	120	453	78	165	32	8	2	101	25	.364
1946 S. Bordagaray, Thr. Riv.	104	353	78	128	27	4	11	83	20	.363
1947 Malcolm Mick, Amsterdam	109	418	98	149	22	2	12	61	31	.357
1948 Eug. Hasson, Pittsfield	112	340	69	125	18	0	27	106	2	.368
1949 Peter Elko, Quebec	104	399	102	139	26	6	6	71	15	.348
1950 Garland Lawing, Quebec	134	438	110	152	33	2	19	141	13	.346
1951 William McMillan, G-J	96	337	67	127	23	9	7	69	42	.377

Attendance

City	1936	1937	1938	1939	1940	1941	1942	1946	1947	1948	1949	1950	1951
Amsterdam	*	*	25,672	39,346	41,051	37,738	36,627	78,915	88,876	90,790	83,449	49,026	30,837
Auburn	*	*	16,178	*	10,040	*	*	*	*	*	*	*	*
Brockville	???	6,242	*	*	*	*	*	*	*	*	*	*	*
Cornwall	*	*	23,687	24,285	*	*	*	*	*	*	*	*	*
Gloversville	*	24,113	*	*	*	*	*	*	*	*	*	*	*
G'ville-J'town	*	*	29,178	25,485	39,613	34,495	46,957	50,436	75,279	61,736	83,638	48,448	36,807
Kingstown	*	*	*	19,849	*	*	*	*	*	*	*	*	16,961
Ogdensburg	???	27,827	27,016	*	*	*	*	*	*	*	*	*	*
Oneonta	*	*	*	*	39,851	46,951	34,411	56,381	53,008	51,204	63,217	45,911	32,503
Oswego	???	21,076	16,522	25,448	16,478	*	*	*	*	*	*	*	*
Ottawa	???	15,949	24,827	33,993	*	*	*	*	*	*	*	*	*
Ott.-Ogdens.	*	*	*	*	29,373	*	*	*	*	*	*	*	*
Perth	???	*	*	*	*	*	*	*	*	*	*	*	*
Perth-Corn.	*	19,194	*	*	*	*	*	*	*	*	*	*	*
Pittsfield	*	*	*	*	*	32,239	34,411	64,913	67,644	52,986	56,674	28,668	39,820
Quebec	*	*	*	*	*	47,179	46,569	65,557	85,876	144,156	176,779	123,352	*
Rome	*	18,387	51,363	57,654	36,395	42,828	19,819	58,371	58,463	75,103	40,331	34,535	23,454
Schenectady	*	*	*	*	*	*	*	53,239	146,227	146,421	115,966	76,853	*
Smiths Falls	*	14,197	*	*	*	*	*	*	*	*	*	*	*
Three Rivers	*	*	*	*	*	36,143	30,766	72,097	59,961	80,747	76,672	46,339	*
Utica	*	*	*	*	*	*	*	*	*	*	*	*	*
Watertown	???	*	*	105,394	89,669	51,000	83,443	*	*	*	*	*	*
Playoffs	*	11,044	17,140	18,059	33,314	37,163	31,812	48,970	56,739	34,168	32,949	21,712	11,800
Totals	65,000	158,029	231,583	349,513	335,784	365,736	369,223	494,893	635,030	703,143	696,726	453,132	180,382

Records

TEAM RECORDS

Most Championships — Amsterdam, 3 (1938, 1939, 1942)
Most Playoff Championships — Oneonta, 4 (1941, 1942, 1948, 1951)
Managed Most Champions — Steve Yerkes, 2 (1936, 1937)
Best Winning Percentage — Oneonta, .709 (1951)
Worst Winning Percentage — Auburn, .231 (1940)
Biggest Lead — Quebec, 14½ games (1949)
Most Games Won — Quebec, 97 (1950)
Fewest Games Won — Auburn, 28 (1940)
Most Losses — Auburn, 93 (1940)

INDIVIDUAL BATTING

Highest Batting Average — Austin Knickerbocker, Oneonta, .406 (1941)
Most At Bats — George E. Clark, Jr., Three Rivers, 565 (1949)
Most Hits — Austin Knickerbocker, Oneonta, 202 (1941)
Most Runs — Frank "Chick" Genovese, Oneonta, 145 (1941)
Most Doubles — Eddie Sawyer, Amsterdam, 53 (1941)
Most Triples — Frank Malzone, Oneonta, 26 (1949)
Most Home Runs — Maurice Van Robays, Ogdensburg, 43 (1937)
Most Sacrifices — Oscar Fleischman, Oswego, 29 (1939)
Most Bases on Balls — Garland Lawing, Quebec, 168 (1950)
Most Strikeouts — Arnold Spence, Gloversville-Johnstown, 135 (1949)
Most Stolen Bases — Jim Whalley, Ottawa, 64 (1939)
Most Games Hit Consecutively — Dale Long, Oneonta, 28 (1947)

INDIVIDUAL PITCHING

Best E.R.A. — Xavier Rescigno, Smiths Falls, 1.56 (1937)
Best Percentage — Roy Partlow, Three Rivers, .909 (1946)
Most Wins — George McPhail, Oneonta, 24 (1951)
Most Strikeouts — Harry Markell, Schenectady, 280 (1948)
Most Bases on Balls — Frank "Blacky" Rochevot, Ottawa and Cornwall, 218 (1938)
Most Games — Loren Stewart, Gloversville-Johnstown, 56 (1950)
Most Games Started — Alexander Danelishen, Quebec, 32 (1949)
Most Complete Games — Frank Rochevot, Ottawa-Cornwall, 27 (1938); John Dickenson, Cornwall, 27 (1938); Harry Kuntashian, Oswego, 27 (1940)
Most Shutouts — John Masuga, Pittsfield, 7 (1949)
Most Innings Pitched — Frank Rochevot, Ottawa-Cornwall, 278⅔ (1938)
Most Balks — Robert Jeffries, Pittsfield, 5 (1951)

Most Wild Pitches — Mike Naymick, Oswego, 37 (1938)
Most Hit Batsmen — Edward Carr, Ottawa, 25 (1937)
Most Consecutive Games Won — Albert "Duke" Farrington, Amsterdam, 13 (1938)

TEAM FIELDING

Best Percentage — Amsterdam, .964 (1942)
Worst Percentage — Rome, .937 (1937)
Fewest Errors — Ottawa, 150 (1936)
Most Errors — Amsterdam, 307 (1949)

TEAM BATTING

Highest Team Batting Average — Rome, .310 (1939)
Lowest Team Batting Average — Kingston, .226 (1951)

Yearly Standings

1936

Team	Won	Lost	Tied	Pct.	Manager	Parent Club
Perth	50	30	3	.625	Steve Yerkes	Buffalo
Ottawa	53	37	4	.589	Walter Masters	None
Brockville	43	36	2	.544	Jess Spring	Red Sox
Ogdensburg	38	45	3	.458	Knotty Lee/ Bernard Fasulo	None
Watertown	35	52	1	.402	Admiral Martin	Bees
Oswego	32	51	3	.386	John Dashner/ Blaine Kunes	Buffalo

Shaughnessy Playoffs
Brockville 3, Ottawa 1; Perth 3, Ottawa 2; Perth 3, Brockville 0

1937

Team	Won	Lost	Tied	Pct.	Manager	Parent Club
Perth-Cornwall	69	37	2	.651	Steve Yerkes	Buffalo
Oswego	67	40	1	.626	Blaine Kunes	Indians
Gloversville	68	42	1	.618	Admiral Martin	-----
Ogdensburg	55	47	3	.539	Knotty Lee	-----
Smiths Falls	57	49	0	.538	John Haddock	Yankees
Rome	40	59	3	.404	Joe Brown	-----
Brockville	30	69	1	.303	Jess Spring	Red Sox
Ottawa	32	75	3	.299	Clair Foster	Bees

Shaughnessy Playoffs

Gloversville 3, Perth-Cornwall 1; Ogdensburg 3, Oswego 1; Ogdensburg 4, Gloversville 3

1938

Team	Won	Lost	Ties	Pct.	Manager	Parent Club
Amsterdam	79	40	4	.664	Admiral Martin	Yankees
Cornwall	74	47	0	.612	Steve Yerkes	Buffalo
Ogdensburg	66	52	6	.559	Knotty Lee	-----
Gloversville-Johnstown	63	62	2	.504	John Roser	-----
Rome	61	63	6	.492	Wm. J. Buckley	-----
Oswego	54	69	2	.439	Riley Parker Max G. Ziel	Indians
Auburn	49	68	4	.419	John Cimpi	-----
Ottawa	38	83	4	.314	Clair Foster/ George Army	-----

Shaughnessy Playoffs

Amsterdam 4; Gloversville-Johnstown 0; Cornwall 4, Ogdensburg 0, Cornwall 2, Amsterdam 1*
*One game tied. Series abandoned because of inclement weather.

1939

Team	Won	Lost	Tied	Pct.	Manager	Parent Club
Amsterdam	81	41	5	.664	Eddie Sawyer	Yankees
Oswego	69	53	3	.566	Blaine Kunes	Senators
Rome	68	54	7	.557	Admiral Martin	-----
Cornwall	62	56	1	.525	Steve Yerkes/ Emil Graff	Toronto
Ogdensburg	60	58	4	.508	Knotty Lee	-----
Ottawa	55	69	3	.444	Wally Schang	-----
Gloversville-Johnstown	46	77	3	.374	Elmer Yoter	Dodgers
Utica	45	78	2	.366	Amby McConnell	

Shaughnessy Playoffs

Rome 4, Perth-Cornwall 0; Amsterdam 4, Oswego 0; Rome 3, Amsterdam 2

1940

Team	Won	Lost	Tied	Pct.	Manager	Parent Club
Ottawa-Ogdensburg	84	39	2	.683	Cy Morgan	Phillies

1940 *(cont.)*

Team	Won	Lost	Tied	Pct.	Manager	Parent Club
Gloversville- Johnstown	72	53	6	.576	O. Blakeney	Pirates
Amsterdam	70	53	5	.569	Eddie Sawyer	Yankees
Utica	69	56	2	.552	E. Jenkins	-----
Oneonta	62	63	2	.496	Lee Riley	-----
Oswego	58	63	4	.479	Art Funk	-----
Rome	50	73	2	.407	Admiral Martin	-----
Auburn	28	93	1	.231	Knotty Lee	-----

Shaughnessy Playoffs

Gloversville-Johnstown 4, Utica 1; Amsterdam 4, Ottawa-Ogdensburg 1; Amsterdam 3, Gloversville-Johnstown 2

1941

Team	Won	Lost	Tied	Pct.	Manager	Parent Club
Oneonta	78	46	1	.629	Emil Barnes	Red Sox
Amsterdam	68	54	1	.557	Paul O'Malley	Yankees
Rome	66	58	2	.532	Lee Riley	-----
Pittsfield	62	59	5	.5124	Art Funk	-----
Three Rivers	63	60	3	.5122	Wally Schang	-----
Quebec	57	67	2	.460	Admiral Martin/ Roland Gladu	Dodgers
Gloversville- Johnstown	54	70	0	.435	O. Blakeney	Pirates
Utica	45	79	0	.363	Frank Zubik	Buffalo

Shaughnessy Playoffs

Oneonta 4, Rome 2; Pittsfield 4, Amsterdam 3; Oneonta 4, Pittsfield 2

1942

Team	Won	Lost	Tied	Pct.	Manager	Parent Club
Amsterdam	77	46	1	.626	Shakey Kain	Yankees
Gloversville- Johnstown	67	54	1	.554	Mickey Hornsby	Browns
Utica	66	54	0	.550	Red Marion	Springfield
Oneonta	68	56	2	.548	Emil Barnes	Red Sox
Pittsfield	63	52	1	.504	Shano Collins/ Rabbit Moore	Buffalo
Three Rivers	56	66	1	.459	Justin Kennoy	-----
Quebec	55	67	0	.451	Mel Simons/ Roland Gladu/ Charlie Small	Rochester
Rome	38	85	0	.309	John Griffiths	Phillies

Shaughnessy Playoffs

Amsterdam 4, Gloversville-Johnstown 3; Oneonta 4, Utica 1; Oneonta 4, Amsterdam 3

Six of 8 clubs had working agreements, 2 received help

1946

Team	Won	Lost	Tied	Pct.	Manager	Parent Club
Three Rivers	72	49	0	.5950	F. Bordaragay	Dodgers
Pittsfield	69	47	2	.5948	Tony Rensa	Indians
Rome	72	52	0	.581	Woody Wheaton	Tigers
Oneonta	68	54	0	.557	Red Marion	Red Sox
Amsterdam	61	58	1	.513	Sol Mishkin	Yankees
Gloversville- (Johnstown)	53	67	1	.442	Ben Huffman	Browns
Schenectady	45	75	1	.375	Bill Cronin	Phillies
Quebec	41	79	1	.342	J. Segrue/ Tim Murchison/ John Inktehofer	Cubs

Shaughnessy Playoffs

Three Rivers 4, Rome 3; Pittsfield 4, Oneonta 3; Three Rivers 4, Pittsfield 1

1947

Team	Won	Lost	Tied	Pct.	Manager	Parent Club
Schnectady	86	51	1	.628	Lee Riley	Phillies
Gloversville-Johnstown	74	65	0	.532	Stan Rogers	Browns
Amsterdam	73	67	2	.521	Sol Mishkin	Yankees
Oneonta	70	67	2	.511	Red Marion	Red Sox
Pittsfield	71	69	0	.507	Tony Rensa	Cleveland
Three Rivers	65	69	2	.485	Lou Rochelli	Dodgers
Rome	67	72	3	.482	Ed Boland/ Adam Bengochea	Tigers
Quebec	45	91	3	.331	Buck Desorey/ Tony Ravish	-----

Shaughnessy Playoffs

Schenectady 4, Amsterdam 3; Gloversville-Johnstown 4, Oneonta 1; Schenectady 4, Gloversville 1

1948

Team	Won	Lost	Tied	Pct.	Manager	Parent Club
Rome	79	57	0	.581	Clyde Smoll	Tigers
Three Rivers	78	60	0	.565	Ed Head	Dodgers
Oneonta	72	65	2	.526	Red Marion	Red Sox
Pittsfield	69	67	1	.507	Gene Hasson	Indians
Schenectady	69	68	1	.504	Lee Riley	Phillies
Gloversville-Johnstown	68	69	0	.496	Jim McDonnell	Browns

1948 *(cont.)*

Team	Won	Lost	Tied	Pct.	Manager	Parent Club
Amsterdam	57	80	0	.416	Jim McLeod	Yankees
Quebec	56	82	0	.406	Tony Ravish	Giants

Shaughnessy Playoffs

Oneonta 4, Rome 3; Pittsfield 4, Three Rivers 1; Oneonta 4, Pittsfield 1

1949

Team	Won	Lost	Tied	Pct.	Manager	Parent Club
Quebec	90	48	0	.652	Frank McCormick	-----
Oneonta	75	62	0	.547	Ed Popowski	Red Sox
Three Rivers	75	64	0	.540	George Scherger	Dodgers
Pittsfield	74	65	0	.532	Gene Hasson	Indians
Amsterdam	67	71	1	.486	Mayo Smith	Yankees
Gloversville-Johnstown	65	74	0	.468	Jim Cullinane	Browns
Schenectady	58	80	1	.420	Dick Carter	Phillies
Rome	48	88	0	.353	Clyde Smoll	Tigers

Schaughnessy Playoffs

Quebec 4, Three Rivers 0; Oneonta 4, Pittsfield 2; Quebec 4, Oneonta 0

1950

Team	Won	Lost	Tied	Pct.	Manager	Parent Club
Quebec	97	40	0	.708	Geo. McQuinn	-----
Schenectady	88	46	2	.657	Dick Carter	Phillies
Oneonta	86	52	0	.623	Ed Popowski	Red Sox
Amsterdam	72	65	1	.526	Mayo Smith	Yankees
Gloversville-Johnstown	57	81	0	.413	Jim Cullinane	-----
Rome	51	86	0	.372	Wm. Gates/ Wm. Booker/ Emil Gail	Tigers
Pittsfield	49	86	1	.363	Lloyd Brown	Indians
Three Rivers	46	90	0	.338	Geo. Scherger	Dodgers

Shaughnessy Playoffs

Quebec 4, Oneonta 1; Amsterdam 4, Schenectady 2; Quebec 4, Amsterdam 0

1951

Team	Won	Lost	Pct.	Manager	Parent Club
		FIRST HALF			
Oneonta	37	17	.685	Owen Scheetz	Red Sox
Pittsfield	37	18	.673	Dick Carter	Phillies

1951 *(cont.)*

Team	Won	Lost	Pct.	Manager	Parent Club
Amsterdam	32	24	.571	Frank Novosel	Yankees
Gloversville-Johnstown	26	29	.473	Al Barillari	Milwaukee
Rome	25	33	.431	Buck Etchison	Athletics
Kingston	11	47	.190	Henry Camelli/ Joel Kern	-----

			SECOND HALF		
Oneonta	46	17	.730	Owen Scheetz	Red Sox
Pittsfield	35	24	.593	Richard Carter	Phillies
Amsterdam	30	32	.484	Frank Novosel	Yankees
Gloversville-Johnstown	26	32	.448	Al Barillari	Milwaukee
Kingston	22	37	.373	Joel Kern/ John Sosh	-----
Rome	21	38	.356	Buck Etchison	Athletics

			OVERALL		
Oneonta	83	34	.709	Owen Scheetz	Red Sox
Pittsfield	72	42	.632	Richard Carter	Phillies
Amsterdam	62	56	.525	Frank Novosel	Yankees
Gloversville-Johnstown	52	61	.460	Al Barillari	Milwaukee
Rome	46	71	.393	Buck Etchison	Athletics
Kingston	33	84	.282	Henry Camelli/ Joel Kern/ John Sosh	-----

Shaughnessy Playoffs

Oneonta 3, Amsterdam 1; Gloversville-Johnstown 3, Pittsfield 2; Oneonta 3, Gloversville-Johnstown 1

Ballparks

City	Ballpark	LF	CF	RF	Capacity*
Amsterdam	Mohawk Mills Park	279	406	309	3,200
Auburn	Falcon Park	330	409	335	2,200
Brockville	Fulford Field	275	400	450	2,000
Cornwall	Cornwall Ath. Grds.	360	407	400	3,000
Gloversville-Johnstown	Glovers Park	330	405	330	3,000
Kingston	Dietz Stadium	?	?	?	3,000
Massena	Alco Field	?	?	?	?

Ballparks (cont.)

City	Ballpark	LF	CF	RF	Capacity*
Ogdensburg	Winter Park	260 ?	450	386	1,800
Oneonta	Neahwa Park	337	403	341	3,000
Oswego	Otis Field	550	585	428	2,000
Ottawa	Lansdowne Park	400+	350	348	10,000
Perth	P.C.I. Park	353	431	353	1,400
Pittsfield	Wahconah Park	352	362	333	4,000
Quebec	Municipal Stadium	317	372	317	7,500
Rome	Colonels Park	360	380	320	3,500
Schenectady	McNearney Stadium	320	390	320	5,000
Smiths Falls	Can. Pac. Rec. Fd.	270	410	400	2,500
Three Rivers	Municipal Stadium	317	372	317	6,000
Utica	Braves Field	389	503	400	5,000
Watertown	Fair Grounds Park	300	350	300	3,000

*Maximum capacity; capacities were often smaller when park opened.

Players with Major League Experience

AMSTERDAM

Player	Year	Position	Major League Teams
Zeke Bella	1951	outfielder	Yankees
John Blanchard	1951	catcher	Yankees, Kansas City, Milwaukee
Lew Burdette	1947	pitcher	Yankees, Braves, Cardinals, Cubs, Phillies, Angels##
Allie Clark	1942	2nd base	Yankees, A's, Cleveland, White Sox
Joe Collins	1942	1st base	Yankees
Bill Drescher	1942	catcher	Yankees
Karl Drews	1941	pitcher	Yankees, Browns, Phillies, Cincinnati
Ford Garrison	1938	outfielder	Red Sox, A's
Bob Grim	1949	pitcher	Yankees, Kansas City, Cleveland, Cincinnati, Cardinals
Herb Karpel	1939	pitcher	Yankees
Bill Kennedy	1941	pitcher	Cleveland, Browns, White Sox, Red Sox, Cincinnati
Dick Kryhoski	1946	1st base	Yankees, Detroit, Browns, Baltimore, Kansas City
Danny McDevitt	1941	pitcher	Yankees, Brooklyn, Minnesota, Kansas City
Joe Murray	1946–47	pitcher	A's
Vic Raschi	1941	pitcher	Yankees, Cardinals, Kansas City
Mel Queen	1939	pitcher	Yankees, Pittsburgh
Kenny Sears	1938	catcher	Yankees
Spec Shea	1940	pitcher	Yankees, Washington

AMSTERDAM *(cont.)*

Player	Year	Position	Major League Teams
Mayo Smith	1949–50#	outfielder	Phillies * ** ##
Gus Triandos	1950	catcher	Yankees, Baltimore, Detroit, Phillies, Houston
Vince Ventura	1939	pitcher**	Washington

BROCKVILLE

Joe Krakauskas	1936	pitcher	Washington, Cleveland

CORNWALL

Frank Colman	1939	pitcher/ph*	Pittsburgh, Yankees
Dick Fowler	1939	pitcher	A's
Phil Marchildon	?	pitcher	A's, Red Sox
Whitey Platt	1939	outfielder	Cubs, White Sox, Browns

GLOVERSVILLE-JOHNSTOWN

Chuck Harmon	1947 & 49	outfielder	Cardinals, Phillies
Ben Huffman	1946#	catcher	Browns*
Earl Jones	1942	pitcher	Browns
Joe Lutz	1946	1st base	##
Jack McKeon	1950	catcher	##
Packy Rogers	1947#	infielder	Brooklyn*
Frank Sacka	1948	catcher	Washington*

OGDENSBURG

M. Van Robays	1937	outfielder	Pittsburgh

ONEONTA

Bob Aspromonte	1950	infielder	Brooklyn, Los Angeles, Houston, Atlanta, Mets**
Ivan DeLock	1947	pitcher	Red Sox, Baltimore
Joe DeMaestri	1949	shortstop	White Sox, Browns, A's, Kansas City, Yankees
Vance Dinges	1942	outfielder	Phillies
Dick Fowler	1940	pitcher	A's
A. Knickerbocker	1941	shortstop	A's
Dick Littlefield	1947	pitcher	Red Sox, White Sox, Detroit, Browns, Baltimore, Pittsburgh, Cardinals, Giants, Cubs, Milwaukee

ONEONTA *(cont.)*

Player	Year	Position	Major League Teams
Dale Long	1947		Pittsburgh, Browns, Cubs, San Francisco, Yankees, Washington
Emmet O'Neil	1941	pitcher	Red Sox, Cubs, White Sox
Frank Malzone	1949	shortstop	Red Sox, Angels
Eddie McGah	1941	catcher	Red Sox
Stan Partenheimer	1942	pitcher	Red Sox, Cardinals
Earl Rapp	1941	outfielder	Detroit, White Sox, Giants, Browns, Senators
Lee Riley	1940#	outfielder	Phillies
Robert G. Smith	1950	pitcher	Red Sox, Cardinals, Pittsburgh, Detroit
Hal White	1941	pitcher	Detroit, Browns, Cardinals
Sammy White	1949	catcher	Red Sox, Milwaukee, Phillies

OSWEGO

Player	Year	Position	Major League Teams
Bob Lemon	1938	3rd base**	Cleveland##
Bill Kalfass	1939–40	pitcher	A's*
Mike Naymick	1938	pitcher	Cleveland
Frank Skaff	1939	2nd base	Brooklyn,* A's##
Vince Ventura	1940	pitcher**	Washington

OTTAWA

Player	Year	Position	Major League Teams
Walt Masters	1936#	pitcher	Washington,* Phillies, A's
Wally Schang	1939#	catcher	A's,* Red Sox,* Yankees,* Browns,* Detroit*

OTTAWA-OGDENSBURG

Player	Year	Position	Major League Teams
Homer Howell	1940	catcher	Pittsburgh, Cincinnati, Brooklyn
Geo. Jumonville	1940	shortstop	Phillies
Paul Masterson	1940	pitcher	Phillies
Bill Peterman	1940	pitcher	Phillies
Specs Podgajny	1940	pitcher	Phillies, Pittsburgh, Cleveland

PERTH-CORNWALL

Player	Year	Position	Major League Teams
Danny Carnevale	1937	3rd base	##

PITTSFIELD

Player	Year	Position	Major League Teams
Gene Hasson	1948#	1st base	A's*
Brooks Lawrence	1950	pitcher	Cardinals, Cincinnati
Jim Lemon	1948	outfielder	Cleveland, Washington, Minnesota, Phillies, White Sox##
Hal Naragon	1947	catcher	Cleveland, Washington, Minnesota##
Tony Rensa	1946–47#	catcher	Detroit,* Phillies,* Yankees,* White Sox*

PITTSFIELD *(cont.)*

Player	Year	Position	Major League Teams
Al Rosen	1946	3rd base	Cleveland##
Dick Tomanek	1950	pitcher	Cleveland, Kansas City

QUEBEC

Player	Year	Position	Major League Teams
Peter Elko	1949–50	3rd b/ of	Cubs*
Moose Erickson	1949–50	pitcher	Detroit
Roland Gladu	1941–42	3rd base	Braves
Butch Lawing	1949–50	outfielder	Giants,* Cincinnati*
Frank McCormick	1949#	1st base	Cincinnati,* Phillies,* Braves*
George McQuinn	1950#	1st base	Cincinnati,* Browns,* A's,* Yankees*
Charlie Small	1942#	outfielder	Red Sox*

ROME

Player	Year	Position	Major League Teams
Peter Elko	1950	3rd base	Cubs*
Lynn Lovenguth	1947–48	pitcher	Phillies, Cardinals
Dale Matthewson	1942	pitcher	Phillies
Peter Elko	1950	3rd base	Cubs*
Lynn Lovenguth	1947–48	pitcher	Phillies, Cardinals
Dale Matthewson	1942	pitcher	Phillies
Lee Riley	1941#	outfielder	Phillies
Hal White	1937–38	pitcher	Detroit, Browns, Cardinals

SCHENECTADY

Player	Year	Position	Major League Teams
Tommy Lasorda	1948	pitcher	Brooklyn, Kansas City##
Lynn Lovenguth	1946	pitcher	Phillies, Cardinals
Duke Markell	1948	pitcher	Browns
Bobby Micelotta	1950	shortstop	Phillies
Steve Ridzik	1946–47	pitcher	Phillies, Cincinnati, Giants, Cleveland, Washington
Lee Riley	1947–48#	outfielder	Phillies*
Carl Sawatski	1946	outfielder**	Cubs, White Sox, Milwaukee, Phillies, Cardinals
Barney Schultz	1946	pitcher	Cardinals, Cubs, Detroit##

SMITHS FALLS

Player	Year	Position	Major League Teams
Xavier Rescigno	1937	pitcher	Pittsburgh

THREE RIVERS

Player	Year	Position	Major League Teams
Hank Biasatti	1942	1st base	A's
S. Bordaragay	1946#	1st base	Brooklyn*
Pete Gray	1942	outfielder	Browns
Billy Hunter	1948	shortstop	Browns, Baltimore, Kansas City, Cleveland##
Danny O'Connell	1947	3rd base	Braves, Giants, Washington
Lou Rochelli	1947#	3rd base**	Brooklyn*

THREE RIVERS *(cont.)*

Player	Year	Position	Major League Teams
Jean Pierre Roy	1941	pitcher	Brooklyn
George Scherger	1949–50	2nd base	##
Larry Shepherd	1941	pitcher	##
George Witt	1950	pitcher	Pittsburgh, Angels, Houston

UTICA

Regie Otero	1942	1st base	Cubs##

*Played with major league team prior to Can-Am service
**Played different position in majors than in Can-Am League
#Playing manager
##Saw service as major league coach, manager or general manager

Bibliography

NEWSPAPERS

Albany *Knickerbocker-News*
Albany *Times-Union*
Amsterdam *Evening Recorder*
Berkshire *Eagle*
The Dorp Sporting News
Gloversville & Johnstown *Leader-Republican*
Gloversville & Johnstown *Morning Herald*
Ogdensburg *Journal*
Oswego *Palladium-Times*
Rome *Sentinel*
Schenectady *Gazette*
Schenectady *Union-Star*
The Sporting News
Utica *Observer-Dispatch*
Watertown *Daily Times*

BOOKS

Allen, Lee. *The Hot Stove League*. New York: A.S. Barnes, 1955.
Barber, Red. *The Broadcasters*. New York: Dial Press, 1970.
Beverage, Richard. *The Hollywood Stars: Baseball in Movieland 1926–1957*. Placentia, Calif.: Deacon Press, 1984.
Boynton, Nat. *Media Rare: Adventures of a Grass Roots Newsman*. Maynard, Mass.: Chandler Press, 1988.
Brooks, Ken. *The Last Rebel Yell*. Lynn Haven, Fla.: Seneca Park, 1986.
Chrisman, David F. *History of the International League 1919–1960*. Self published, 1981.
_____. *History of the Piedmont League*. Self published, 1986.
_____. *History of the Virginia League*. Self published, 1988.
Clifton, Merritt. *Disorganized Baseball*. Richford, Ver.: Samisdat Press, 1982.
Crissey, Harrington E., Jr. *Athletes Away*. Philadelphia: Archway Press, 1984.
Etkin, Jack. *Innings Ago*. Kansas City, Mo.: Normandy Square Publications, 1987.
Finch, Robert L., Addington, L.H., and Morgan, Ben M. *The Story of Minor League Baseball*. Colombus, Ohio: National Association of Professional Baseball Leagues, 1952.
Gerlach, Larry R. *The Men in Blue: Conversations with Umpires*. New York: Viking, 1980.

Goldstein, Richard. *Spartan Seasons: How Baseball Survived the Second World War*. New York: Macmillan, 1980.

Gropman, Donald. *Say It Ain't So, Joe!* Boston: Little, Brown, 1979.

Hart, Larry. *Tales of Old Schenectady, Volume II*. Scotia, New York: Old Dorp Books, 1977.

Holway, John B. *Blackball Stars*. Westport, Ct.: Meckler Books, 1988.

Honig, Donald. *The Man in the Dugout*. Chicago: Follett, 1977.

Kahn, James M. *The Umpire Story*. New York: J.P. Putnam's Sons, 1953.

Karst, Gene, and Jones, Martin J., Jr. *Who's Who in Professional Baseball*. New Rochelle, N.Y.: Arlington House, 1973.

Keetz, Frank M. *Class C Baseball: A Case Study of the Schenectady Blue Jays in the Canadian-American League 1946–1950*. Schenectady, N.Y.: Self published, 1988.

Kubek, Tony, and Pluto, Terry. *Sixty-One: The Team, the Record, the Men*. New York: Macmillan, 1987.

Lasorda, Tommy. *The Artful Dodger*. New York: Arbor House, 1985.

Linthurst, Randolph. *The Newark Bears: The Final Years*. West Trenton, N.J.: self-published, 1981.

Marazi, Rich, and Fiorito, Len. *Aaron to Zipfel*. New York: Avon, 1985.

_____. *Aaron to Zuverink*. New York: Avon, 1985.

McKeon, Jack. *Jack of All Trades*. Chicago: Contemporary, 1988.

Mead, William B. *Even the Browns*. Chicago: Contemporary, 1978.

Obojski, Robert. *Bush League: A Colorful, Factual Account of Minor League Baseball from 1877 to the Present*. New York: Macmillan, 1975.

Rappoport, Ken. *Diamonds in the Rough: Life in Baseball's Minor Leagues*. New York: Grosset & Dunlap, 1979.

Riley, James A. *The All-Time All-Stars of Black Baseball*.

Robinson, Jackie. *I Never Had It Made*. New York: G.P. Putnam's, 1972.

Ryan, Bob. *Wait Till I Make the Show*. Boston: Little, Brown, 1974.

Seymour, Harold. *Baseball: The Golden Age*. New York: Oxford University Press, 1971.

Society for American Baseball Research. *Minor League Baseball Stars*. 1978.

_____. *Minor League Baseball Stars Volume II*. 1985.

Stern, Chris. *Where Have They Gone?* New York: Grosset & Dunlap, 1979.

Thorn, John, and Peter Palmer, eds. *Total Baseball*. New York: Warner, 1989.

Tygiel, Jules. *Baseballs' Great Experiment: Jackie Robinson and His Legacy*. New York: Oxford, 1983.

Whiting, Robert. *The Chrysanthemum and the Bat*. New York: Avon, 1983.

GUIDES

Spalding Guides
Sporting News Guides

Index